A CHRISTIAN
WORLDVIEW

Rev. Msgr. Chester P. Michael, S.T.D.

INFINITY
PUBLISHING

Copyright © 2012 by Rev. Msgr. Chester P. Michael, S.T.D.

ISBN 978-0-7414-7962-4 Paperback
ISBN 978-0-7414-7963-1 eBook
Library of Congress Control Number: 2012916338

Printed in the United States of America

Published November 2012

INFINITY PUBLISHING

Toll-free (877) BUY BOOK
Local Phone (610) 941-9999
Fax (610) 941-9959
Info@buybooksontheweb.com
www.buybooksontheweb.com

This book was first published in 2002 by Monsignor Chester P. Michael's non-profit organization, *The Open Door, Inc.* In 2010 Monsignor Michael and the Board of Directors made a decision to use a publisher's services to mass-market the book. The book you hold in your hands is the result of that decision.

Many have benefitted from Monsignor Michael's work through *The Open Door, Inc.*, most especially the attendees of his retreats, and students of *The Spiritual Direction Institute* (SDI) in Charlottesville, Virginia. The *Spiritual Direction Institute* is a two-year program which began in 1989 and continues today to enrich the lives of seekers. Monthly meetings and four weekend retreats offer a venue and a supportive environment for spiritual development within the Catholic Christian tradition. Enrollment is open to all.

Inquiries concerning SDI and retreats should be sent to The Open Door Inc., P.O. Box 855, Charlottesville, VA 22902 or to Al Mirmelstein at amirmelstein@nlrg.com or Patty Huffman at palhuffman@yahoo.com. More information may be found at www.ChesterMichael.org

IN MEMORIUM

Casimir (Casey) E. Norrisey

January 31, 1923 – January 14, 2002

Friend – Coworker – Business Manager

.

TABLE OF CONTENTS

INTRODUCTION.. 1

1. WORLDVIEW... 4

    A New Worldview... 5
    How Worldviews are Born............................... 7
    A Secular Worldview.. 9
    The History and Origin OF Today's Secular Worldview 10
    Changing our Worldview............................... 12
    The Importance of Each Individual 13
    What is Wrong with our Modern Secular Worldview?............. 15
    Ultimate Reality.. 16
    The Deist Worldview...................................... 18
    The Apocalyptic Worldview 19
    Fundamentalist Worldview 19
    Ptolemaic Worldview..................................... 20
    Copernican Worldview 21
    Einsteinian Worldview.................................... 21
    Developing A Christian Worldview 21
    An Aquarian Worldview for Today's World............. 24
    Where to Begin?... 25

2. SELF-PRESERVATION AND SURVIVAL 28

    Worldview after September 11, 2001....................... 28
    Threat of World-Wide Terrorism 29
    Idolatry of our American Way of Life 30
    Worship of the All-Powerful, Security State 31
    Worship of Pleasure 31
    The Fallen Spiritual Powers of our Institutions and Organizations 32
    Nuclear Proliferation 34
    World Hunger and Destitution 35
    Ecological Pollution 36
    Diminishing Natural Resources..................... 37
    Repressing our Unconscious Shadow 38

3. MODERN DEMONS AND THEIR REMEDIES 40

Worldview of Today's World 40
Redeeming Our Demons 46
Rereading Genesis Three 49

4. BEATITUDES 52

Worldview of Jesus 52
The First Beatitude 53
The Second and Eighth Beatitudes 60
The Third Beatitude 67
The Fourth Beatitude 74
The Fifth Beatitude 81
The Sixth Beatitude 88
The Seventh Beatitude 96

5. MISSION OF CHRIST, MISSION OF CHURCH 103

Worldview of Christ & Church 103
Twelve Aspects of the Mission of Christ 104
Mission of the Church 108
Pyramid Church Structure 109
The Ptolemaic Church 110
Horizontal Church Structure 111
The Copernican Church Model 113
Co-Relational Church Structure 114
The Einsteinian Church 116
Three Worldviews of the Christian Church .. 120

6. GOD'S PLAN FOR THE HUMAN RACE 122

Worldview of God 122
Five Bases of Prayer 125

7. Using the Bible in Prayer 128

Worldview of the Bible 128
Lectio Divina 133
Ignatian Prayer 134
Prayer of the Liturgical Year 135
Augustinian Prayer 135
Thomistic Prayer 136
Franciscan Prayer 137
Centering Prayer 137

The Lord's Prayer 138

Conclusion 139

8. CELEBRATING COVENANT WITH EUCHARIST 141

Place of Eucharist in Worldview 141

Dimensions of the Mass 143

Berakah — Thanksgiving — Eucharist.......................... 145

Parallels between Passover and Eucharist 147

Development of the Christian Eucharist 148

Lost Symbolism of the Eucharist............................. 150

Recapturing Personal Meaning in the Eucharist 152

The Eucharist as an Extension of Jesus' Incarnation and
Resurrection 155

9. SACRAMENT OF PENANCE FOR ADULTS........................ 158

Place of the Sacrament of Penance in Worldview.................. 158

10. OPENNESS TO THE HOLY SPIRIT 164

Place of Baptism and Confirmation in Worldview.................. 164

Awakening our Sleeping Giant 164

Activating the Graces of Confirmation 167

The Role of the Holy Spirit in God's Plan 167

11. LITTLE WAY OF SPIRITUAL CHILDHOOD..................... 170

Worldview of the Saints 170

The Little Way... 172

Consequences of Littleness..................................... 173

Simplicity and Authenticity.................................... 175

Unlimited Confidence in God.................................... 176

Immense Desires.. 178

12. LAW OF POLARITY: BALANCE OF OPPOSITES................ 181

Need of Balance in Worldview 181

Balance Among the Three Commandments of Love............... 183

Balance Between the Awesome and the Fascinating
Aspects of God.. 186

Balance Between Nature and Grace 188

Balance Between This Life and Life After Death.................... 190

Balance Between Self-Development and Renunciation........... 193

Balance Between Fulfillment and Diminishment.................... 196

Balance Between Spiritual Childhood and Spiritual Maturity . 197

Balance Between Consciousness and the Unconscious 199
Balance Between Femininity and Masculinity 199
Balance Between Perceiving and Judging Functions 200
Balance Between Action and Contemplation 201
Balance Between Change and Status Quo 202
Balance Between Counsel and Fortitude 204
Balance Between Freedom and Submission 204
Balance Between Meekness and Mercy 206

13. SEVEN TRUTHS LEADING TO LIFE **208**
Necessary Aspects of our Worldview 208
All is One 208
Honor One Another 209
Honor Oneself 210
Love is a Divine Power 211
Surrender Personal Will to Divine Will 211
Seek Only the Truth 212
Live in the Present Moment 214
Conclusion 215

14. DREAMS AND THEIR SIGNIFICANCE **217**
A Way to Discern God's Will in our Worldview 217
Understanding the Language of Dreams 219
Putting Dreams in Their Proper Perspective 221
Subjective Interpretation of Dreams 222
Dialoguing With Dream Characters 224
Dialoguing with Animals and Nightmare Characters 226
The Meaning of Different Images in Dreams 229
Objective Interpretation of Dreams 231
Completing Unfinished Dreams 233
Using Commonsense in Interpreting Our Dreams 234

15. HEALING MINISTRY **237**
Correcting Our Worldview When It Goes Astray 237
Four Methods of Healing 238
Areas that May Need Healing 240
Healing of Memories 241
Healing the Family Tree 243
Agnes Sanford's Prayer for Healing of Memories 244
The Wounded Healer 245
Ministering to Dysfunctional Families 247

    Examples of Dysfunctionalism.. 248

16. JOURNEY OF FAITH..**250**

    Carrying Out God's Plan for Us and the Whole Human Race.. 250
    The Uniqueness of Our Call.. 253
    Desert Journey... 254

17. WHERE TO BEGIN? **257**

    Faith... 258
    Hope 259
    Charity 260
    Prayer 261
    Almsgiving 262
    Fasting 263
    Holiness 265

APPENDIX A: PERSONAL GROWTH PLAN **266**

BIBLIOGRAPHY..**268**

INDEX **272**

INTRODUCTION

This book is a follow-up volume to *A Guide Book for Spiritual Direction and Adult Religious Education*. It covers a portion of the material used in the two-year training course of the Spiritual Direction Institute (SDI). This book discusses the different aspects of a Christian worldview applicable to the times in which we live today. Any valid worldview must attempt to discern God's plan for the human race as well as God's plan for each of us. We believe that our all-wise God has a definite plan and purpose for each of us. It is our task to discern our God-appointed plan each day, each year of our life. One of the best ways to discern God's plan is to use a daily Personal Growth Plan. We suggest such a plan in Appendix A. The final chapter of this book offers some suggestions of where to begin to carry out our God-appointed destiny on earth.

The first chapter discusses the all-importance of discerning our worldview, our way of looking at all reality. This includes our way of looking at God, as well as the whole of God's creation. Chapter four looks at the worldview of Jesus as seen in the eight Beatitudes. Chapter five discusses the worldview of Jesus as seen from the viewpoint of Christ's mission on earth and of the mission of Christ's church. Chapters two and three suggest the needed changes in our worldview as a result of the events of September 11, 2001.

Other chapters discuss the place of the Bible and the Sacraments in any authentic worldview. We also look at the worldview of the saints as seen in the life of one saint, St. Therese of Lisieux. Other chapters discuss the need of balance in our worldview, the necessary aspects of a valid worldview and the way dreams can help us discern a worldview in accord with God's will. A chapter on Healing Ministry suggests some of the ways to heal a worldview that has gone astray. All of us have a tendency to wander away from God's destiny for us.

In chapter sixteen we suggest the use of the six Cs to help us on our journey of faith in carrying out God's plan and destiny for us as individuals as well as for the whole human race. The six Cs are Call – Conversion – Covenant – Celebration – Consolation – Commission. We need to repeat these six steps again and again as we climb the spiral staircase leading to an eternal union of love with God. The daily Personal Growth Plan keeps us on the right track leading to God.

The final chapter suggests that we begin each day with an increase of faith, hope and charity. By our practice during the day of prayer, almsgiving and fasting we will fulfill our God-appointed destiny and carry out God's plan for us and for the whole of God's creation.

God is constantly calling us to a closer union of love. God's plan for the human race is to expand the family circle of heaven to include all of us and the whole of creation. Our journey of faith is to identify God's plan and destiny for us, and then to follow it as best we can. The fulfillment of this divine plan is what Jesus calls the Kingdom of God.

God loves us unconditionally and exceedingly. We can say that God is head over heels in love with each one of us. God wants to share with us all the treasures and benefits which the three Persons of the Holy Trinity share. A Christian worldview accepts this plan of God, and acts accordingly. Faith uses our power and freedom of choice to accept God's plan and God's love, and to make a return of unconditional love to God. Trust in God is to feel secure in the midst of all the uncertainties of life because we are safe in the arms of God. Charity is our response of love to God's love.

Another way of considering love is the three religious practices of prayer, almsgiving and fasting. Prayer contributes to our intimacy with and love of God. Almsgiving is an example of our love and ministry to other human beings. Fasting deals with the need of a loving self-discipline regarding ourselves.

A final way of considering love is to think of it as referring to the four relationships with God, neighbor, self and the whole of creation. In each of these areas we are called and challenged by God our Creator to practice unconditional love. This means that we consistently put the legitimate needs of others above our own selfish desires.

CHAPTER 1

WORLDVIEW

[handwritten: Refer to P. 120-121]

*[handwritten: * - taken on faith]*

Worldview refers to those unproven and unprovable assumptions one makes regarding all reality, but especially ultimate reality. Ordinary human reason proves one statement to be true by asserting another more basic statement. This more basic statement is then proven correct by a still more basic statement. This process of human reasoning has to stop somewhere. The final statement is accepted as true on blind faith. We satisfy our consciences by stating that the truth of this final statement is self-evident. What we mean by this is that we are ready to accept the truth and validity of this final statement on blind faith without having to prove it. These assumptions of truth, which we accept on faith without further proof, constitute our total worldview.

Different people have different worldviews, depending upon which statements regarding truth and reality they consider to be self-evident, and therefore not needing any further proof. In the past there have been long periods of human history when the overwhelming majority of educated people of that period had the same worldview. In other words, most of one's neighbors accepted as true the same set of self-evident statements. As a result, people were able to live at peace with their worldview without feeling the need of further proof of these so-called "self-evident" truths.

Today the situation is quite different. There is a variety of worldviews from which each of us must choose one that seems most in accord with truth and reality. For the past hundred years or more learned persons have been engaged in "demythologizing" many or most of the "self-evident" truths accepted by people of the past. They recognize these "truths" as human assumptions taken on blind faith.

4

Therefore, they have felt free to disregard these old worldviews and construct new worldviews. To emphasize the tentative value of these new worldviews, they label them as "theories." *uncertain*

Everyone has a worldview but most people are unaware of the tentative nature of their worldview. Almost everyone has certain authorities whom they trust and whose word they accept as truthful and in accord with reality. The tragedy is that the authorities most people today accept as trustworthy are anything but trustworthy. The prime example of this is the blind acceptance by most Americans of the ultimate value of the three "Ps" of Power, Possessions and Pleasure. These three "Ps" are creations of God and are limited goods but not absolute goods. When we make them absolute values we turn them into idols and we become idol worshipers. Yet this is the secular worldview of most Americans and the Western world. In order to save the human race from collapse it is necessary that our thinking processes be scrutinized and changed.

The previous statement is a very strong assertion. There is a real danger of the collapse of our modern world if we persist in following our secular worldview. Power, Possessions and Pleasure are not absolute values. We are guilty of worshiping a false god when we make these three limited goods into absolute goods. We are no longer living the truth. We are living a falsehood. Just as all the civilizations and societies of the past collapsed when they persisted in worshiping a falsehood, we can expect the same fate if we persist in following the prevailing worldview.

A New Worldview

What are the chances of our changing our present secular worldview into one more in accord with the truth? In my opinion there is a fifty-fifty chance that we will succeed. It is the same chance that Jesus took when he attempted to convert the wrong worldview of the religious authorities of his time. He did not completely succeed, but he began the

Christian movement which for two thousand years has slowly converted countless millions of people to a new worldview. We have the assurance of the Risen Christ that we will never be alone, that He will always be with us to help us bring about the conversion of the human race to a valid worldview. Jesus states this promise in the final verse of Matthew's Gospel, "All power in heaven and on earth has been given to me. Go, therefore, and make disciples of all nations,…teaching them to observe all that I have commanded you. And behold, I am with you always until the end of time."

Great movements begin with a single person. Mother Teresa began her world-wide movement by leaving her religious community and going alone to live with the poor. Her example encouraged some of her former students to join her, and thus began the Missionaries of Charity. Gandhi and Martin Luther King, Jr. began two movements that changed the face of history in India and the United States. Pope John XXIII began, almost alone, the reform movement in the Church that became the Second Vatican Council.

It is foolish to think that we can bring about a change in the worldview of others by our human efforts alone. We need only to remind ourselves that all power in heaven has been given to Jesus Christ and that he has promised never to abandon us. Having that assurance, let us call on God to bless our efforts, to expand the borders and territory of our ministry to include all those who have adopted a secular worldview. We go forward with the assurance that the powerful hand of God will always be with us to help us and protect us from evil. We pray that in our efforts we will not cause unnecessary pain to anyone.

Before we can hope to change the worldview of others, we need first of all to take a good, hard look at our own present worldview. Living as we do, among so many people who have adopted a secular worldview, it is to be expected that we will be somewhat contaminated by this false worldview. Are we guilty of making Power, Possessions and Pleasure into absolute goods, and thus guilty of idolatry? Let us use the antidotes of Prayer, Almsgiving and Fasting in order to heal ourselves of the disease of the secular worldview.

There is a variety of worldviews that have been adopted by sincere Christians during the past two thousand years. Some of them have much value in helping us to adopt a worldview that meets the needs of the world today. Others need to be rejected as going in the wrong direction from the Kingdom of God, as taught by Jesus in the Gospels. We must study closely all the teachings of Jesus regarding the Kingdom of God. We need to study the insights of wise men and women of past ages and of the present to discern the proper worldview for our times. Let us be open to changes in our present worldview which will respond to the needs of our time. For example, what is the proper Christian attitude towards nuclear energy and nuclear war? Jesus in the Gospels says nothing about nuclear power since it did not then exist.

One by one we need to study each of the worldviews proposed by people of the past and of the present. We accept those elements which seem to be in accord with truth and reject those that are not, as we are able to discern them. Ultimately our worldview will require us to accept certain assumptions about truth and reality on blind faith. We call this "*remythologizing.*" We no longer call these new assumptions "self-evident" but simply theories of what seems, at present, to be the closest to truth and reality as we are able to comprehend. Having constructed our "new" personal worldview, we then base our life upon it until a new theory is discovered that seems to be more in accord with truth and reality. Humility and truth require us always to be open to new insights into truth that will lead us to update our present worldview.

How Worldviews are Born

In order to live on earth we must make decisions each day. As rational, thinking beings, these decisions should be based on a solid foundation of truth. For most of us and in most instances, this will be true in accordance with actuality as far as our conscience and common sense can determine. However, all of the decisions of life are based ultimately on certain assumptions that we take on faith. When we get to the rock bottom choices, we invariably will discover that there will always be at least several different options. No matter which direction we choose to go, there will always be some uncertainty and some unproven and unprovable premises. Absolute, uncontestable proof or truth is impossible here on earth with our present limited knowledge, yet we must stop somewhere and make an act of blind faith in the truth or value of a particular option. For example, believing in the existence of God and believing that life goes on after death are both acts of blind faith on our part as Christians. We have some indication of the truth of both of these statements, but no absolute proof. This then becomes the assumption on which we base our whole philosophy of life and out of which we make our decisions and conduct our life. Therefore, our philosophy of life is actually based on a series of unproved and unprovable assumptions. These assumptions constitute the particular worldview of life to which we adhere.

Most people never take the time or perhaps do not have the intellectual curiosity or capability to think through their attitudes toward life until they come to the ultimate unproven assumption or option on which they base their personal philosophy of life. Instead they simply go along with the society or culture in which they live, and adopt the prevailing worldview. If the worldview of the culture in with they live has not changed for generations and is not questioned by others, most people never even refer to the foundation upon which they have based their life and decisions. However, the situation changes when a culture or civilization is in the process of changing to a new way of life. Then many thinking people begin to question the assumptions that they take on faith and upon which their view of life is based. Today we live in just such a time of upheaval, when the ideas and attitudes of the previous several centuries are being superseded and are no longer acceptable to large segments of the population. People everywhere are beginning to question those suppositions upon which, without previously realizing it, they have based the decisions governing their life. They are taking a long, hard look at the other options which they might choose and which could change their whole worldview. Ultimately, as we have said, our life is based on a certain blind faith, a leap of belief whereby we choose to accept one particular assumption over others as trustworthy. What then are the unprovable assumptions upon which today's prevailing worldview is based? Are these the options that we want to choose?

A Secular Worldview

The prevailing worldview of our present Western society is very secular and temporal. The visible, physical world is assumed to be the most important concern of our life. In fact, the present physical world is the only concern of the majority of Americans. Seldom do they seriously advert to a possible life beyond this world. They may not openly and deliberately deny the possibility of life beyond death, but simply ignore it. Getting ahead here on earth is the prevailing determinant upon which they base their life. This is called "*secular humanism*" or simply "a secular worldview." It is based on the assumptions that material goods and physical pleasure are the highest possible goals for human beings and that the physical sciences are the only way of attaining certitude.

Countless Americans do believe in a life after death and base many of their major decisions on faith in eternity. But the prevailing atmosphere in which we, in America, live today is secular; this mundane view of life influences the decisions we make, much more than we are aware. In fact, because it has been the prevailing worldview since the French Revolution, we are constantly and daily being influenced by it without our realizing it.

In the course of an average week, how much time and energy do we give to the concerns of this present, physical, materialistic world as compared to the time and energy given to the concerns of the spiritual world, of God, of prayer? Would it not be fair to say that at least nine-tenths of our waking hours is given to the things of the secular world? How many people actually tithe their time and give one-tenth of every day to the concerns of the spiritual world? Is not the prevailing atmosphere in which we live based on the unconscious assumption that this present world and its problems and benefits are what really matter? And so, without any qualms of conscience, we give almost all of our time, energy and attention to the pursuit of materialistic, earthly goals.

The History and Origin OF Today's Secular Worldview

Since the Renaissance and the Industrial Revolution, Western society has been affected by a secular worldview. This was a reaction to the medieval worldview which put an exaggerated emphasis on spiritual values to the neglect of the physical world. When one aspect of reality is over-emphasized, compensation occurs by the emergence of an opposite extreme. Conveniently, the people of the Renaissance Period found a whole philosophical system ready at hand to justify the new secular worldview. The philosophy of Aristotle, introduced into the West by Arabian philosophers and adopted by St. Thomas Aquinas and the Scholastics, insisted that all knowledge came through the senses, and through reasoning based on sense experiences. This amounted to a virtual denial of the experience of the inner world of the spirit. Justification was found for the secular worldview which placed almost exclusive emphasis upon the physical world, and denied the value of the inner world of the spirit. A climax to this emphasis on reason and the physical world was reached when the Goddess of Reason was crowned on the high altar

* 14 - 19ᵗʰ Century - transition from medieval to modern world.

** Began about 1760 in England - Replace hand tools with power driven tools.

10

of Notre Dame Cathedral in Paris during the French Revolution.

For the past two centuries secular values have been given precedence over spiritual values. The Christian churches continued to preach the priority of spiritual values over material values, but those who took the teachings of the Christian Gospel seriously, and lived a life in accord with the values of Jesus Christ, became more and more a minority of Christians. Throughout this period of Rationalism and Materialism, there have been counter-cultures among different minorities of citizens who have insisted on the priority of spiritual and religious values. The generally accepted worldview, however, was that the material and temporal world was where the action was, and what really mattered. This was the unconscious assumption accepted by most people even though many of them continued to be Sunday church-goers. During the week, the majority of their decisions were based on the unconscious assumptions of an exclusively secular worldview. Religious people found themselves torn between two loyalties: to the immediate, secular world and to the teachings of Jesus and the Gospels. Sometimes, they chose to follow the Christian worldview, but more often than not, the secular worldview was the winner of their affections.

As a result of the priority given to the material over the spiritual world, most research and progress during the past several centuries has been in the physical sciences and in the ever deeper and broader enmeshment in the material world. We have to think only of today's high state of technology in electronics, nuclear physics, astronomy, etc., as compared to the progress of religion and the interior life in order to see how far physical science has outstripped metaphysical inquiry. This has brought us to a very dangerous impasse. We presently have at our disposal virtually unlimited physical power in nuclear energy, but we lack the spiritual qualities and strength to know how to handle properly these powers. The problems of ecology, of the environment, of proper use of nuclear energy are a

[handwritten margin note:] being to speak in my real spiritual dialect of meeting.

[handwritten note at bottom:] concerned ε abstract thoughts or subjects such as existence, causality, or truth.

11

direct result of the secular worldview which Western society has advocated for the past several centuries.

During the past forty years or so there has been a gradual disillusionment with this secularist worldview. Nevertheless, it still has a profound influence on the majority of people in Europe, Japan and North America, even when they outwardly profess to acknowledge a spiritual dimension to reality. We keep looking at the world with the rose-colored glasses of this-worldly values. Today most people perceive their life and their world through the spectacles of materialism and rationalism. These faulty assumptions are especially dangerous since they operate unconsciously. Most people pay little attention, and don't realize that they are operating out of certain unproved and unprovable assumptions.

Changing our Worldview

We must be careful not to condemn the secularist view as a wholly unworthy one. To do so would make us fall back into the same mistake as our medieval ancestors. Modern secularism is the final stage of several centuries-long reaction against the one-sidedness of medieval Christendom which exalted spiritual values at the expense of the values of this world. Today we are experiencing a revolution against the secularist worldview which could be as decisive and world-shaking as the Renaissance and the Industrial Revolution which brought an end to the Middle Ages. We need to recognize that we live in two worlds: the physical and spiritual, the outer and inner, and establish a healthy, creative tension between the two polarities.

One of the great mistakes of this modern secularist era is the exaggerated confidence which modern man places in such a frail instrument as human reason. We can never make human reason an absolute standard for discerning truth. It simply cannot bear such a tremendous burden. Yet, this has been the blind and taken-for-granted faith of modern man. In actuality such confidence in human reason

WORLDVIEW *Something that a person cannot conquer; achieve, etc*

has brought about its own nemesis. Growing numbers have become disillusioned with science and technology, and with the wealth and comfort of our affluent society. People are hungry for the things of the spirit. We realize afresh the truth of St. Augustine's words: "Our hearts were made for Thee, O God, and they shall not rest until they rest in Thee."

A worldview does not change automatically, nor does change occur simultaneously in a whole society, nation, or civilization. A change in worldview begins with individuals who, one by one, become convinced of discrepancies in the assumptions upon which their present or previous attitudes were based. Alert persons begin to study all the possible options available for developing their own theory about the welfare of the world. Each of these options must be carefully *selected* investigated in order to arrive at the best possible choice of the available ideas. Now these assumptions should be carefully considered and culled, allowing one to choose those options that present the best available evidence of being true. These ultimate foundations for our worldview are called "assumptions" because they are based on faith and cannot ever be absolutely proved. Ultimately we have to stop somewhere, and the place we stop requires an act of faith in the trustworthiness of the assumptions we accept. We must then try to keep an open mind to new evidence that might arise or be suggested to us. Should new evidence convince us of a better way of viewing reality, we must be ready and willing to change our worldview.

The Importance of Each Individual

During a very uncertain era of history, like the present one, when we are unable to cope with the problems presented by adherence to our old materialistic, scientific, rationalistic worldview, it is almost impossible to exaggerate the important role each individual plays in determining the future direction of the world. Whichever direction the world and society goes will be determined by a comparatively small number of people who present some very clear and strongly convincing statements about a new worldview.

These persons will be the leaders who take present and future generations in one particular direction rather than another. Those who have the strongest convictions and the most convincing arguments will decide the future course of society and the world. They will create for us our new worldview.

Not a single person among us should ever say that he or she is unimportant in this present time of upheaval during the demise of the old and the birth of a new worldview. A person with strong convictions, even if uneducated, can have a tremendous influence. It is a sociological fact that most people are very insecure and uncertain in their faith and beliefs and that most people are strongly influenced by the thinking and convictions of the people among whom they live. Therefore, one person with strong and vociferous views can lead a whole community or even a whole nation in either a good or an evil direction. The proof of this is the influence that one man, Adolph Hitler, had over a whole nation for an entire generation. The same is true for Gandhi and Martin Luther King, Jr., both of whom influenced and changed the course of history in their respective countries of India and the United States.

What then is the course of action for us as individuals or as small groups of like-minded persons? As mentioned earlier, the first step is to study our present secular worldview in order to discover the flaws and good points in the assumptions upon which this view of life is based. The second step is to study all the possible indicators that might lead to a different worldview. We should look carefully at all the reasons for and against each of them. Ultimately, we will have to choose and make a leap of faith, at least tentatively for the time being, by embracing one particular option or assumption. Every available source of knowledge should be used. This includes not only our own intelligence and common sense but the combined intelligence of sincere, seeking, honest persons expressed in vocal debate or in the written word. We must never neglect to seek help from God through prayer. Whatever our final decision, it will always involve a risk, a blind leap of faith; but that is the basic condition in which we live; and it is unrealistic to expect anything else. All of life is based on faith, hope, and trust. All of life is ultimately humanly insecure.

What is Wrong with our Modern Secular Worldview?

That an abundance of material goods and pleasures can fully satisfy the human heart is one faulty assumption of the secular worldview. By ignoring the inner world of the spirit and giving God and religion a very obscure place in the schema of priorities and values, modern secularism has made a greater mistake than did the medieval world with its over-emphasis on the spiritual. Furthermore, by exaggerating the ability of human reason to attain truth, modern science has denied the value of personal, spiritual experience. This has resulted in an over-emphasis on the head and intellect, and a neglect or denial of the heart and personal values. In actuality, modern capitalistic societies and communist governments have the same secular worldview, with one exception. Communist society denies the value and freedom of the individual citizen, while capitalistic countries still emphasize the value and freedom of individual citizens. It is true that many capitalistic countries give certain lip service to God, religion and even Christianity. However, this has gradually become less and less until now we are experiencing attempts to eliminate all forms of religion from public life by relegating religion to the private, personal sphere alone.

The limitedness of the secular worldview can be shown by taking a look at the results of several centuries of following the secular way of life. The nuclear arms race was a direct result of adopting this worldview. Today in America much more faith is put in the nuclear bomb to protect us from our enemies than is put in God and His Divine Providence. This is reaching the ultimate of actual idolatry of something material, namely, nuclear armament. Some people will object to the use of the word "idolatry" to express our dependence on nuclear deterrence for bringing peace to the world. However, an idol is that which we worship because we place our ultimate faith and trust in it. Have we not placed this confidence in our nuclear stockpile? To assert that the majority of Americans today put more faith and trust in God, prayer and religion than they do in the nuclear build-up would be the height of foolishness and falsehood. The nuclear bomb is a god that we worship and upon which we depend for our security. If you do not believe that, take a look at how much of our hard-earned money is spent on the military.

Today's blind alleys of escape into drugs and alcohol, the reckless cults of sexual excesses, the mounting suicide rate, the various attempts to become lost in fantasy and oblivion are all results of the adoption of a purely secular view of life. The ecological crisis, the rape of our natural resources and the breakdown of our environment are other dead ends into which a secular worldview has led us. The difference between the standard of living of those who possess power as compared with 90% or more of the world's population of the poor, powerless, and oppressed becomes greater with each passing year. This in turn gives rise to violence, revolution, terrorism, and war. The world situation has become more and more desperate each year. Today's terrorist attacks are the ultimate threat to our American way of life.

Ultimate Reality (7)

Before choosing which worldview to follow we need to make a decision regarding ultimate reality. In today's world there are at least six different options regarding ultimate reality. In almost every community we will find sincere, intelligent persons adhering to each of these options. Whichever option one chooses regarding ultimate reality will influence the particular worldview one accepts.

Carl Sagan

① The first option regarding ultimate reality might be called the *"nameless void."* Those who choose this option would be atheists who experience total despair regarding the future of the world and the human race. For them there is no life after death, just a nameless void. The second option is that of agnostics who admit that ultimate reality is some sort of ②*impersonal force.* They may even claim to believe in God but deny God as a person. They simply recognize that ultimate reality is some sort of a nameless, impersonal force or energy. *Stephen Hawkins*

The third option is quite popular among many people *do not* today. It is the claim that the ③*physical universe* with its *believe* billions of galaxies is ultimate reality. Materialists, *in a* Communists, Marxists and a host of other educated persons *soul* today choose this option. It is probably the most popular option among the faculties and teachers of our secular colleges. This results in many of their students adopting this option. This explains why so many college students stop believing in God. *(Seeing is believing)*

The fourth option is also popular in all of our secular colleges and universities. It is that the *human race* is ultimate reality. These are the secular humanists who make a god out of the three "Ps" of Power, Possessions, and Pleasure. This is the religion of the majority of people in this country and in the Western World. It is the religion behind the policies of most of our industrial system as well as the decisions of our government. People who choose this option may still profess to believe in God but the actions and decisions of their whole life show clearly that they have made the human race their ultimate reality. *Put may faith in nuclear deterrents that God* *secular humanist*

The fifth option is that of theists and all believers in a *personal God.* This would include the Christians who deny the divinity of Jesus as well as Jews, Muslims, Buddhists, Hindus, and other believers in a Supreme Being. The sixth option is that of *Christians who believe in the divinity of Jesus Christ.* They believe that God came down to earth in the person of Jesus Christ and took on a human nature. Among these Christian believers we can distinguish at least six different worldviews, all of them claiming to be Christian worldviews. The names I will give to these Christian worldviews are ① Deist, ② Apocalyptic, ③ Fundamentalist, ④ Ptolemaic, ⑤ Copernican and ⑥ Einsteinian. There are many sincere Christians who adhere to each of these worldviews. In my opinion the first four must be rejected because they are not in accord with the needs of our time. It is only the last two that seem worthy of adoption. In this chapter I will briefly describe each of these seven worldviews. In Chapter five, under the heading of "Mission of the Church," I will describe how the Ptolemaic, Copernican and Einsteinian worldviews affect our understanding of Church structures.

The Deist Worldview *(Thomas Jefferson)*

(i) (Deny miracles)

The Deist believes in a "clock-maker God" who creates the world and then leaves it entirely up to us to work out our salvation without any interference from God. According to this view, once God created the world, creatures have to carry on as best they can without any miraculous help from God. The Deist denies the presence of miracles in the physical, material world and attempts to explain away all miracles in the Gospels by suggesting some natural event occurred. For example, Louis Evely in his book *That Man is You* explains away the miraculous feeding of the five thousand by claiming that Jesus preached such a powerful sermon that everyone shared their food with others so that all had enough to eat. Rudolph Bultmann, the German biblical scholar, attempts to explain through natural causes all the miracles of the Gospels. Rabbi Kushner in *Why Do Bad Things Happen to Good People* adopts this position. Thomas Jefferson and many founding fathers of our country were Deists.

Does not believe in miracles.

For the past several centuries many physical scientists have followed the Deist position and attempted to explain all physical phenomena by purely natural causes. A great many Christians unconsciously adopt this Deist position and deny God the right to countermand the laws of nature. By so doing they have a difficult time explaining the Incarnation. It seems obvious that a true Christian who believes in the Gospels could never adopt the Deist position.

The Apocalyptic Worldview (Rapture)
(wiping out of the world)

Many sincere Christians have adopted an Apocalyptic worldview. This is understandable in view of the presence of so much violence and evil in today's society. The Apocalyptic position is that the present situation of the human race is so evil that God will once again be forced to destroy most of the human race just as in the time of Noah. A few faithful persons will be saved to build a new human race after the world-wide chastisement and destruction. This was the worldview of the first generation of Christians. We can see this reflected in several chapters of the Gospels: Matthew 24, Mark 13, Luke 21 and in the following books of the New Testament: II Thessalonians, II Peter, Jude and Revelation. Several of the prophetic books of the Old Testament had this apocalyptic worldview: Daniel, Habakkuk, Joel, Zephaniah, and Zachariah.

Read

This has been the worldview of groups of Christians throughout the past two thousand years. It was how the Jehovah's Witnesses and Seventh Day Adventists originated. As we begin the third millennium many modern day Christians are adopting this worldview. They could possibly be right despite the fact that all previous Apocalyptists were mistaken about the imminent end of the world and the second coming of Christ. I choose to believe in a new intervention of God's grace which will lead us to a higher level of faith. I think the second coming of Christ is still in the far future. Very prevalent today

Fundamentalist Worldview (Baptist Church)

Countless sincere modern-day Christians adhere to a Fundamentalist worldview. They insist on a strict literal interpretation of all the words of the Bible. They refuse to accept a symbolic meaning of biblical words. The creationist

(Read: Fr. Raymond Brown)

Christians maintain that the Garden of Eden actually existed just 6000 years ago and the world was created in just six 24-hour days. They believe Noah's flood occurred just 3,000 years before the birth of Christ and that it literally covered the whole earth, even the highest mountains. This literal, fundamentalist interpretation of the Bible was followed by the authorities of the Roman Catholic Church until Pope Pius XII issued his encyclical, *Divino Afflante Spiritu* on September 10, 1943. Until that date Catholic biblical scholars attempted to explain all the texts of the Bible in a literal way.

(1979)

John Paul II

adapted

Today many Catholics, along with a great many Protestants, adhere to a fundamentalist worldview. It is no longer the official view of the Catholic Church or Catholic biblical scholars. However, the new Catholic Catechism does follow this literal interpretation of the first books of Genesis. The present position of the Church is that there are many forms of literature in the Bible, including fiction. Stories like Jonah in the belly of the whale and the book of Job were invented to teach a moral lesson.

Ptolemaic Worldview *(Greek / Arabic)*

In second century, A.D., the Egyptian astronomer, Claudius Ptolemy, developed a theory of astronomy to explain the apparent movement of the sun, moon and stars around the earth. The earth was seen as a stationary globe, the center of the universe. This Ptolemaic worldview was adopted by the whole Western world until 1543 when Copernicus and Galileo proved it to be false. However, the Christian Church continued to adhere to the Ptolemaic worldview since this was the worldview of the Bible. The Church condemned Galileo as a heretic and forced him to recant. In Chapter five we will see how this Ptolemaic worldview influenced the structures and teachings of the Church. We still see this influence in the new Catholic Catechism issued in 1994.

God (Human beings are the center of the universe)

Pope

Bishops — *the earth* *Pray obey* *vertical / pyramid*

clergy

laity

Horizontal view [handwritten]

Vatican adopted [handwritten]

- Copernican Worldview (Heliocentric) [handwritten annotation]

The divorce between the Church and the natural sciences continued for four hundred years until the Second Vatican Council. The Council attempted to bring about the needed changes in Church teaching and structures to fit the Copernican worldview. In Chapter five we will see the results of this new worldview on the structures and theology of the Church. "The institutions, laws, and modes of thinking as handed down from previous generations do not always seem to be well adapted to the contemporary state of affairs" (*The Church in Modern World*, article 7).

Co-relational [handwritten]   *(Evolutionary World view)* [handwritten]

- Einsteinian Worldview
the end [handwritten]

One document of the Council went beyond the Copernican worldview and adopted the worldview of Albert Einstein. Schema 13, *The Church in the Modern World*, suggests a universe of ever evolving relationships instead of static, unchangeable substances. Instead of the expanding universe of the Copernican worldview it advocates a converging universe leading to an Omega point of union in the universal, cosmic Christ. Thus we have a co-relational dimension along with the three dimensions of past, present and future. The real absolutes are transcendental aspects of God: love, truth, justice, unity, beauty. The only sin is the failure to love. In Chapter five we will show how this new worldview affects Church teachings and structures.

How everything are one another related [handwritten margin note]

400 yrs from in the process of change + becoming Jewish to world view 50 to 451 Israel world view [handwritten]

Developing A Christian Worldview

It is quite possible that a fully authentic Christian worldview will contain elements of truth from a variety of worldviews. It is the task of every Christian to study all options and understand and adopt the truth that might be present in each worldview. In adopting a Christian worldview, we must be careful not to make the same mistake as the medieval Christians. We must give the physical, material world its just dues, for it does have

21

considerable value. Both the Old and New Testaments emphasize the importance of this present world. As long as we are on earth, we must work out our eternal salvation through a ministry to the needs of the human race. Jesus Christ, the Incarnation of God on earth, is our model.

In choosing a Christian worldview, we must also be careful to take into proper consideration today's situation as compared with the world conditions in the time of Jesus or in any previous period of world history. Two thousand years ago Jesus of Nazareth did not have to contend with a nuclear bomb threat, nor with a serious ecological crisis, nor with a population crisis. Therefore, the worldview expressed by Jesus and the early Christians will be somewhat different from ours today. However, there is much we can learn from the worldview of Jesus as seen in the Gospels and as understood and followed by the first generations of Christians. By comparing a worldview of the Gospels with the modern secular worldview, we can determine the suitable assumptions to replace modern rationalism and secularism.

One of the very first assumptions that we need to make to adopt a Christian worldview is that a simpler lifestyle is indicated. The first Beatitude expresses this succinctly: "Blessed are the poor in spirit, for theirs is the Kingdom of God." In no way did Jesus deny the value of material goods and physical pleasures. He seemed completely at home at the marriage feast at Cana and apparently never turned down an invitation to dinner. In fact, his enemies accused him of being a wine bibber and glutton. Nevertheless, he insisted on the primacy of the spiritual and the values of the inner spirit. He insisted on justice, charity, mercy, forgiveness, meekness and love, and gave them precedence over material wealth or physical pleasure. He made use of the goods of this world insofar as they were needed to live decently on earth; but he insisted that we not make a "god" out of money or mammon. This was the simple lifestyle that Jesus both practiced and preached. Any authentic Christian worldview must help us to do the same.

22

A Christian worldview is God-centered rather than ego-centered. There will be a detachment from both worldly power and material wealth. There will be a dependence upon the power and presence of God to bring about a change of attitude in self and in others. The power of God is available not only for the practice of the love of God but also for the practice of loving service to one's fellow human beings. It will not be a self-righteous goodness that looks down with disdain on those who are less fortunate than oneself but will show great love and mercy towards those caught by the powers of evil, poverty and oppression. In a Christian worldview the love of neighbor will be so heroic and unselfish that it will include the willingness to lay down one's life for the sake of another human being. It is the way of non-violence and at the same time a bold confrontation of evil by truth, even though it may result in persecution and death to self. The Christian attitude is not a mealy-mouthed, "Uriah Heep" type of humility and meekness; rather it is strong, courageous, self-sacrificing and a bold proclamation of truth, justice, charity, mercy and love. It will be a balanced union of the physical and spiritual, of bread and word. It will possess the healing power of God to release those held captive by evil powers. It will proclaim a release from the slavery to this present material, physical world. It will constantly hold out hope for better things to come.

Jesus summed up his own worldview in the phrase, "Kingdom of God." He insisted that his purpose for coming on earth, his destiny, was to begin the establishment of this God-centered Kingdom on earth. He said that anyone who wished to be his follower must also make this his or her primary goal in life. To bring about the Kingdom of God, Jesus said that both he himself and his disciples must be ready and willing to take up their cross each day. By "cross," Jesus was referring to the symbol of crucifixion, which would inevitably be the lot of those who opposed the prevailing worldview of the time. In other words, anyone who chose the worldview of Jesus could expect suffering, opposition, persecution—perhaps even death itself—from those who resisted giving up their old worldview to adopt the Christian worldview. Actually, when we study the worldview of the Sadducees and Pharisees living in the time of Jesus, we discover that, basically, their worldview was the same as the modern secular worldview. They also ignored the inner world of the spirit and put all their eggs in one basket of the goods of this present physical world: worldly power, material goods, money and worldly prestige.

carrying 2 pails of water - polarity / balance

✕ *An Aquarian Worldview for Today's World*

The situation in today's world is somewhat different from that two thousand years ago in Palestine or in the Roman-Greek Mediterranean world of early Christianity. In the time of Jesus there was no clear understanding of virtue and goodness. Therefore, it was necessary to emphasize the "light" at the expense of "darkness." For perhaps the first thousand years of Christianity, or even for all of these years since the time of Christ, this emphasis on goodness, light, virtue and truth was indeed necessary. It was the only way to isolate "goodness" so that it could be fully recognized for what it really was. However, the result of this emphasis on light, truth, goodness and virtue was that darkness, untruth, evil and sin were repressed, driven underground and even denied. Such an imbalance with over-emphasis on one side and repression of the other side will sooner or later result in what Carl G. Jung called "*enantiodromia*," where we find ourselves going to the opposite extreme. That seems to be the situation in the world today where darkness and evil are emphasized to the neglect of light and truth.

Many modern thinkers are saying that we are now in the process of entering a new age of the world, an Age of Aquarius, the Water-carrier. The water-carrier is usually pictured as carrying two pails of water suspended from a board or rope across his shoulders. The symbolism is that of a balanced tension or polarity between two opposite realities. This would seem to be the challenge facing us today. We must find a way of carrying not only the burden of goodness but also the burden of our evil upon our shoulders. Rather than denying or repressing the presence of evil within our life and ourselves and projecting this evil on our enemies, we must take back our projections, recognize and accept ownership for the evil that belongs to us. It will be in the creative tension between our evil shadow and our professed virtue that we will find the energy to create a new age in the world. Therefore, the Aquarian worldview is somewhat different from the Christian worldview taught by Jesus and the writers of the New Testament. However, Jesus seems also to provide for such a balanced worldview. He told the Pharisees and Herodians, "Render to Caesar the things that are Caesar's and to God the things that are God's." (Mark 12:17)

It will be no easy task for us today to discern and apply this new balanced worldview. We can learn very much from a study of the Gospels and Epistles of the New Testament and from the lives of Christian saints; but it would be a mistake to adopt literally the same solution that Jesus and the saints of past centuries have found successful. We live in a world today different from that in which Jesus and the saints of earlier centuries lived. We must become creative in studying both the examples of the past and the situation of the present and then discern the best possible solution. Since Jung and his followers have been able to interpret many of the teachings of Jesus and Christianity in a language that is understandable to people today, Jungian depth psychology will be one of the great helps in discernment. A combination of Jungian depth psychology and the Christian Gospel is probably the easiest path to the discovery of a new, Aquarian worldview suitable to our times. Of course, there is room for any number of possible ways to combine new and old insights. As Jesus states in the Gospels: "Every scribe who is learned in the Kingdom of God is like the head of a household who can bring from his storeroom both the new and the old" (Matthew 13:52).

Where to Begin?

To develop a new, Christian, Aquarian worldview that is suitable to our time requires us to start somewhere. A starting point is all we dare suggest. The final scope of our endeavors remains to be worked out and will probably require the combined efforts of many people over several generations. But, at least, we can begin. A consideration of our own spiritual life with its weaknesses and strengths, and the habitual human practice of projection would seem to be an excellent place to begin. Every one of us, individually as well as nations, races and groups, fall victim to this habit of projection. So true is this that one of the best ways for us to discover our personal or national shadow is to take a look at those faults in other persons and nations which most upset us, and cause us to become disturbed emotionally.

Both the medieval and the modern secular worldviews made similar mistakes in emphasizing only one side of reality, while ignoring, neglecting and even denying the reality or value of the other side. A better worldview that will suit the new era in which we find ourselves would acknowledge a balance between opposite poles of truth. An important balance needed today is recognition of the balance between good and evil in each one of us as well as in every nation and every institution. In the past, many Christians have over-emphasized the presence of good and denied the evil in themselves. Others have gone to the opposite extreme and over-emphasized the presence of evil. An Aquarian worldview would seek to recognize and acknowledge the presence of both. This balance would be more in accord with truth and therefore be a more suitable worldview than either our modern secularism or the medieval Christian worldview.

Secondly, studying the projection of evil upon others is the quickest and probably the easiest and most authentic way to become conscious of the shadow side of our personality. This repressed shadow is not all evil but represents that vast potential for good within our inner being that is still undeveloped. Another psychological fact that Jung and others have discovered is that when we repress and neglect to use this potential for good, it has the tendency to join forces with whatever evil is lurking in our unconscious. Therefore, even the good values of our shadow become tainted through repression, and non-use or non-recognition.

So, where to begin to construct a Christian, Aquarian worldview? Begin with yourself. Take a good, long, hard look at those faults that most upset you in other individuals and other groups. With the help of a trusted friend or spiritual director, try to discern if and how these same faults are present unconsciously in your own life and conduct. Recognize the tendencies toward these faults in yourself. "There, but for the grace of God, go I." Accept ownership for these faults and evil tendencies. Then try to respond to this repressed, unconscious shadow of yours in two ways. (1) Stop being negative and critical of those faults in others. Develop a positive, merciful, forgiving, tolerant attitude toward them. (2) With the help of a friend or spiritual director, try to discern how you can transform and convert the energy of your own repressed faults into something good and productive, of benefit to others. This will take lots of wisdom, grace from God, strenuous efforts on one's own part and the assistance of others. But any progress made in these two areas will be a positive contribution toward establishing an authentic, Christian, Aquarian worldview for yourself and for those around you. Once we accept the reality of our evil side and keep a balanced tension between it and our good side, it no longer remains a destructive evil but becomes a creative source of energy for life, love, truth and mercy.

CHAPTER 2

SELF-PRESERVATION AND SURVIVAL

Worldview after September 11, 2001

There are a number of global issues facing the human race today which need to be addressed and resolved if we are to survive. The events of September 11, 2001, were a wake-up call not only for our country but for the whole human race. The danger is that most of us will not heed this wake-up call and will try to continue living the way we have been living in the past. There are at least ten global issues which we need to resolve if the human race is to survive and prosper. All of these ten issues are the direct result of our worship and idolatry of the three "Ps" of Power, Pleasure and Possessions. In order to survive we need to have a real metanoia, a turning away and conversion from the worship of our false idols, and a return to a worship and service of the true God.

The situation facing us today is similar in many ways to the state of the Roman Empire in the 4th and 5th centuries. They failed to heed their wake-up call and, as a result, the Roman Empire and Roman civilization collapsed in the Barbarian invasions. The same fate awaits us today unless we address and find a way to resolve the global issues facing us. These are the issues:

1. Threat of world-wide terrorism
2. Idolatry of mammon—worship of American way of life
3. Worship of power—all-powerful, security state
4. Worship of pleasure—"if it feels good, do it"
5. Fallen spiritual powers of our institutions and organizations

6. Nuclear proliferation—nuclear war, nuclear bombs
7. World hunger and destitution
8. Ecological pollution
9. Diminishing natural resources
10. Repression of our unconscious shadow

Threat of World-Wide Terrorism

In dealing with the terrorists we are dealing with a group of religious-oriented people who are convinced that our American and Western culture is a serious threat to God's Kingdom on earth. They see the destruction of this culture as greatly pleasing to God. They are so convinced of this that they are willing to die in defense of their religious beliefs. We call it religious fanaticism but it is the same sort of total dedication that we find in the Christian martyrs who rejoiced in sacrificing their lives in the Roman arena. The big difference is that Jesus taught non-violence while this fanatic Islam group approves of violence as a way to foster the spread of the worship of Allah.

The wake-up call of the events of September 11 is a call to us to change our ways, and repent of worship of the three "Ps" of Power, Pleasure and Possessions. Seeing that God allowed this to happen to us might awaken us to recognize our sins and bring about true repentance. "For those who love God, all things work together for good." Will most Americans miss this call to repentance? If history is any indicator, probably so. For those of us who do heed this call, it means a serious examination of our conscience to see where we are guilty of idolatry and worship of the false idols of Possessions, Power and Pleasure.

The likelihood is that the terrorists will continue their religious campaign to put an end to 'idolatrous' Western and American culture. Even as we succeeded in capturing and putting to death Osama bin Laden, it is likely that other terrorist leaders will rise up to take his place. The terrorists today may do for us what the Barbarian tribes did to bring an end to Roman civilization. The terrorists pose a real threat to our whole American way of life. Either we bring about a religious conversion of our idolatrous ways or the terrorists may be the spark that ignites a world-wide revolution against the nations of the First World.

Idolatry of our American Way of Life

Much of our American way of life is an example of the idolatry of mammon. We literally worship our high standard of living, and feel no guilt in constantly seeking to raise this material standard. Our American way of life also includes an exaggerated emphasis on freedom. We have taken something that is a limited good and made it into an absolute good. Thus we turn freedom into an idol which we worship and are prepared to go to war to protect. Freedom of choice in the area of abortion is an example of turning the limited good of freedom into an absolute good. There is only one absolute good and that is God. Any time we make something other than God into an absolute good we become guilty of idolatry.

How many Americans are ready and willing to forego their high standard of living to live a more simple lifestyle? How many Americans are willing to make an equal distribution of the goods of the earth among the billions of 'have-nots' in the Third World? We are willing to be generous to an extent, as long as it does not pinch our resources too much. Very few of us are willing to go the whole way and make the sacrifices necessary to have an equal distribution of the wealth and goods of the world. Therefore, for the most part, our country, at the present moment, is not ready to experience a conversion from our idolatry of mammon. We are where Jesus was during his public ministry when most of the people were unwilling to make the sacrifices needed to bring about the Kingdom of God on earth. How did Jesus respond to this lack of the peoples' response? He offered his life on the cross. This was the first step in the conversion of the human race to God. Two thousand years later, a few persons have taken the needed steps to practice unconditional love of God and our neighbors. Most of us are still waiting for some miracle of grace to bring about our conversion to God and love.

Worship of the All-Powerful, Security State

We Americans take delight in being the most powerful nation in the world. We worship this power so much that we are willing to go to war to keep our power. Almost half of the total national budget is spent on the military. Seldom does anyone in America question this attitude towards power. We fail to see how we repress our own evil shadow and project it upon other nations. Like money and possessions, we have made power into an absolute good and thus turned it into an idol whom we worship.

What kind of a conversion do we need to experience in order to divorce ourselves from this idolatrous worship of power? We need to change our list of priorities and take power and possessions off their pedestal, and replace them with God and love. We need to share our power with the powerless of the world. We need to listen to the cries of the oppressed throughout the world and find a way to give them more power. Power is good and necessary, just as freedom is good and necessary for a full life. However, power and freedom are not absolute goods. We are not allowed to do anything we choose with our freedom and power.

Worship of Pleasure

Our worship of pleasure is what the terrorists see as corrupting their own people, especially the youth. Pleasure has become an absolute good in much of our American culture. "If it feels good, do it." We reject any constraints upon our pursuit of pleasure. We see this especially in the breakdown of sexual morality. Almost all the old traditions about what is sinful in sexual matters have been rejected by most Americans. Drugs and alcohol are other examples of the worship of pleasure in our American culture. Our media glorifies pleasure.

What is the conversion needed to forego the worship of pleasure? We need to emphasize the value of self-discipline. Fasting is the traditional name given to the conversion of the god of pleasure. Fasting is more than sacrificing the pleasures of eating and drinking. It means bringing our will under the control of the will of God in the whole area of bodily pleasure. Pleasure is one of God's gifts to the human race. God wants us to have pleasure in our life. However, just as in the case of power and possessions, pleasure is a limited good. If it becomes one of our top priorities in life, we become guilty of idolatry. Through self-discipline we need to bring our pursuit of pleasure under control.

The Fallen Spiritual Powers of our Institutions and Organizations

Walter Wink, in his trilogy of books on the fallen spiritual powers, makes a good case of the need to engage and convert these spiritual powers of freedom, possessions and pleasure. They are present in our earthly institutions and organizations. They form the soul of these institutions. They were created good by God but, like the fallen angels, they are no longer in God's service. They have become a god onto themselves. They now work for their own glory rather than the glory of God. They need to be identified, unmasked and engaged in a loving, non-violent way. They need to be brought back to obedience in love of God.

There is a heavy price to pay to convert these fallen powers. It is the same price Jesus paid by his death at the hands of these same powers. These powers are extremely powerful and both openly and secretly control many of the decisions made by earthly institutions. They are actively at work in our churches as well as other earthly organizations. They have exerted this control for thousands of years and are most reluctant to lose control. They are prepared to kill and destroy any individual or group which threatens them.

Jesus recognized the hold these powers had over the religious institutions of his time. This recognition by Jesus may have occurred during his transfiguration on Mount Tabor. St. Luke's Gospel says that Moses and Elijah appeared to Jesus and spoke to him about his coming exodus in Jerusalem. This could well have been the moment in Jesus' life when he became fully convinced that he would have to sacrifice his life in order to begin the process of redeeming these fallen spiritual powers. When Peter objected to this kind of talk, Jesus not only reprimanded Peter and called him a devil, but insisted that his followers must also take up their cross and die.

The Christians of the first three centuries realized that in order to convert these spiritual powers of evil, they must be willing to suffer death. Unfortunately in the 4th century Constantine adopted the Christian Church and henceforth the Church became more and more a servant of the secular state. The Christian Church has never completely lost its vocation of martyrdom. Throughout these past 1700 years there has been a number of Christians who resisted the inroads of the fallen powers and have been willing to lay down their lives to redeem the fallen powers. Walter Wink makes an excellent case of the need to love these fallen powers and work to redeem them, not to destroy them. The resurrection of Jesus is our proof that one day we will succeed in redeeming and saving these same powers. However, this redemption will not be accomplished by violence but by non-violent, redeeming love. Gandhi in India, and Martin Luther King, Jr. in this country provide examples of how the power of non-violent, redeeming love triumphs over the fallen powers of freedom, possessions and pleasure.

The experience of September 11th shows us the extremes to which people will go who are under the guidance of these fallen, spiritual powers. Just as Caiphas and the Jewish Sanhedrin put to death Jesus in the name of their God, Yahweh, so the terrorists carried out their nefarious deeds in the name of their God, Allah. The right way to react and respond to these terrorists is not by more violence on our part. Violence begets more violence. We must respond the same way that Jesus responded to Caiphas and the Sanhedrin. We must be willing to lay down our lives in order to redeem and transform the evil powers that possess these terrorists. We need, of course, to do all that we can to protect ourselves from acts of terrorism. If we can apprehend the terrorists, we need to bring them to a court of justice. Then by unconditional love we need to seek to convert them to authentic love. However, Jesus was unsuccessful in converting Caiphas and the Sanhedrin. So we can expect many failures and few successes in this work of conversion by love. This is the way Jesus went and this is the way a true follower of Jesus must go.

Nuclear Proliferation

For over fifty years the whole human race has been living under the threat of a nuclear war, nuclear proliferation, nuclear winter and the possible extinction of the whole human race. For many decades we were just five or ten minutes away from such a nuclear war. For the past decade we have been spared the constant threat of nuclear destruction at the hands of Russia. However, both Russia and the United States still have many thousands of nuclear bombs that could destroy all life on earth. Gradually more and more nations have developed a nuclear arsenal that could wreak havoc on the whole earth. China, India, Pakistan and Israel have all developed nuclear bombs. The more widespread this nuclear proliferation, the more opportunity exists for terrorists to obtain control of a nuclear device. It is possible that a nuclear bomb could be stored in a terrorist's suitcase as they freely travel the world. We know that some sort of biological germs or poison could also enter our country in the suitcase of a terrorist. When we are dealing with men as desperate as those who did the bombings on September 11th, we realize that we are far from safe from more terrorist attacks. Regardless of what measures the government might take to protect us, our whole country is in real danger of future terrorist attacks. Even as we remove bin Laden, there are many hundreds of other terrorists that are ready and willing to take his place.

In the face of such dangers what can we do to protect ourselves? Here is where our faith and trust in God must enter. We believe that God is still God, and in control of the whole of creation. We believe that God has a plan to establish His Kingdom of love upon earth. We believe that God is all-powerful, all-good, all-loving, all-wise and always faithful to His promises. We can hope and trust that God will not allow the terrorists or the fallen powers to totally frustrate God's plans in our regard. It is certainly evident that God is willing to allow terrorists to do the things they did on September 11th. But if we see this as a wake-up call for us to be converted from our sinful ways, then great good could come from these events.

World Hunger and Destitution

According to recent figures, the population of The United States is about five percent of the total population of the world, yet we are using between 35 and 40 percent of the world's resources. The group of Seven Industrial Nations (United States, Britain, France, Italy, Japan, Germany and Russia) contains 20 percent of the total population of the world, yet they have use of 87 percent of the wealth of the world.

The average, middle-class American family has an annual income of about $40,000. That would be about $770 per week. According to James Flanigan, chief financial writer for the Los Angeles Times, the average weekly income for the different countries in the Mid-East is as follows: Israel and Kuwait - $320, Saudi Arabia - $120, Lebanon - $100, Turkey - $62, Iran - $34, Egypt - $28, Jordan and Syria - $20, Iraq - $2, Palestinians and Afghanistan even less than $2.

As each year passes, the rich get richer and the poor get poorer. Literally billions of people in the Third World of Asia, Africa and Latin America live in destitution, and are on the verge of starvation at all times. Billions go to bed hungry every night. Many millions die of starvation each year. In the face of such a disproportion of the goods and resources of the world, it is my opinion that our high standard of living in the United States is probably our greatest sin.

What then should we do in order to repent of our sin? I think we are called to adopt a very simple lifestyle. We should limit ourselves to necessities that we need in order to carry out our obligations to God, our families, our work, etc. We live in the most fertile country in the world. There is enough unused arable land in railroad rights of way in the mid-west to feed most of the starving people of the world, if it were properly cultivated. We need to cut back on our consumption of meat, especially red meat, since the amount of grain needed to produce one pound of meat could feed a number of poor families for a whole month.

Ecological Pollution

I defer to experts such as Father Thomas Berry to provide the proof of the terrible pollution of water, air and soil that is caused by our modern industrial system. The depletion of the ozone layer in our atmosphere, the climate change of our planet, the disposal of nuclear waste and other poisonous waste are some of the results of our present worship of the fallen powers. There seems to be real danger of irreparable harm to our whole planetary life if we continue the same reckless way we are going. Yet our American government has turned a deaf ear to the many warnings from environmentalists. Those persons and corporations who profit from this pollution seem to be calling most of the shots.

What can we do to put a stop to the ecological pollution of our planet? We live in a democratic society where our government leaders are elected by the citizens of this country. We need to make our voices heard in the halls of Congress and the White House as well as at state and local levels. How many letters of protest have you written to your elected representatives during the past year? Past ten years? We need, first of all, to accurately inform ourselves of the exact nature of this rape of our planet. I would suggest getting some of the books written by Father Thomas Berry, and educate yourself in this area. Then get busy and make your voice heard in halls of Congress, the White House, state offices, etc.

Diminishing Natural Resources

According to the environmentalists, our need to maintain our high standard of living in America is resulting in a tremendous consumption of all the natural resources of our planet. This begins with the tremendous consumption of the oil resources. If this continues at the present rate, we will exhaust our useable oil resources within a couple of centuries, perhaps a couple of generations. The same is true of the tropical forests and other natural resources. This exhaustion of the earth's natural resources is occurring despite the fact that the vast majority of the people of the world do not benefit from this rape of mother earth. Most of these resources are being used to help us of the Western world to maintain our present high standard of living.

We must lower our present high standard of living or we will be in danger of facing extinction. God has given us an intellect that is able to recognize the wrong directions we are presently taking. The American way of life that we cherish is in danger of being lost to future generations of the human race. It is possible to lead a happy life without the luxuries we now take for granted. But if we hope to bequeath to future generations the same happiness we now enjoy, there is need of some drastic curtailments in our present way of life. God can bring good out of evil. Perhaps God is using the events of September 11th to awaken us from our lethargy and bring about the needed changes of direction in our whole American way of life.

Repressing our Unconscious Shadow

Sigmund Freud, Carl Jung and others were able to uncover the vast world of the Unconscious. The name given to it is *shadow*. There is both a positive shadow and a negative shadow. The positive shadow is the vast potential for good that we have not yet brought into conscious awareness. The negative shadow is the vast potential for evil that is present in our unconscious inner self but has not yet become conscious. All that is unconscious needs to be brought into consciousness and be put to use in a positive, loving way. The shadow is a Pandora's Box that can do much harm if its contents are brought too quickly into consciousness. Our task then is to find a way to gradually make conscious the positive and negative shadows and use them in a loving, constructive way. We do this by finding a way to use the energy of the shadow in unconditional love.

We need help from God and our fellow human beings in order to use, in the right way, the energy of the positive and negative shadow. We need to pray daily for the needed grace to bring into consciousness whatever positive and negative energy it is God's will for us to experience. God has a plan and an earthly destiny for each of us. We need the energy of both our positive and negative shadow to carry out God's plan. We also need God's power so that we are able to use, in a positive, loving way, these energies of the unconscious shadow. We need, especially, God's help to transform our negative shadow energy into the positive energy of love. We call this God-given energy "grace." We need to ask for this grace each day. The necessity of asking is not to inform God of something He does not know, but to keep us humble and aware of our need of God's help. Since grace has a short shelf-life, we need to go back to God every day to ask for a fresh supply of grace in order to actualize the energies of our shadow and then to use them in the positive way of love.

The terrorists who carried out the evils of September 11th were using the energies of their unconscious negative shadow. They failed to convert this energy into love. Instead they used it to hate America and all we stand for. We need to pray every day, not only for ourselves that we will make good use of the energy of both positive and negative shadow in a loving way. We need also to pray for all the terrorists in the world that they will accept the God-given grace to use the energy of their unconscious shadow in the positive way of love and not of hate. This prayer for our enemies is the first step of love of enemies which Jesus teaches us in the Sermon on the Mount. The second step is to pray for the grace to practice unconditional, non-violent love for all of our enemies.

CHAPTER 3

MODERN DEMONS AND THEIR REMEDIES

Worldview of Today's World

There is a real danger that we will spend all our efforts towards conquering our external enemies while neglecting the many demons which we harbor within our unconscious psyche. We need the honesty and humility to face the personal demons which endanger us and make use of the proper remedies to exorcise them. These modern demons were originally good, but by our neglect they have become fallen evil powers. It would seem that whenever an originally good power is not used in accord with God's plans, it turns into an evil power or demon. Rather than attempt to destroy such demons it is now our responsibility to convert them back to their original good purpose for which God created them. The Biblical term for such a conversion of evil into good is *exorcism*. A more modern term would be "remedy" or simply "healing." This recognizes that these demons are still basically good and not totally evil.

Jesus and the people of his time had a very simplistic attitude towards evil, and towards Satan and demons. They attributed all evil, including bodily sickness and disease, to demons. Today after 2,000 years of experience, we have a more sophisticated attitude towards evil and sickness. We realize that bodily sickness can result from many other sources than Satan and demons. For example, the case in the 17th chapter of Matthew's Gospel is clearly a case of epilepsy. It is not true to claim that all epilepsy is directly caused by possession of evil spirits. It may result from a virus, germs or a mix-up of genes.

Even though today we are aware of other causes of illness than possession by evil spirits, we must not make the mistake of denying the reality of evil spirits in our society. These modern demons are subtle and hidden, but nevertheless are real and powerful and able to do great harm. The seven capital sins of pride, envy, greed, sloth, lust, gluttony, and anger might be seen as modern-day demons that need to be overcome by faith, trust, prayer and fasting. I would add three other modern demons: fear, negativity, deceit. These ten demons have the power not only to harm our spiritual life but also to cause, at least partially, many illnesses of the body. These are psychosomatic illnesses.

There are three other demons that cause great harm in today's world. They are the three "Ps": Power, Possessions and Pleasure. The three temptations which Jesus experienced during his forty days in the desert are examples of what might be called "desert demons." All of these three "Ps" are creations of God, and so are basically good. The problem is that they are so good and attractive that we have a tendency to idolize them and make them top priorities in our life. When we do this we take something that is of limited value and make it an absolute or top goal in our life. These three "Ps" then become the false gods whom we worship. Instead of remaining good, they now become demons that lead us astray from God, and from the God-given destiny of our life on earth.

There are many other blessings and good things in our life that we turn into demons when we place them as one of our top priorities. We do this whenever we become excessively attached to these God-given blessings. The modern name we give to these excessive attachments is *addictions*. It is safe to say that all of us are excessively attached to one or more of the good things of God's creation. Therefore, all of us might think of ourselves as addicts. When we allow ourselves to become excessively attached to any of God's creations, we take something good and turn it into a demon or evil spirit. No longer is it one of

God's blessings, but a curse. We need then to find an antidote or remedy that will enable us to free ourselves from the addiction, and once again make it one of God's blessings.

DEMONS	ANTIDOTES
Power	Prayer
Pleasure	Self-discipline, fasting
Possessions	Almsgiving, ministry to others
Pride	Humility
Greed	Detachment, simple life style
Envy	Love
Lust	Sacrifice
Gluttony	Self-denial
Sloth	Hard work
Anger	Charity, forgiveness
Fear, insecurity	Trust
Deceit, half-truths	Honesty
Negativity	Positive attitude
Ignorance	Education
Confusion	Simplicity
Mediocrity	Generosity
Procrastination	Sacrament of present moment
Refusal to forgive	Forgiveness, pray for enemies
Hatred of enemies	Love of enemies
Violence, eye for eye	Non-violence
Credit cards	Monthly payment

DEMONS	ANTIDOTES
Lottery, gambling, casino, slot machine	No gambling
TV, Internet, Computer and Video games	Self-denial
Shopping Mall, clothes, jewelry, luxuries	Sacrifice
Sports, Hobbies, Golf, Spectator sports	Balance
Liquor, Tobacco, Food, Ice Cream, Coffee	Moderation
Books, Gadgets, Computers, SUVs, big cars	Balance
Stock Market	Love of the poor
Work, job, management position	Balance
Spouse, children, friends	Unconditional love

Demons are present not only in those areas that are obviously evil, but also in the good things of God's creation whenever we use them to excess. There is the constant need of balance and moderation. This moderation will express itself in the three main antidotes of Prayer, Fasting and Almsgiving. Through prayer, we bring balance to our attitude towards freedom. Through fasting and self-discipline, we bring balance to our love of pleasure. Through almsgiving and charity towards others, we bring balance to our excessive attachment to money and earthly possessions. Without these antidotes we become possessed or obsessed by many demons.

In his book, *The Shattered Lantern,* Ronald Rolheiser suggests three other demons that possess the modern world. They are Narcissism, Pragmatism, and Unbridled Restlessness. Narcissism is an excessive preoccupation with one's self. According to Rolheiser, "Pragmatism is a way of life that asserts that the truth of an idea lies in its practical efficacy. What that means is that 'what is true' is what works." Restlessness results from feeling pressured from all sides so that we experience perpetual tiredness leading to burnout.

The antidote for Narcissism is centering our life in God, God's will and loving service to others. As Jesus says, "I have come not to be served but to serve, and to give my life in ransom for many" (Mark 10:45). The antidote for Pragmatism is to put 'being' ahead of 'doing' in our life. Faithfulness is more important than success. The antidote for restlessness is to make room in our life for leisure and contemplation. In all three of these areas the goal is balance and moderation. We need to have a certain concern for ourselves. We need to be practical in our efforts to succeed in life. We must be willing to endure a certain amount of tiredness and even restlessness. This means that we are never fully satisfied with our present situation, but always strive to be better with moderation and not excessive anxiety.

Jesus taught the human race a whole new way of handling evil in the world. Before the Incarnation of Jesus two thousand years ago, the normal way to handle evil was by what we call "redemptive violence." The Old Testament expressed this method of redemptive violence as "an eye for an eye, a tooth for a tooth" (Exodus 21:23). Jesus did away with this old way of transforming evil. He taught his followers to love enemy, return good for evil, and go the way of non-violence. He practiced this new method of overcoming evil, and paid for it by his death on the cross.

For three hundred years the followers of Jesus sought to practice this love of enemy. However, things changed when Constantine adopted Christianity as the religion of the Roman Empire. Augustine sought to justify the abandonment of Jesus' teaching by composing the rules for a just war. From the 4th to the 20th century, the Christian churches preached this new doctrine of a just war. It is only in the past century that we have rediscovered the Gospel teaching of Jesus about love of enemy and the way of redemptive sacrifice. The majority of those who claim to be followers of the Gospel of Jesus still cling to the ways of God in the Old Testament. Most Christians are still in need of conversion to the Gospel teaching of Jesus regarding non-violence and love of enemies.

In the presence of enemies we have a choice of three options: flight, fight, or the way of Jesus. Flight is for cowards, and in most instances this is not a worthy option. Fight is the way of redemptive violence. It is the way the leaders of our country have chosen to meet the terrorists who endanger us. It was the way that God seems to have approved and recommended for the Chosen People in the Old Testament. It is the way of the just war theory which St. Augustine developed in the 5th century. Until recent times it has been the way taught by most Christians. The Quakers seem to have been the only group immune to this way of redemptive violence until the peace movements of the past century. Gandhi in India, Martin Luther King, Jr, Dorothy Day and the Catholic Worker Movement in this country are examples of a return to the non-violent teachings of Jesus in the Gospels. Gradually, more and more Christians have been converted to this third way of relating to our enemies. It is clearly the way Jesus teaches in the Sermon on the Mount. Walter Wink, in his trilogy of books on the Powers, has made an important contribution in the development of thought on the importance and truth of subscribing to loving, non-violent confrontation of evil.

Redeeming Our Demons

In his book, *Engaging the Powers*, Walter Wink insists that the demonic powers, present in all our institutions and in all of our personal lives, are not totally evil. They were all created good by God. God cannot create anything evil. However, by the many wrong choices made by our ancestors during the past million or so years, these powers have fallen and have become demons. Rather than seeking to destroy these demons, we need to convert them back to the original purpose for which God created them. This conversion can be accomplished only through great love on our part, and the willingness to suffer. Once they are redeemed, they cease being demons and become angels of light for ourselves and others. Jesus began this task of redemption two thousand years ago. He willingly paid the price of his crucifixion in order to convert the demons of his time. However, Jesus did not complete the work of redemption of the powers and demons. He, the head of the Mystical Body, *began* the work of redemption. Jesus challenges us, members of his Mystical Body, to continue this work of redemption. We are called upon to take up our cross and follow Christ. The work of redemption and the establishment of the Kingdom of God upon earth must go on until all the powers and demons have been converted. By the look of things, that goal is probably many thousands of years in the future.

How then do we convert these fallen powers and demons into loving angels and helpers? It will be done only by the practice of unconditional love on our part, and the willingness to suffer and die in the same way Jesus did. We must love our enemies, which means we must love the demons and fallen powers which, at the present time, oppress us. We must never think of them as *completely* evil. They were all created good and still retain this divinely created goodness in the depths of their being. We must search out this goodness in them and by our love for them help them to actualize this basic goodness into real, earthly goodness. There is a heavy price that we will pay in order to bring about this conversion of evil and hatred into love and goodness. The fallen powers will resist our efforts of conversion the same way they resisted Jesus' ministry to them. Many of us will need to pay the price of persecution and death just as Jesus did. It will never be easy. But we are assured by Jesus that the same Holy Spirit that helped him to undergo crucifixion will be present to help us love, suffer and die.

The antidotes suggested earlier are simply positive ways of loving the demons which now oppress us. Perhaps we should stop calling them demons and call them the fallen powers. However, Jesus, in the Gospels, speaks of them as evil spirits. We must realize that evil is the absence of love and goodness. It is the vacuum which is created when we fail to carry out the commandments of love to which all of us are called. However, "nature abhors a vacuum." This vacuum of love and goodness does not remain idle but becomes an evil power, an evil spirit, a demon. All of the energy and power that God originally created to be used in love now takes a new direction toward hatred and away from love. In other words, the energy that God created for love never remains idle. Either we use it for the purposes of love for which God created it, or it becomes an evil power.

Walter Wink suggests that the life of each demon has three stages. Every demon was originally created good, since the all-good God cannot create evil. We presently do not know any details of the life of evil spirits in the original good stage of their life. The Bible speaks of Satan and other evil spirits as "fallen angels." They misused the power of freedom that God had given them to love. Instead they used this freedom to rebel against God and God's plans for them. "I will not serve," is the way the Bible describes the fall of Satan and the evil spirits.

At the present time we are experiencing the second stage in the life of the evil spirits. They continue to rebel against God's will. They continue to misuse the gift of freedom in the opposite direction from love. Walter Wink suggests that the Bible hints at a third stage in the life of evil spirits when they will be redeemed and brought back to the original purpose for which God created them—namely, to love, to use their freedom to do God's will. Thus they will fulfill God's original plan and purpose in creating them.

We need to go to the Gospels and study exactly how Jesus treated the evil spirits or demons of his time. He clearly showed that he had total control of them. They were totally obedient to his words. He ordered them to depart from a person and stop afflicting their victims. He even permitted them to enter into a herd of pigs feeding on the hillside. However, we have no case of Jesus sending these demons back to a hell-fire where they will suffer for all eternity.

Walter Wink suggests that Jesus' death and resurrection was not only to redeem human beings but also to redeem these fallen angels. Nowhere in the Bible do we find such a suggestion. However, St. Paul in Colossians 1:20 states: "Through him (Jesus) God was pleased to reconcile to himself **ALL THINGS** whether on earth or in heaven, by making peace through the blood of his cross." "All things" may include demons and evil spirits. This would be the third stage in the life of these fallen powers. All of us are called by God to continue this work of the redemption of these demons. Again, St. Paul in Colossians 1:24 states, "I am now rejoicing in my sufferings ... and in my flesh I am completing what is lacking in Christ's afflictions." This redemption of the fallen powers seems to be the primary purpose for the Incarnation of Jesus and for our own ministry on earth. We will do our part in the work of redemption of the fallen powers in the same way that Jesus redeemed them. Like Jesus, we must confront and challenge these demons in a loving, non-violent way. Like Jesus, we must be willing to sacrifice our lives in order to redeem them.

Today we have at least two examples in recent history of the success of redeeming the fallen powers. They are Mahatma Gandhi and Martin Luther King, Jr. Like Jesus, they paid for their success in redeeming the evil powers by giving up their lives. The stories of all the martyrs throughout history, both Christian and non-Christian, illustrate the path each of us is called by God to take in redeeming the fallen powers. The Church has always insisted that besides the red martyrs who shed their blood, we have a host of white martyrs who sacrificed their lives.

Rereading Genesis Three

We need to reread the description of the original fall of the human race described in the 3rd Chapter of Genesis. The story of Adam and Eve eating the forbidden fruit is a perfect illustration of how the human race has repeatedly misused God's gift of freedom and disobeyed God's plan and destiny for the human race. In my opinion, I cannot conceive of our good God creating a *Tree of the Knowledge of Good and Evil* in the Garden and then forever refusing to allow human beings to eat its fruit. The sin of Adam and Eve described in Genesis was their decision to eat first of the fruit of the *Tree of the Knowledge of Good and Evil* before eating sufficiently of the fruit of the *Tree of Life*.

If we think of the fruit of the *Tree of Life* as symbolizing love, and the fruit of the *Tree of the Knowledge of Good and Evil* as symbolizing knowledge, the Book of Genesis clearly teaches us that we must always put love before knowledge. Adam and Eve made the mistake of putting knowledge ahead of love, and thereby sinned. We can be sure that if they had obeyed God and eaten first of the fruit of love, the time would have come when they would have been sufficiently mature to eat of the fruit of the knowledge of good and evil.

The whole history of the human race is an endless series of our making the same mistake as did Adam and Eve. Again and again we have put knowledge ahead of love and thus lacked the maturity to handle properly this new knowledge. We have an example of this lack of order in our developing the knowledge of nuclear energy before eating sufficiently of the fruit of love. Once again we have made the same mistake as did Adam and Eve. We have made knowledge the top priority in our life instead of love.

We seem to be on the verge of being cast out of our Garden of Paradise for our sin just as Adam and Eve were cast out of the Garden of Eden for their sin. We might think of the wonderful world in which we live today as a Garden of Paradise, our Eden. By our abuse and misuse of all the resources of planet earth, we are today in danger of losing it all and being cast out of our Paradise. It takes little imagination to see how this could happen if even a small percentage of the stockpile of nuclear weapons were exploded. The name "*nuclear winter*" has been given to this modern-day example of God casting us out of our Garden of Eden.

We have not yet experienced a nuclear winter. There is still time for us to redeem our fallen powers. There is still time for us to make love the top priority in our lives instead of knowledge. The tree of life and love is still alive and available for us to eat its fruit. Only God knows whether we will take advantage of this present period of grace, or will we like Adam and Eve and so many others in human history allow this opportunity to slip through our fingers. Only God knows how much time today's human race has before it will be cast out of our Garden of Eden, the modern world with all its technology (i.e. knowledge of good and evil). We almost lost the opportunity to repent and redeem the fallen powers during the Cuban missile crisis 40 years ago. Are the events of September 11 the beginning of our modern world being cast out of the Garden of Eden? Or will we take heed of the lesson of Genesis Three, and repent of our misdeeds and make love the top priority of our lives? The tree of life is still with us. There is still time to eat of the fruit of this tree of life and love.

We Christians have no excuse for our failure to eat sufficiently of the fruit of love on the *Tree of Life*. We need only to study the Gospels in order to see how Jesus went about the work of redeeming the fallen powers. The mission of Jesus' life on earth two thousand years ago is the mission of the Church today. In the next chapter we will look at the worldview of Jesus as presented in the Beatitudes. In the following chapter we will look at the twelve aspects of the mission of Christ. Then we will see how the Gospel teachings of Jesus reveal our mission, our God-given destiny, the purpose for our creation and existence on earth.

CHAPTER 4

BEATITUDES

Worldview of Jesus

The eight beatitudes best describe the worldview of Jesus. Therefore, these same beatitudes give us the model we need to follow as disciples of Jesus Christ. This is how Jesus lived his life on earth, and this is the way we must try to live.

At the beginning of the Sermon on the Mount, which is found in Matthew 5:2-11, Jesus gives the new laws of the Kingdom of God on earth. In his Gospel, Matthew constantly contrasts the old Moses of the Exodus with Jesus, the new Moses of the Kingdom. Just as Moses received the Ten Commandments from God on Mount Sinai, so Jesus, the new Moses, gives his followers the new laws of the Kingdom of God on a mountain in Galilee. These new laws have come to be called the Beatitudes, because they begin with the word, "Blessed."

Probably, Jesus himself never gave all eight beatitudes together in one single teaching. More likely Matthew, or some other early follower of Jesus, culled these eight laws of the Kingdom from the various teachings Jesus gave in the course of his public ministry.

Not everything in the Beatitudes is original with Jesus. There are many passages in the Old Testament which are precursors of the new laws of the Kingdom. Jesus gathered these gradual revelations of God to the prophets and sages of the Old Testament and added new insights of his own. The result is like a tremendous new thunderbolt of truth similar to the thunder and lightning on Mount Sinai.

The Beatitudes are paradoxical with truth that flies in the face of conventional wisdom, yet they give a practical method for shaping our lives and destinies into the holiness and wholeness we long for and seek.

The First Beatitude

"How happy are they who know they are spiritually poor, the Kingdom of God is theirs."

Poverty of spirit is the realization of our total dependence upon God. As St. Paul puts it: "What have you that you have not received?" The spiritually poor are those who expect nothing from this world but who expect everything from God. They look to God alone for the fulfillment of all their basic needs. They cast themselves upon God's loving care and become "beggars of the spirit" before God. The poor in spirit are willing to ask humbly of God all that is needed, to be totally dependent upon God's mercy, and to be keenly aware of their need of help from God.

We must therefore be unpretending and honest enough to know who we are, to know our limitations, to accept our weaknesses and our need of God. In this sense, the first Beatitude is talking about authenticity. To be an authentic person is to realize, vividly, our great neediness as a creature, and our poverty without the gifts and blessings of God.

The words of this first Beatitude can also be taken to mean those who are poor in their own estimation, and who admit that they are nothing of themselves. In that sense, this Beatitude can refer to the disposition of the humble. A humble disposition is the opposite of the conceited and hard-hearted disposition of those who imagine they are better than others, and that this goodness is due to their own efforts and not to God. God promises that those who are humble, detached, and poor in spirit will possess the Kingdom of God. In exchange for detachment from the things of this world, they will receive a special claim upon God's promise of present and eternal possession of His Kingdom.

The basic disposition or requirement for anyone choosing to follow the way that leads to the Kingdom of God is total detachment from everything that is not the will of God. In practice, this total detachment toward everything of this world means the willingness to be content with what is needed, with only what is necessary to carry out our ministry and our vocation on earth, and to be willing to do without the luxury of things that are not essential to our vocation.

Another way to speak of poverty of spirit is to say that the first Beatitude is a call to live a very simple lifestyle. In that sense, this Beatitude goes contrary to much of modern advertising's emphasis on amassing more goods, and obtaining as many pleasures as possible. If we had a truly Christian culture, the structure of modern advertising would be drastically changed and the amount of money spent on advertising greatly decreased. In this first Beatitude, Jesus is telling us that happiness will be found not by increasing our desires, but in just the opposite way, by decreasing our desires, and by being detached from everything that is not essential to our vocation or ministry in life.

The detachment asked by this first Beatitude is not only from material things, but also from our own will, from our likes and dislikes, and from everything but God and God's will. St. John of the Cross tells us that it makes no difference whether a bird is tied down to earth by a slender thread or a heavy chain, for it is impossible for the bird to fly away until the detaining thread or chain is broken. And, similarly, by detachment we must break any thread that ties us down to earth or to our selfishness.

"Blessed are the poor in spirit, for theirs is the Kingdom of God." Notice the use of the present tense in the promise that Jesus makes. Only those who are truly detached from the things of this world will find happiness upon earth, according to Jesus. It is only when we have reached the point where we are uninterested in the things of this earth, except for those things that are needed to carry out God's will in our regard—only then will we find true peace and happiness, which is really the beginning of heaven. Detachment gives us freedom, and only the person who is free from wants and desires can be happy. Putting it another way, the detached person is free of care, free of anxiety, free of worry and fear regarding the future, trusting in God and trying to do God's will.

Detachment from the things of this world does not mean that we refuse to enjoy creature comforts whenever it seems clear that such is God's will for us. Rather it is the willingness to do without them or to give them up the moment we become convinced that God's will is calling us in another direction. Detachment means we do not look back on the things that we have to give up, but keep our eyes always ahead on the will of God. It means that we are able to relinquish the things of this world without regret, without self-pity, without envy of those who have them, without anger, resentment or bitterness. We hold loosely to everything, ready to let go of everything at the moment it becomes clear that God wills for us to let go.

In order to know whether or not we have this kind of detachment, and in order to increase whatever detachment we now have, it is essential that we practice frequent self-denial of the joys and pleasures of this world, not totally but at least in some little way every day. William James, the great psychologist at Harvard at the beginning of the last century, said that if we wish to keep alive the spirit of detachment and to experience a freedom of the spirit we need to practice at least one act of self-denial every day. Perhaps this is what Jesus means when he says that we must take up our cross each day and follow him.

Poverty of spirit is primarily the attitude we have toward things of this world—our willingness to not know how or where our present and future needs will be fulfilled, the willingness to depend upon God's providence to supply our needs from day to day. Detachment gives us the freedom, the openness and readiness to move in any direction that God wills for us, to change, to let go, to give up all that is near and dear to us. Jesus says: "Anyone putting his hand to the plow and looking back is not fit for the Kingdom of God" (Luke 9:62).

We must train ourselves to be content with a minimum of the goods of this world. By detachment and self-denial we make room in our lives for God and the things of God. We learn to put the priorities in our life in proper order. We come to the realization that we were born to serve the whole of creation, and not merely that little portion of life which we possess. Life is bigger than the individual, more than these earthly possessions. Just as we are told in the second chapter of the Epistle to the Philippians that Jesus "emptied himself," so we must be willing to divest ourselves of everything that is not in accord with God's will.

It is not a case of masochistically diminishing our enjoyment of pleasure but rather of sacrificing temporary pleasures for the higher, better, more permanent joys of life. Self-denial of earthly pleasure, including bodily pleasure, is required to liberate the higher powers within us. We have only so much energy and so much time, and if all or most of our time and energy is given to amassing and preserving things, there is none left for the things of God. A constant stripping of the things near and dear to us is needed in order to be open to the higher values. For example, there needs to be a balance in our life between feasting and fasting. There should be as much fasting in our life as there is feasting. Or, putting it another way, in our life there should be as many experiences of going to extremes in fasting too much as there are of going to the extreme of feasting too much. Yet we know that practically all of us have, many times, over-eaten; but how many of us can say that, even once in our life, we have made a mistake in fasting too much, in practicing too much self-denial? Actually, we need to test the upper limits at both ends, both in self-indulgence and in self-denial to be able to come to true and honest balance and detachment. Yet the ordinary experience is that we have many experiences of self-indulgence but very few of self-denial, and we never discover the optimum point of greatest spiritual and psychological growth.

When Jesus speaks of the happiness and the blessedness of the poor, he does not mean that every poor person is going to heaven, and that every rich person is going to hell. Jesus is not primarily interested in the external condition of a person, but in our internal disposition. That is why Matthew translates this Beatitude as "blessed are the poor in spirit, blessed and happy are they who are detached from the things of this world," who have not made a god out of money and material possessions. How fortunate are those people who do not depend primarily on the things of this world for their happiness, but depend directly and primarily upon God.

The only really happy people on earth are those who are detached from material possessions, and whose only desire is to please God and do God's will in all things. When we put our effort to amassing more and more of the goods and pleasures of this world, we find that we are never satisfied. The more we get, the more we want; and it seems the more precarious becomes our possession of what we have. Whereas if we put our dependence upon God and the doing of God's will, we find that as we go on in life the realization of God's loving care becomes more and more obvious and present. We become more and more free, and much more happy.

Jesus guarantees our security, in a most paradoxical way, by demanding that we give up all our personal security and abandon ourselves into God's hands. In that sense this is similar to what God asked of Abraham in the twelfth chapter of Genesis when he told him, "leave the place where you now are and go to the place that I will show you." As in the case of Abraham, God also asks us to live from day to day in total dependence upon His graciousness, in daily vulnerability to God, in radical vulnerability to the transcendent element of life.

It is clear in the Gospels that Jesus showed a preference for the poor, for the oppressed, for the lowly (the *anawim* as they are called in the Old Testament), for those who have nothing to expect from this world, and who do not fit into its structures. Such people, Jesus insists, are people who are most easily able to cast themselves upon God's loving care, and the Kingdom of God comes to such persons more easily. God wills to be present with them in a very special way by the inbreaking of His love, mercy, healing and forgiveness. God promises to comfort and satisfy people who are keenly aware of their nothingness and their helplessness, and are willing to cast all their care on God.

To live up to this Beatitude, we must be willing to be ignored, passed over by others, not taken seriously by them, willing to be laughed at, made fun of, ridiculed, forgotten. If we can accept this lowly condition in the right spirit, without anger or bitterness, or rebellion, we will find a tremendous freedom in this state and be able to give our attention to the really important matters in life. No longer are we dependent on the approval of others, but we are dependent upon God.

Poverty of spirit is a perfect preparation for prayer since it requires of us the faith, trust and dependence upon God that is necessary for good prayer. Without poverty of spirit, we are tempted to depend too much on ourselves. Poverty, without hope and trust in God, will lead to despair, frustration, discouragement, a breakdown of our inner spirit, a loss of peace and joy, and fear and anxiety for the future. To follow the spirit of the first Beatitude there must be a willingness to live for the present moment, and make the most of it without undue concern about the future and how we are going to handle the problems of tomorrow. Poverty in spirit and trust in God must grow hand in hand in proper balance. One without the other will not bring happiness. The two together are needed.

In the Gospel, Jesus set a good example of what is meant by poverty of spirit, and we know that he insisted that his disciples follow a similar path of poverty. Jesus depended upon the good will of the people among whom he worked. He told one person "the Son of Man has nowhere to lay his head." For his daily bread he depended upon the free will offerings of the people to whom he preached. The disciples of Jesus found this teaching about poverty just as difficult to understand and accept as we do today. For example, in the tenth chapter of Mark, Jesus told the rich young man that if he wished to be perfect, he must go and sell everything he had and give the money to the poor. Only then would he be able to come and be a disciple of Jesus. Because this rich young man was attached to his things, he turned away sad from this request of Jesus. When he went away, Jesus looked around and said to his disciples: "How difficult it is for the rich to enter the Kingdom of heaven!" The disciples marveled at his words. Jesus repeated: "My dear children, how difficult it is to enter the Kingdom of God. It is easier for a camel to pass through the eye of a needle than for a rich man to enter the Kingdom of God." With that the disciples were completely overwhelmed, and exclaimed to one another, "Who, then, can be saved?" Jesus fixed his gaze on them and said, "With men, it is impossible; but not so for God. With God, all things are possible" (Mark 10:21-27).

If, then, we wish to live up to this first Beatitude, we must depend upon God's help. It is something that we are unable to accomplish by our own efforts. To practice the detachment from worldly goods and worldly pleasures which is required for a disciple of Jesus, we must become beggars of the spirit, which is another way to translate this Beatitude. "Blessed and happy are the beggars of the spirit." Daily we must beg God for the necessary help, desire and grace to practice the detachment that the Gospel asks of us, and to depend constantly upon God's loving care. This is the best and the only insurance policy that will bring us the freedom and happiness we call the Kingdom of God.

The Second and Eighth Beatitudes

"Blessed are those who mourn, for they shall be comforted."

"Blessed are those who suffer persecution for the sake of justice and holiness, the reign of God is theirs."

In John 12:24, Jesus tells us "Unless the grain of wheat falls to the earth and dies, it remains alone. But if it dies, it produces much fruit." Each one of us has a hard shell of selfishness around our heart, just as the grain of wheat has an outer shell around its inner life. Only if the hard shell is broken or removed is the grain of wheat able to produce fruit and to come alive.

In each of us, a hard, egocentric, selfish shell stands between our conscious life and our inner self where the Holy Spirit dwells. Unless we are willing to have the barrier removed, we keep God in prison within our inner self and He is unable to break out, to penetrate and to influence our external activities. If, however, we allow grace to break open this hard shell, we become a transparent being. We become so open to God's Spirit that it shines through our every thought, word, deed and emotion. This was the way Jesus lived his life. He was totally open to the Holy Spirit. This is the goal of every disciple of Jesus.

How then do we break open this hard shell which stands between our outer nature and our inner self? There is but one way: suffering. Not just any suffering, but only that suffering which we have learned to use properly for our spiritual growth. Therefore, we can translate this second beatitude as "blessed or happy or fortunate are they who have learned the true meaning of suffering, for they will find comfort."

Many people see suffering as pure evil, and as something which is to be avoided at all costs. Many people become bitter, resentful, angry, angry at God, or angry at the world when some particular suffering overtakes them and they are not able to see any purpose in it. In other words, if we have not learned its true meaning, suffering is not a blessing but a curse. It becomes harmful to those people who are ignorant of the true meaning of suffering.

If we look back over our life at the different sufferings which have come into our path, we may be able to say that we did make good use of some of these sufferings, that they did break open the pride, the vanity, the selfishness which had formed like a hard shell around our heart. As a result of our own sufferings, we have been more compassionate and more understanding of other people. Those people who go through life without any hardships, without any kind of pain or suffering very often lack compassion, empathy and sympathy for those people who have to suffer. Again, we might think back to certain occasions in our life when something was difficult or caused some kind of pain and suffering and, as a result, we became resentful and angry; we rejected this particular blessing, this particular grace that comes from the second Beatitude.

St. Paul tells in Romans 8:28, "For those who love God, all things work together unto good." This certainly includes the sufferings we have to endure. Continuing in Romans 8:18, Paul says, "I consider the sufferings of the present to be as nothing compared to the glory to be revealed in us." Paul reminds us in this same chapter that we are co-heirs with Christ, that we are children of God by adoption and therefore we are brothers and sisters of Jesus Christ. "But," he says, "only if we suffer with him in order that we may also be glorified with him."

There is a proud streak in the heart of every human being, and this proud streak needs to be broken. To break our willful spirit does not mean that we destroy our will or our ego. If that were to occur, it would lead to a real psychosis. We need a strong will and a strong ego. When we speak of brokenness of the spirit, we are making the same inference as when we speak of "breaking a horse," which means that the will of the horse is submitted to the higher will of the rider. We do not destroy the horse when we "break it"; we enable the horse to be useful and capable of doing many things. Whereas, if that horse were never broken, it would be of no help to humankind.

So, to experience brokenness ourselves means to learn to submit our will, our mind and our whole being to the higher will of God as well as to the needs of our brothers and sisters. There can be no submission to God without a submission of our life to the loving service of others.

As to this mystery of suffering, we will never fully understand its origins. There can be various reasons why we suffer pain. It may be the fault of someone else. It may be our own fault. In other words, it can come from sin or negligence. Very often it is simply a part of the necessary growing pains as we develop, as we leave one stage and proceed to another stage of life. Finally, there certainly are some sufferings which are a result of that cosmic battle that goes on between the forces of evil and of good. The arena for that battle is right here on earth, as the Book of Revelation reminds us. Therefore, we are a part of the struggle of the forces of good to overcome the forces of evil. In this struggle, there is going to be suffering and pain.

Why did the passion and death of Jesus obtain our salvation? It was certainly not to appease God nor was it to ransom us from the devil, as some of the early fathers of the Church thought. The passion and death of Jesus saved us because of the love with which Jesus endured the suffering of the cross, while despising the shame. His love was more powerful than the evil of his enemies' hatred, and thus he turned back the flood of evil in the world. If we could think of this force of evil as a giant river in flood stage and imagine it rushing down a valley and destroying everything in its path, you can grasp evil's tremendous power for destruction. We might think of Jesus, seeing this tremendous flood of evil which had been created by the sins of the human race for many, many generations, as one lonely person who walks right out into the valley, confronts the flood of evil and allows it to overcome him. Or, if you wish, Jesus counteracts the force of the powerful and rampant surge of evil by absorbing it into his own body without lashing back. This is the passion and death of Jesus.

Instead of resenting it, instead of being angry, instead of passing it on to someone else, Jesus returned good for evil. Jesus accepted his passion, accepted this flood of evil in the world, absorbed it into his own body through his passion and death, and passed on love. In that sense, it was through suffering that the back of the force of evil in the world was broken.

As St. Paul says in Colossians 1:24, we, as members of the Body of Christ, must be glad to make up in our own body, by our sufferings, for those sufferings which are still wanting in the sufferings of Christ. In some mysterious way, Jesus takes us into a partnership in overcoming the evil of the world. This gives us a tremendous dignity and really is a tremendous privilege, but there is a price to pay: pain and suffering. Blessed are they who have learned the true meaning of suffering, who are able to take the sufferings that come to them and, following the example of Jesus, return good for evil, return love instead of hatred.

Not all suffering is redemptive, only that suffering that is endured for the sake of God frees us from the captivity of evil. This brings us to the eighth Beatitude which is really another way of looking at the question of suffering.

Usually translated as, "Blessed are they who suffer persecution for the sake of justice, for the sake of holiness," we translate it a little differently: "Happy and blessed and fortunate are they who suffer persecution because they do what God requires."

As St. Paul tells us, "Be not overcome by evil but overcome evil with good." Therefore, the persecution we accept as a result of doing what God requires of us becomes a means of sanctification, if it is accepted in the same way that Jesus accepted the cross. The reward expressed in this Beatitude is "for theirs is the Kingdom of God." Again, note the use of the present tense.

If people are willing to accept the suffering and persecution that comes from doing what God requires of them, and bear this suffering in a loving and forgiving way, without anger and resentment, they will begin to experience the Kingdom of God now, here on earth. We see this in the stories of the martyrs of the first centuries. We read how they went into the arena to be torn to bits by the wild beasts, praising God, singing and rejoicing. They did experience the Kingdom of God on earth, a union with God as we will have in heaven.

Deeply sensitive people suffer more intensely than others. This sensitivity can be turned into a deep concern and compassion for others, thus enabling one to have greater understanding of what others are going through. We can put out our antenna and pick up more easily and quickly those calls for help which come from others who are in need, or in great suffering. We pick up the vibrations of the pain that someone else is suffering, even though it is some sort of psychological or spiritual pain that is not noticeable in an exterior sort of way. If we have experienced brokenness ourselves, and especially if God has given us a very sensitive heart, we are able to minister in a special way to such people. This would be a part of the happiness, the joy, the blessing which comes from our experience of suffering. People who themselves have never suffered are ordinarily not very good counselors for others who are in a state of depression or in other physical or mental agony.

The battle between the cosmic forces of evil on earth and the forces of God, of love and of goodness, goes on right now. Just as Jesus was willing to enter into this struggle, so we too are called upon to contribute some part. Therefore, the anguish we feel at the sight of the evil in the world today—the poverty, the loneliness, the violence, the destitution, the pride, the greed, the lack of better distribution of the resources of the world, the ambitions for power, the abuse of power—can cause real pain, a real suffering, in our being. If we accept this in the spirit of Christ, then in some mysterious way we will make a contribution to the over-all healing of these wounds of the human race.

The closer we come to spiritual maturity and sanctity, the more people around us will consider us to be odd, to be different, to be someone they think is a bit crazy. We know that this is what Jesus had to experience from even his own family and relatives. In Mark 3:21, we are told that Jesus' family and relatives came to take charge of him saying, "He is out of his mind." This can be the lot of the person who today takes absolutely seriously the teachings of Jesus in the Gospels, and tries to live up to the eight Beatitudes. This person is going to be out of step with most of the rest of the world. Therefore, that person can expect persecution, opposition, criticism and is apt to have a hard, difficult time on earth. This is a part of suffering persecution because we do what God requires.

If we take the teachings of Jesus seriously, we will experience suffering of all kinds. For example, we will find ourselves defenseless against the powerful of this world. We will have no defenses except those used by Jesus: namely, love, prayer and forgiveness. Therefore, like Jesus, when we suffer persecution because we do what God requires, we must consistently return good for evil, turn the other cheek, bless and pray for those who persecute us, allow the whole fury of evil to sweep over us, and accept that evil without anger or hatred but always with mercy and love.

As St. Paul says, "We may be knocked down but we will never be knocked out" (2 Cor 4:9). By accepting suffering in the way that Jesus did, our suffering becomes a means of sanctification for ourselves and in some mysterious way brings about the grace of salvation even for the persecutors, even for those who are responsible for our suffering.

If we can understand and appreciate the true meaning of suffering, then in the very midst of such persecution, God will give us an inner peace and comfort us. Jesus says in answer to the second Beatitude: "Blessed are they who mourn, for they shall be comforted."

Another aspect of suffering is that it includes contrition or sorrow for our sins, which we must have in order to fully experience forgiveness. Our heart is squeezed with the pain of our sins. We are broken and bruised in spirit by the knowledge of our sinfulness. Therefore, a part of this Beatitude is to have an abiding sorrow for sin, which Father Faber tells us is a most essential element for our growth in virtue and holiness. We must never forget the fact that we have been sinners and we must never cease to regret that we have been unfaithful to God.

Another kind of suffering comes to persons of certain temperaments, who find it difficult to make changes in their lives, especially in their later years. If we are to continue to grow and become the saint that God wants us to become, there is the need of constant letting-go of the past and pushing on to new things. One way of expressing this is that "we must slay our darlings," which refers to the Old Testament story of Abraham and Isaac. Abraham was asked by God to sacrifice his only son Isaac. Just as Abraham, we must be ready and willing if God should ask us to sacrifice "our little Isaacs," "to slay our darlings," to give up those things to which we have become excessively attached. The result is real pain, agony, anguish, suffering. If we have learned the true meaning of suffering, if we have learned to use suffering in the right way, this kind of sacrifice and pain will be a means of salvation not only to ourselves but also for many others as well.

This Beatitude has nothing to do with melancholy or ill humor. It does not mean that we should be sour and negative toward life. There is a Christian joy in suffering. We rejoice, as did the Apostles, that we are considered worthy to suffer something for Christ. If we have the right intentions, then suffering does not make us miserable. It does not take away our happiness. This is the paradox of the Gospel and of the Beatitudes. "Blessed are they that mourn, blessed are they that have learned the true meaning of suffering, for they shall be comforted." That joy, that comfort, comes right here on earth.

Just as any lover is not satisfied or happy until he has done something difficult to prove his love for the beloved, so we should find great joy and comfort when we are called by God to sacrifice our pleasure and comfort, and to accept some kind of pain or persecution. If we do it in perfect abandonment to God's will, we will be blessed with many graces.

The Third Beatitude

"Blessed are the meek, for they will receive what God has promised."

Having experienced detachment and brokenness, the next step for one who is on a spiritual journey is to develop meekness. Meekness is not weakness even though at times the two may appear to be the same. Meekness actually requires great strength since it means bringing our will into tune with God's will responding instantly to every vibration of the Holy Spirit.

Meekness means to have sensitive ears, alert eyes without blind spots, and a listening heart and mind constantly open to God's inner voice, the creative voice of the Holy Spirit within us. To be meek we must be able to distinguish this creative voice of eternity from the destructive voice of our egocentricity, pride and selfishness. We must be without callousness, dullness, inhibitions and repressions. We must have sensitivity and openness to God's truth and the needs of others, and to the love of both God and neighbor. Meekness is the ability to unite our will with the will of God and also to be sensitive to the will of others. Meekness encompasses the willingness to sacrifice ourselves in order to enter into the life of God and the lives of others.

An example of meekness would be that of two musical stringed instruments, for instance, a piano and a violin. If they are exactly tuned to one another, and if they are in the same room, it is possible to strike any note on the piano and, without anyone touching the strings of the violin, it will pick up the vibrations of the musical note in the air and begin to resound softly the same note as the piano. If we would think of the piano as God's will, and the violin string as our will, we can more easily understand what it means to be a meek person.

Meekness is always a sign of our submission to God's will. All who have been subdued or broken by the tremendous and fascinating image of God our Creator, and who aim to pattern themselves in His image are characterized by meekness. It is, therefore, the opposite of obstinacy, hardness and abrasiveness.

Some of the signs by which we can recognize a meek person would be as follows. First, a meek person is approachable, easy to talk to, accessible. A meek person is a good listener, who is sincerely interested in others and not overly critical and judgmental. Secondly, a meek person is highly sensitive, alert to others, responsive to the needs and feelings of others. A meek person will not be inconsiderate, nor will he/she hurt other people's feelings. A third quality of a meek person is the readiness to cooperate with others, and the willingness to work in harmony with them. A meek person readily confesses one's limitations, mistakes and sinfulness. A meek person usually is able to shed tears rather easily, is easily edified by the good conduct of others, and is always open to receive help as well as give help.

The prime example of meekness is God. Our God is a meek God Who awaits our free will decision, Who tries to conform His eternal plan to our will as far as that is possible, Who even adjusts His will to accord with our free decisions, Who continues to love us, forgive us and help us despite our sins and our negligence of Him.

Just consider these two examples of the meekness of God. Let us think about how we treat God in regard to prayer. We take it for granted that at any moment or any hour of the day or night we can begin to pray and know for certain that God is there waiting and available. God is omnipresent. God does not treat us as perhaps some professional person might by giving us an appointment for many weeks after we have made the initial contact. God is available to listen to us and to respond to our needs and prayers the very instant we decide to enter into contact with him.

Another example of the meekness of God is that we can be certain that when God created each one of us He had in mind a certain plan for our life, certain missions, certain ministries. Now, it is possible that a few of us are so open to God's will, and have such a good training from our parents and teachers that, throughout our life, we never resist the original plan which God has for us. We believe that this was true in the case of Jesus Christ and of his Mother, the Blessed Virgin Mary. We have instances of saints like St. Therese, The Little Flower, who stated that from the age of three she remembers never refusing God anything. These examples of great sanctity are the exception. The likelihood is that all of us have failed to respond to God's original plan for us not just once but many times over. What does God do? He simply readjusts His plans to conform to the situation in which He finds us here and now. God is willing to change or readjust His plans in our regard, not just once or occasionally, but over and over again, even every day. This is what we mean by the "meekness of God."

We also see this meekness in the person of Jesus. He never forces his will on others but waits patiently for their decision. He does not use violence but he offers what God has given him, that is the Kingdom, to those who are willing to receive it. We see the meekness of Jesus in a very special way during the Passion when the Gospels tell us that "he answered not a word."

Moses in the Old Testament is another example of a meek person. In the ninth chapter of Deuteronomy, the writer says that Moses was the meekest of men. An example of the patience of Moses is seen in his relationship with the Chosen People during the forty years that they wandered in the Desert of Sinai. When the Israelites built the golden calf and were worshipping it, God became very angry and said to Moses, "Step aside and I will destroy this people, and I will raise up a new chosen people with you as the head." Moses said to God, "Ah, this people has indeed committed a grave sin in making a god of gold for themselves. If you would only forgive their sin! If you will not, then strike my name from the Book of Life" (Exodus 32:31-32). Moses' meekness was sufficient to turn God's anger away from the people.

We need wisdom to know when to compromise in secondary matters in order to retain what is really important and primary. There are times when we need to conform ourselves to others' wishes, but there are times when we need to stand firm. The gift of meekness, which is indeed a grace from God for which we need to pray, will give us the wisdom to know when to be strong and to stand up for God's rights and for the rights of others, and when to be silent and wait for a more favorable occasion.

It is impossible to practice meekness if we are wrapped up in ourselves. We need to break the hard shell of egocentricity around our hearts and become open to God and others. We must overcome our fears, our insecurity, our inferior complex in order to practice meekness. We must be able to feel secure within ourselves before we can meekly submit our will to the will and desires of others without destroying our inner dignity. Then we will become willing to sacrifice ourselves for God and others. The meek person is willing to make himself the servant of all, the last of all, and finds joy and contentment in this meekness without any loss of human dignity or respect.

We need, first of all, to know and experience our own value and worth, and then to have great self-control and self-discipline, especially over the emotion of anger. According to St. Thomas Aquinas, meekness is the virtue which controls the inordinate movement of anger. It is the virtue by which the passion of anger is brought under strict control of one's reason. Now this does not mean that the meek person will never use the powers of anger. There is a righteous anger, as Jesus showed toward the buyers and sellers in the temple. For the meek person anger will always be a righteous anger that will be used in the pursuit of good for everyone involved, and that will be used for the advancement of the glory of God, and never for the advancement of oneself.

The meek person refrains from violence or force to get his own way. Instead, the meek person is able to adapt himself to whatever circumstances he faces. Meekness respects both the freedom of God and the freedom of others, and does not try to force others to do his will or even to do God's will. Of course, this is what we see in the meekness of God and, in a special way, in the meekness of Jesus.

The meek person refuses to use violence to maintain his own right, even refuses to use force to right a wrong, except when it is absolutely necessary. Considered from this point of view, meekness is a very attractive and appealing virtue. Each one of us desires self-mastery and self-control. When one's temper is brought under perfect control, it becomes our servant in doing good rather than evil. It becomes a power to bring about the will of God and not something that creates disorder, disharmony, quarreling and hatred.

On the other hand, it is not bad to have a very strong temper. It can be a wonderful power for good, provided it can be kept under the control of our reason and subject to God's will in all things. The virtue of meekness does just this to our inclination to anger. Seeing how desirable the possession of the virtue of meekness is, the question of how one acquires this virtue remains.

First of all, one should pray for this virtue. "Jesus, meek and humble of heart, make our hearts like unto yours," is an example of a prayer for meekness. We must pray for humility because it is impossible to practice true meekness unless one is already humble.

Secondly, we must wage a constant battle against our excessive tendency to anger. We must try to control our temper and not allow ourselves to speak when angry, to learn to wait until we have brought our temper under control before making a decision. Meekness means to try constantly to be gentle and patient with others, even those who exasperate us. Meekness means to speak slowly and calmly regardless of the occasion. Try to return good for evil, and to overcome evil with good. This is what our Lord meant by "turning the other cheek."

To be meek means to try to have compassion toward even those who injure us or become angry with us; to feel sorry for the interior harm or external injury this may cause them; and to be unmindful of our own injury. It means to be ready to forgive others, "seventy times seven," as Jesus advises us, to pray for our persecutors, not to nurse grudges, and to refuse to consider the question of revenge. Meekness requires deep humility, the willingness to become little, to suffer misunderstanding and opposition without hitting back, to respond to the violence of others with love.

The meek person knows how to wait patiently for Divine Providence to arrange the right time for everything. Meekness requires patience and silence under opposition, misunderstanding and persecution, but not necessarily always. There is a time to speak up and respond. In such situations the meek person has the wisdom to know when to be silent and when to speak, when to accept and when to react in a very positive way. The meek person knows how to be quiet and wait.

A meek person is willing to step aside, and let others take credit for what one has started. A meek person has the willingness to let go of everything that is near and dear to him and to respond with patience to the demands of others. Meekness means the non-use of power over others when one has an advantage over them. Meekness means gentleness, kindness and love.

A disciplined love of others enables one to sacrifice personal advantage. The questions that are always in the forefront of the mind of a meek person are: "What will do the most good for the most people? What can I say, what can I do, what reaction of mine will accomplish the greatest good?" Of course, that greatest good is God's will. What is God's will, what is God's plan, what will foster the furtherance of the Kingdom of God upon earth? These are the questions that engage the attention of the meek person.

Naturally there will be times when a meek person will make mistakes in speaking up or remaining silent. The meek person is guided by the principle of trying to do or say, or not do or say, whatever seems to create the greatest good for the most people. Therefore, the meek person responds with one's whole being to the needs, desires and sufferings of others, and is readily accessible to them so that they do not hesitate to ask favors, even when those requests require heroic efforts. People can recognize in the meek person a joyful willingness, even a gratefulness, at the prospect of an opportunity to serve others.

The meek person very frequently chooses the last place, the lowest place, thus doing everything possible to make others feel important, needed and worthwhile. According to the promise of the Beatitudes, only the meek will possess the earth and receive what God has promised. Why is this true? Meekness is the way that is most in accord with our real human nature. God created us to love, to serve, to give, to sacrifice ourselves for others. We certainly see this in the life of Jesus when he says, "I have come on earth not to be served but to serve, and to give my life for others." Jesus gives us an example of meekness in a special way at the Lord's Supper when he took a basin of water and washed the feet of the disciples, including those of Judas.

•

The meek person has the farsightedness and insight to be willing to sacrifice temporary or present advantage for the sake of something better in the future. Only the meek are truly creative in building up, rather than impeding, the Kingdom of God, of being positive rather than negative, of being constructive instead of destructive. Why is this true? Only the meek have the vision and the insight to see far ahead and know which direction leads to the Kingdom of God. Without meekness and sensitivity to the voice of God within us and around us, we shall be frequently mistaken in our judgments as to which direction we should go to find the Kingdom of God. Frequently the path that leads to destruction looks as good or even better than the path that leads to the Kingdom. Only the meek will be successful in discovering, in choosing, and in following the right path. Therefore, only the meek will possess the earth, the New Earth, the New Creation, the Kingdom of God. Only the meek will receive what God has promised.

The Fourth Beatitude

"Blessed are they who hunger and thirst for holiness, for they shall be satisfied."

The original translation of this beatitude is, "Blessed are they who hunger and thirst for justice." In this instance, "justice" means giving to everyone what is due to that person. It means, first of all, giving to God what is due to Him. What we owe God is to become saints. That is our destiny, that is what we are called to be.

How does one become a saint? The first step toward attaining sanctity is to desire it intensely, to crave it like someone who, dying of thirst, desires water, or to covet it like a jewel of great price. According to this beatitude, if we wish to become saints, we must be dissatisfied with our present way of life. Discontent with our present spiritual situation means to recognize how far removed we still are from the sanctity to which we are called. We need to hunger for an inner spiritual revolution in ourselves, to pray that our intensity of purpose will grow, and to desire intensely to progress toward perfect justice.

In Chapter 16 of St. Luke's Gospel, Jesus says, "Up to the time of John it was the Law and the prophets. Since then, the Kingdom of God has been preached and by violence everyone is getting in." The violence spoken of here is the kind of recklessness with which a starving person seeks food or a person dying of thirst searches for water. This is the kind of intensity, the hunger, the craving that we should have for spiritual conversion, for growth into something more perfect. We must hunger so much for new growth in holiness that we are willing to pay any price and to make any struggle in order to attain it. This beatitude reminds us to never rest content until we have obtained this holiness.

Justice also means giving to our fellow human beings, to our neighbors, what is due to them, which is to love them at least as much as we love ourselves, but even to go further than that. As Jesus says, "A new commandment I give you, that you love others as I have loved you."

Finally, justice also means to give to ourselves what is due to us, to take the proper care of our bodies, minds, souls, and spiritual life. This is all a part of justice. Therefore, the New American Bible changes the word from justice to holiness. "Blessed are they (or happy are they) who crave for holiness, for they shall obtain it." It is also sometimes translated, "They will be satisfied," or "they shall have their fill."

Of course, this is the great commandment of Jesus: "You should love the Lord your God with all your heart, with all you mind, with all your soul and with all your strength. You shall love your neighbor as yourself" (Mark 12:30-31). Holiness means to give God everything. It includes the willingness to sacrifice everything to do His will, to put God and others ahead of ourselves just as Jesus did. As Jesus said, "I do all the things that please my heavenly Father."

This desire for holiness must persist throughout life. Actually it should increase and intensify as we get older and nearer to our death because we know that we have less time to accomplish this goal of life. With the experience of age, we also learn more of what is required of us to be a saint. This beatitude reminds us that we must never be content with mediocrity or anything less than the best. As someone has said, "If something is worth doing, it is worth doing well."

To accept the call which this beatitude gives us, we should desire not just to be saved and get to heaven, but to be great saints. The desire for the highest possible perfection is an ambition very pleasing to God. God wants to give us everything that our hearts desire, so if we really, intensely, sincerely desire to be saints, and if we are willing to pay the price necessary to obtain sanctity, we can be sure that God will give us the grace, and will grant us this desire. God loves us so much that He will try to live up to whatever desires or expectations we have of Him. In Chapter Six of St. Luke's Gospel, where Jesus is talking about these beatitudes, he makes this statement, "Woe unto you who are satisfied, who are content with things as they are."

In other words, "Woe unto you who have no passionate desire for that which you do not presently possess. Woe unto you who live comfortably enough just now; the day will come when you will discover that you have somehow missed the greatest thing of all."

The greatest barrier to full entry into sanctity is the malady of not wanting or not really desiring it. In this sense, this beatitude is the most demanding, yet at the same time the most encouraging, of all the beatitudes. It tells us of God's sympathy for the struggler. It is not he who thinks he has already attained holiness who counts with God, but rather one who hungers and thirsts for it. That person will be truly blessed.

If we are to persevere in our desires, whatever we desire must be within the realm of possibility and achievability. If a person desires something that seems totally unattainable, he or she will not seriously strive to obtain that desire; and so we must convince ourselves that great sanctity and holiness are attainable for each of us. Why is this true? God has given us His word that He will always be faithful. He would have never made this declaration telling us that we must hunger and thirst with tremendous desire for holiness unless He was ready and willing to give each one of us all the help we need to reach this goal.

In the Old Testament, two attributes of God are emphasized. In the Hebrew, they are *hesed* and *emath*. Hesed refers to God's loving kindness, His willingness to forgive us again and again, His desire to be a mother and a father to us. The second quality, emath, is sometimes translated as truth; more correctly it refers to God's faithfulness to His promises. God's faithfulness to His word gives us assurance that God would never have asked such a desire of us as He does in this beatitude unless He was ready and willing to fulfill that desire.

Modern psychology reminds us that our desires are the parents of our action. Before we can perform any human action, we must first desire it. The stronger the desire to achieve it, the more certain that an action will follow. If we, therefore, have very strong desires to be holy, to give to God our whole life, as it is due to Him, then we can be sure that in time we will become holy, provided we persevere in our desires.

The Fourth Beatitude reminds us that only those who hunger and thirst after holiness will be happy on earth. At first sight this may seem a contradiction until we realize that the closest we can get to perfect happiness on earth is by way of desire. Most of our joys on earth are the joys of anticipation. And so, there is a real happiness when we have this desire and know that God is pleased with it. God will, in due time, fulfill our desire even if it be only in heaven after death.

The saint who best illustrates this beatitude is St. Therese of Lisieux. One of the essential elements of her "little way of spiritual childhood" is that a person must have immense desires. Therese insists that *the little way* must include, along with humility, a bold confidence that God will make saints of us. She states, "I feel the daring confidence that one day I shall become a great saint. I am not trusting on my own merits, for I have none; but I trust in Him Who is virtue and holiness itself."

She further states, "Our dreams and desires for perfection are not mere fancies since Jesus himself has commanded us to realize them saying, 'Be you perfect, as your heavenly Father is perfect.' ... Little children have a right to be daring with their parents, so my excuse is my title, 'a child of God'. Children do not reflect on what they say. Nevertheless if their parents ... are possessed of immense treasures, they do not hesitate to gratify the desires of the little one whom they cherish more than themselves."

God is infinite in greatness, power, goodness, mercy, love and riches. God is able to give to us forever without exhausting His bountiful treasures. His glory is to be able to give without measure. God finds the greatest joy and satisfaction in pleasing His children on earth who come to Him with loving trust. If we want to give joy to God, we will have these tremendous desires and go to Him trusting that He will answer them. Even the most immense desires we have are exceedingly small in relation to what God is able to give us.

Guided by this kind of thinking, Therese formed immense desires and having formed them she dared to articulate them in the simplicity of her confidence in God. She says, "Immense are the desires that I feel within my heart, and with confidence I call upon You to come and take possession of my soul." She insisted that no one should ever despair of reaching the summit of the mountain of love. "God takes delight in showering upon us the greatest favors, and the more weak and helpless we find ourselves to be, provided only that we trust in Him and have good will, the more He will satisfy our desires." If we sincerely want to put God first in our lives, there is no limit to the heights of love and virtue we might attain through God's grace.

We count not on our own efforts and merits but only on the power of the Infinite God. Regardless of our past life, regardless of how many years we may have already wasted, regardless of how many sins we have committed, we can still trust in God's infinite goodness to make a saint of us. God has a very short memory as far as our past faults are concerned. Putting it another way, God is not concerned about our past; He is only concerned about our present. He takes us as He finds us here and now and is ready to grant us the fulfillment of our desires for holiness.

As Jesus told the father of the epileptic son, "If you can believe, all things are possible to those who believe" (Mark 9:23). The more we ask of God, the more He loves to give. God never wearies of giving. He never considers us importunate no matter how far we pursue Him with our requests. We can never ask too much of Him. In fact, the more daring our petitions, the more He is honored.

If we are to take this beatitude seriously, it is important that we reflect on the word justice. "Blessed are they who hunger and thirst after justice, for they shall be satisfied."

As has been said earlier, justice means giving to everyone what is due to them. There is a justice which we owe to God, another form of justice which we owe to ourselves, and a third form of justice which we owe to our fellow human beings.

We have already discussed at some length what we owe to God—that we owe God everything, every bit of our life; to love Him with all our heart, mind, strength, and will; and to attain that holiness or total sanctity to which He is calling us.

As to the justice which we owe to ourselves, we are under an obligation to make the necessary effort to fulfill our potential for good. Many psychologists claim that the average person achieves only about twenty percent of his potential for good. In other words, the average person could put into effect five times more good during his life on earth than what is usually accomplished.

To give what is fair and just to ourselves would mean that we will try to discover the untapped potential for good which is laying fallow below the level of our consciousness. We will do everything that we can to develop our mind, will, emotions, and imagination. We will develop all of our functions and faculties: thinking, feeling, sensation and intuition, as highly as possible. We will attain the wholeness and maturity to which we have been called and of which we are capable. We should have a hunger and a thirst for this wholeness and maturity and each day be ready and willing to do whatever is necessary to develop our potential for good.

The third area of justice (to our fellow human beings) is what we call social justice. This beatitude tells us we must have a tremendous craving to see that every human being has what is due. We know very well that a considerable portion of the human race is denied justice. For example, many people under autocratic oppression are denied the freedom which is needed for a human being to live a full life. People of the Third World are deprived of even the necessities of life. There are destitute people who are deprived of the basic essentials of food, water, clothing and shelter. Even here in our own country many people are denied the right to work. These are instances of social justice upon which we must labor so that everyone will have a sufficiency of the goods of this world and an opportunity to grow and develop their intellectual, cultural, spiritual and physical life.

The task of social justice is simply overwhelming. There is so much injustice in the world that no one of us feels capable of changing the situation totally; but this beatitude challenges us to do something to bring social justice to all. This beatitude calls each one of us to give everything we possibly can of our efforts, time, energy and our material possessions to see that many of the people in the world will receive everything that is due to them. To labor and strive for this goal is what it means to be a saint in the modern world. We cannot please God, and we cannot attain sanctity by cutting ourselves off from the suffering members of the human race. Our Lord says, "What you do to the least of these, you do it unto me; and what you fail to do to them, you fail to do unto me" (Matt 25:40, 45).

The Fifth Beatitude

"Blessed are the merciful, for they shall obtain mercy."

We might also translate this beatitude a bit differently. "Blessed are they who show mercy, for mercy shall be theirs," or "Blessed are they who show mercy to others, for they shall have mercy shown to them."

This beatitude and the third beatitude have a great deal in common. Mercy is to our neighbor what meekness is to God. In speaking of meekness, we said it means to be open and sensitive to God's will, to every vibration of grace which comes to us from the Holy Spirit. Mercy, on the other hand, means to be open and sensitive to the needs of our neighbor, to every call for help, either conscious or unconscious, that comes to us from another human being. Therefore, it refers to the sympathy, the understanding and the empathy that we might have for the needs and for the suffering of others.

According to this beatitude, we will receive mercy to the extent that we show mercy to others. This, of course, is expressed vividly in Chapter 18 of St. Matthew's Gospel where Jesus tells the story of the two servants. One servant owed his master an immense debt of perhaps as much as twenty million dollars. He asks the master to give him more time to repay; and the master, feeling compassion, forgives the man of his debt. And, then, Jesus tells us that this particular servant meets on his way out a fellow servant who owes him just a few dollars, a very small sum. The second servant asks the first servant to give him time and he will repay the amount; but the first servant refuses and casts him into prison. "When the master heard about it, he sent for the first servant and said to him, 'You worthless wretch, I cancelled your entire debt when you pleaded with me. Should you not have dealt as mercifully with your fellow servant as I dealt with you?' In anger, the master handed him over to the torturers until he paid back all he owed. My heavenly Father will treat you in exactly the same way unless each of you forgives his brother from his heart" (Matt 19:23-35).

Mercy means the willingness to forgive "seventy times seven," which means unlimited forgiveness. Having received so much forbearance and clemency from God ourselves, we need to show a similar compassion to others. In the Lord's Prayer, we are told to pray that God will forgive us our trespasses or debts as we forgive those who have trespassed against us. And, if this were not enough, at the end of the Lord's Prayer Jesus repeats this condition. "If you forgive the faults of others, your heavenly Father will forgive you yours; but, if you do not forgive others, neither will your Father forgive you" (Matt 6:14-15).

Mercy is a mature state of mind characterized by an openness to others. The more accessible and responsive we are to our fellow human beings, the more responsive we will be to God. Our fellow human beings are constantly sending out calls for help. Mercy means to be attuned to these vibrations sent out by others and to be ready to respond to their calls for help. One identifies with the sufferings of others, and is understanding and sympathetic towards his neighbors' calamities.

Mercy is a form of healing, and we should be just as willing to heal the evil in others by our mercy and our forgiveness as Jesus is willing to heal our sins. We may not have the gift of physical healing that Jesus did; but all of us have the gift of spiritual healing through mercy and forgiveness.

The mercy, which we are told to practice in this beatitude, includes a merciful judgment of others. In the Sermon on the Mount (Matthew 7:1-2), Jesus tells us, "Do not judge, for with the same judgment you judge others, so you will be judged yourselves." That God will treat us in approximately the same way that we treat others, is a teaching of Jesus that we need to drill into our consciousness, over and over again. Once we really believe and accept this, then regardless of what others might do against us, or how difficult it might be for us to show mercy and forgiveness, we will be obligated to show it. Otherwise, we cannot expect mercy, love and forgiveness from God.

Mercy requires an overcoming of our inhibitions, repressions and blind spots in regard to other people. The more fully our personality is integrated, the more mature we are, the more sensitive we will be to the needs of our neighbor. We will be able to pick up the vibrations, the calls for help and the cries for mercy which come forth from others. To do this, we must forget ourselves and take even a greater interest in others and their welfare than we do in our own. If we spend our energy and our time doing all that we can to take care of the needs of others, we can be sure that God will take care of us and our needs.

The merciful person forgets his or her own suffering, and thinks primarily of the welfare of others. The merciful person is willing even to suffer unjustly for the sins of others, if thereby some good is accomplished. We know that this is what Jesus did in the Passion; he suffered for our sins thereby obtaining our salvation.

Mercy, then, means the willingness to put aside our own needs, to forego present ambitions for ourselves, to sacrifice present advantages for a more lasting future good, not just for ourselves but for the whole human race.

It is impossible for us to practice mercy if we are totally wrapped up in ourselves, or if we are filled with fear, insecurity, selfishness and pride. Mercy, of its very nature, requires us to go out of ourselves and to minister to the needs of others. To be able to do this, we need to feel very secure within ourselves and to be convinced of God's mercy for us. We need to recognize our own value, worth and significance in God's eyes so that we are free to sacrifice ourselves for others and become the servant of all. Just as Jesus washed the feet of the disciples at the Last Supper, without losing his dignity or the respect of the disciples, so too, when we become mature, whole and holy, we can stoop down and be of humble service to others, without losing our self-respect or losing the respect of others.

In Chapter 12 of St. Matthew's Gospel, there is a quotation from Isaiah 42. "Here is my servant (Jesus) ... the bruised reed he will not crush; the smoldering wick he will not quench." This describes something of the gentleness, meekness and mercy that Jesus showed to the people of his time, and this should also describe the mercy and gentleness that we show to others. One must be very careful not to break the bruised reed. The reed is a very slender, fragile plant which can be easily broken; and if the reed is bruised, it requires great care to bring it back to life.

In the course of our daily life, we meet many "bruised reeds," people who have been hurt, crushed, bruised, or wounded in one way or another. If we want to practice this beatitude, we will show the same gentleness and mercy that Jesus showed to the outcast and the sinner so that we can heal that wound, and restore that bruised reed to health.

The other image Jesus uses, quoting Isaiah, is the smoldering wick. In that time, the wick of the oil lamp was made of flax which would hold a spark very long after its flame had been extinguished. If a person breathed upon that spark very gently, it was possible to rekindle a flame. Whereas, if one blew too hard upon that smoldering wick, one would extinguish it completely. There is a spark of divinity, a spark of goodness, a spark of love in every one of us. If we want to show mercy, we must treat each person in the same way one would treat a smoking wick, the flame of which one wishes to rekindle. Very gently, breathe upon that broken spirit, the smoking flax and rekindle the fires of love and goodness that are there.

Henri Nouwen has written a book, *The Wounded Healer*, reminding us that if we are to practice healing and mercy to others, we will be able to do so only if we are aware of our own wounds and need for healing. So it is with this beatitude; if we are to practice it, we must not be afraid to face up to our own need of mercy and healing.

In the traditional teaching of the Church, we have what are called the "corporal and spiritual works of mercy." The corporal works of mercy are based primarily on Matthew 25:31-46, where Jesus describes the last judgment. He says that when the Lord comes to judge us, "he will separate us as the shepherd separates the sheep from the goats. He will place the sheep on his right hand, the goats on his left. He will say to those on his right, 'Come, you have my Father's blessing! Inherit the Kingdom prepared for you from the creation of the world! For I was hungry and you gave me food. I was thirsty and you gave me drink. I was a stranger and you welcomed me, naked and you clothed me. I was homeless and you sheltered me. I was sick and in prison and you visited me.' The just, of course, will answer: 'Lord, when did we see you hungry, or thirsty, or naked, or homeless, or sick and in prison and visit you?' And our Lord will answer, 'As often as you did it for one of my least brothers and sisters, you did it for me.'"

The above excerpt from Chapter 25 of St. Matthew's Gospel forms the basis of the corporal works of mercy. Traditionally, a seventh has been added, "to bury the dead"—to take care of giving a proper and respectful burial to the bodies of the dead.

And, then, somewhere in the development of Christian teaching, a second set of works of mercy, the spiritual works of mercy, was added. They are: to console the sorrowful, to instruct the ignorant, to counsel the doubtful, to admonish the sinner, to bear wrongs patiently, to forgive all injuries, and to pray for the living and the dead.

These fourteen works of mercy—the seven corporal works which have to do with our physical needs, and the seven spiritual works which have to do with our spiritual needs—cover quite well the scope of this beatitude. The corporal works of mercy are quite understandable as they are given above, but let us consider the spiritual works.

To console the sorrowful: This does not mean only to go out to others at the time of death of a loved one, but also to reach out to those who are experiencing some kind of trouble, who are filled with unhappiness for one reason or another and offer some form of consolation. Very often this can be done just by our presence, just by letting that person know that we care, just by giving them a telephone call, just by making a visit or writing a note to them. If we are given words with which to console the sorrowful, so much the better, but just their knowing that we care for them brings the most consolation.

To instruct the ignorant: There are so many people who sincerely want to do what is right but, through no fault of their own, they lack the proper knowledge and education. When we help someone to come to the correct knowledge of God, we are showing great mercy to that person. Religious education, especially adult religious education, is one of the greatest acts of mercy anyone can perform.

To counsel the doubtful: Many people are insecure and not sure what to do. They need the help of a third party to decide what is best for them—to counsel them. We think of the Holy Spirit as the Divine Counselor. If we ourselves are filled with the Holy Spirit, we will be God's instrument in bringing the advice and the help of the Holy Spirit to enable others to overcome their doubts and rise above their insecurity.

To admonish the sinner: This is no doubt the most difficult of all of the works of mercy to perform. The sinner is anyone who is doing something clearly and manifestly wrong. Perhaps, they are doing harm to themselves or others by some kind of addiction. It is a work of mercy to admonish them by helping them to realize the harm they are doing, and to help them experience a conversion, a change of direction in their life. For example, if we know of an alcoholic or of someone who is clearly becoming too dependent on alcohol or drugs, or who has some other chemical addiction, our particular work of mercy is to go to that person to intervene. Perhaps, we will need the assistance of another who may be better equipped to accomplish this. We will admonish in a firm, but loving, gentle, serious and strong way, what that person needs to change in his or her life. Before one attempts to admonish another, one must seek the help and grace of the Holy Spirit through prayer, approach the situation without undue haste and arm oneself with an abundance of common sense.

To bear wrongs patiently: This spiritual work of mercy means that one is able to accept patiently, gently and lovingly the wrong done against us. Our exemplar for this is Jesus in his reaction to the events of the trial before Pilate, and during his Passion. As he was bearing the terrible pain of the crucifixion, Jesus said: "Father, forgive them, for they know not what they do" (Luke 23:34).

To forgive all injuries: This has been already discussed in our willingness to forgive seventy times seven, to forgive others as we expect God to forgive us.

To pray for the living and the dead: To spend time every day sending out waves of love, mercy and forgiveness to people all over the world, as well as to the people who have already died, is a practice we need to adopt. We have tremendous power to help others just by our prayers. So, it is a work of mercy to send constant petitions to God for the needs of others.

To be merciful to another means to seek the highest possible good for that person. In this sense, mercy goes beyond mere forgiveness of an injury that another has shown to us. It means to love the offender so much that we want the highest possible good for that person. We can see, then, that mercy is at the very heart of sanctity, and the height of charity. It implies a complete forgetfulness of self. We forget about the obligation of justice that the other person owes us. We think purely and simply what is good or best for the other.

This, however, does not mean that we allow the other person to continue to practice something evil or unjust. It may be the best for that person that we confront him with the wrong-doing, that we speak up and point out very clearly what is wrong with their actions. This would be particularly true for people who are doing wrong things without being fully aware of the harm that is being done.

Mercy does not contradict justice, but goes beyond the demands of simple justice. It becomes a form of higher justice. By showing a similar mercy to our fellow human beings, we make a return to God for all He has done for us. In that sense, we might compare mercy to a gentle rain which comes down from heaven and, falling upon the parched earth, softens the hard clay of selfishness and pride. It warms and vivifies the soil, cleanses and purifies, renews and fructifies, and the person upon whom it falls blossoms with new life.

We can compare the mercy we show to others to the gentle, healing touch that Jesus, the Divine Physician, used throughout his public ministry. Jesus is the model we must study, and try to follow in practicing mercy.

The Sixth Beatitude

"Blessed are the pure of heart, for they shall see God."

The reward or fruit which comes from purity, i.e., to see God, is the thing that all of us desire. We want to see God right now during our life on earth, and if we are pure of heart, we shall indeed do just that.

To see God means to see God's hand, His will, His wisdom and His providence at work in all of the events of our daily life; to see God's love and purpose even in our sufferings and failures, in the tragedies and the disasters that happen around us; to see God in every thing and in every one. To see God is to understand His workings in and through us and His purposes in history. Therefore, it means the absence of blindness as to the path that we should be traveling in following God's will. To see God is to know, in every situation, what God wants us to do, where to go, how to act, what to say, when to keep quiet, when to act and when not to act. To see God is to experience the direct hand of God guiding us in all of the details of our life: in our thoughts, desires, words and actions.

In this sense, to see God is a combination of three of the gifts of the Holy Spirit. The Gift of Counsel helps us to know the right thing to say and do both for ourselves and for others on every given occasion. The Gift of Knowledge is the ability to see the hand of God, the Divine Providence of God, at work in all the events of our life and of history. The Gift of Understanding enables us to penetrate the very mysteries of God, Himself, as they are present to us in creation. This, then, is the fruit of this beatitude.

How do we obtain this vision of God here, on earth? According to the teaching of this beatitude, it is through purity of heart or, as the New American Bible translates it, by being "single-hearted." Purity of heart is to our interior life what poverty of spirit is to the exterior life. In the first beatitude, poverty means we must be detached from all external things like money and property. In purity, we present to the Lord an empty heart which is open and ready to receive whatever the Lord wishes to send us.

In this sense, the pure hearted person is like the Virgin Mary. Why did Jesus Christ come to earth, born of the Virgin Mary? Mary presented to the Lord a pure heart, open, receptive and ready for this gift of life from God. "Be it done to me according to your word." Like the Virgin Mary, we must be ready, open, and receptive to God's word whenever He sees fit to send it into our soul. What happened two thousand years ago at the Incarnation is something that is meant to happen again and again. The work of Incarnation must continue, but it cannot continue without us. Just as the first Incarnation depended not only on the will and choice of God, but also upon the single-hearted attitude of Mary, so the completion of the work of redemption depends upon the availability of pure hearts in the world that are single-minded, desirous of doing the will of God, and are ready and willing to be open to the reception of a fresh outpouring of the Word of God.

The more free and single-minded hearts that are available to the Lord, the more quickly will the whole world be incarnated into that union of God and humanity, which we call the Kingdom of God. In that sense, the Word of God is just waiting for other Marys—pure, simple, empty hearts ready to give their exclusive attention to accepting the seed of God's Word. By cherishing it within their hearts, they will help it to grow until it is ready to be born again into the world. God's Word needs to find many pure hearts like Mary's, pure hearts which will accept this new seed of life, and bring forth Jesus Christ into the world today.

Just as there is a close connection between the two beatitudes of meekness and mercy, so there is also a close connection between the second beatitude regarding suffering, and the sixth beatitude of purity of heart.

Our hearts become pure to the extent that we have learned the true meaning of suffering. Our mourning will become an experience of inner growth and perfection of our motives if we learn to accept suffering simply and honestly as a fact of existence, without bitterness or self pity, with patience and openness to whatever new insights the suffering can give us. Through practice of the second beatitude of "those who have learned the true meaning of suffering," we will be able to perceive the deeper meaning behind our suffering and see the loving hand of God at work in these sorrowful events. Through suffering, our hearts become purified. We are able to develop that singleness of purpose which enables us to see God in all the events of life. As St. Paul says, "For those who love God, all things work together unto good" Romans 8:28.

Purity of heart requires the same absence of egocentricity which characterizes the meek and the merciful. Purity of heart presupposes the same absence of blind spots and inhibitions and the same simplicity and authenticity which characterize the poor in spirit. In this sense, it is impossible to practice to perfection any one of the beatitudes without also practicing the other seven.

The virtue of purity of heart has a dynamic quality. It is either growing or decreasing all the time. It grows through experience. Perhaps half of our experiences in life are negative; probably half of the things that happen to us are the opposite of what we would choose. This means that we shall experience suffering, pain, disappointment or failure. In other words, we are compelled to learn the true meaning of mourning and suffering.

How can we increase our purity of heart in spite of all the suffering which is an unavoidable factor in human life? The problem is how we can suffer without becoming egocentric, negative, bitter, resentful and angry. The answer is by trying to see God and God's hand and purpose within, behind and beyond our difficulties. We will try to look at our present predicament from the stand-point of eternity, the view-point of God. With the help of the Holy Spirit, and especially with the Gifts of Knowledge and Understanding, we can discover the deeper reasons for our suffering and see that God can indeed bring good out of everything provided we try to love Him. Seeing God is more than just sensing some contact with eternity. It presupposes a humble acceptance of the evils found in life, and our forgiveness of those who have wronged us, have caused our suffering.

A pure heart is a heart that is free of everything opposed to Love. Throughout the Old and New Testament of the Bible, as well as in ordinary usage, when we speak of the heart, we are often not referring to that physical organ within our body but symbolically to the power of a human being to love. A pure heart, therefore, is a heart that is free of all foreign matter other than love.

Pierre Teilhard de Chardin has a beautiful description of the pure heart in his book, *The Divine Milieu*. He says that if we are to progress in holiness and wholeness, the first quality we need to possess is purity of heart. Here is how he defines purity of heart: "Purity in the wide sense of the word is not merely abstaining from wrong, nor is it even chastity which is only a remarkable instance of it. Purity is the rectitude and the impulse introduced into our lives by the love of God sought in everything we do and everything that happens. A person is spiritually impure who, lingering in pleasure or shut up in selfishness, introduces within oneself and around oneself a principle of slowing down and division in the unification of the universe in God" (Part III, 3.B i, page 112).

Teilhard further describes this concept of purity of heart: "One is pure, who in accord with one's place in the world, seeks to give Christ's desire to consummate all things precedence over one's own immediate and momentary advantage. Still more pure is the one who, attracted by God, succeeds in giving that movement an impulse of Christ's for unity an ever greater continuity, intensity and reality, whether one's vocation is in the material zones of this world or whether one has access to regions where the divine gradually replaces all other earthly nourishment. Thus understood, the purity of a person is measured by the degree of attraction that draws one to the Divine Center or, by what comes to the same thing, by one's proximity to this Center. Christian experience teaches us that this is preserved by recollection, by prayer, by purity of conscience, purity of intention and the sacraments" (Ibid.).

Teilhard's favorite expression for the Kingdom of God was "Christ, the Omega Point." The text he used to describe this Omega Point is from I Corinthians 15:28: "When finally all has been subjected to the Son Jesus, he will then subject himself to the One Who made all things subject to him, so that God may be all in all."

In Matthew 6:22, Jesus says: "If your eye be single, then your whole body will be filled with light." What does it mean to have a "single" eye? It means to have eyes only for God and God's will. As Jesus said: "My meat is to do the will of Him Who sent me, to perfect His work." A single eye means to be single-minded, single-hearted, just as was Jesus. "I do always the things that please my heavenly Father." "Not my will but Thine be done." He teaches us in the Lord's Prayer to say, "Thy will be done on earth as it is in heaven." A single-hearted, single-minded, single-eyed person is one who has but one desire: to please God and to do whatever God desires. It means to have sight for but one thing: God, God's will, God's work, God's Kingdom. Purity of heart, therefore, means a singleness of purpose, an absence of any other motive in our heart except the love and service of God. One is free of selfishness, pleasure-seeking, and every foreign desire except the will of God.

As Teilhard continues in *The Divine Milieu*, "Purity is the straight-forwardness introduced into our lives by seeking the love of God in everything we do and above every other thing." It means having a desire for only one thing, to unite the whole of creation with God, through love.

The singleness of purpose recommended in this beatitude gives a person a tremendous power. However, we have to be careful because this power, which comes from a single-hearted way of life, can be used for either good or evil. We have as an example, Hitler, a person who was very single-minded, who used that tremendous power not only to win over most of his fellow countrymen to his ideas, but was also able to do a great harm to the whole world. Our singleness of purpose, therefore, must always be directed toward the common good.

We know that the leaders of the world who have accomplished great things were motivated by a singleness of purpose. One example is the Wright brothers, who were simple bicycle repairmen living in Dayton, Ohio. Orville and Wilbur Wright decided that they were going to make a heavier-than-air machine which would fly! With that singleness of purpose, they became the prime instruments to bring about the tremendous revolution in transportation and communication which the advent of the airplane and air travel has accomplished.

We see the singleness of purpose of one person, Mother Teresa. Although for the first half of her life she lived as a middle-class nun teaching the upper-class people of India, she felt a call from God, a singleness of purpose, to do something for the poor. Finally, her single-minded persistence enabled her to get from Church authorities the necessary permissions to leave her religious congregation, to go and live among the poor and to begin that work of mercy which has spread all over the world through the Missionaries of Charity.

We see what singleness of purpose can do in the person of Gandhi, who had the determination to free India of British rule. In spite of countless adversities, he was able to accomplish this. We can see this same singleness of purpose in Martin Luther King, Jr., who was able to turn the tide of racial prejudice in the U.S., and bring into existence new laws which have helped to overcome centuries of racial injustice.

In the same section of *The Divine Milieu* referenced above, Teilhard quotes from one of the novels of Robert Hugh Benson, who tells of a visionary coming upon a lonely chapel, which he enters to find one nun praying. "All at once he sees the whole world bound up and moving and organizing itself around that out-of-the-way spot, in tune with the intensity and the inflection of the desires of that puny praying figure of the nun. Through her prayer the convent chapel had become the axis about which the whole of humanity revolved. That contemplative person sensitized and animated all things because of the purity of her heart. Her faith was operative because of that singleness of purpose with which she dedicated her life to God." Benson's novel is fiction, of course, but it illustrates the power of singleness of purpose in the area of prayer. We too have power to do great good in the world today, provided we have this singleness of purpose or purity of heart, and we use it for God and the extension of love.

To develop purity is a never-ending task. We could think of the heart as a jar of dirty water muddied with many foreign objects that interfere with its purity. It is impossible to empty that jar and to begin anew with fresh clean water. Rather we must continually pour clear water—loving desires, loving acts, loving words—into this jar, our heart. And just as a jar of dirty water is gradually cleansed through the addition of pure water, over time one's heart is totally cleansed of imperfections through the addition of love. By making our hearts clean and pure we make them available to God. He can come down, as He did to the pure heart of Mary, and once more become incarnated, present today.

If our hearts are free of all defilement and imperfection, we shall be able to recognize God in a thousand places which we have formerly overlooked. Those who are pure of heart *shall see* God. We shall see Him daily in all the events, even the most unlikely ones. We shall see Him in others, in every person that we meet. We shall see God in every word of Scripture. When our heart is not pure, we are filled with many external distractions so that we miss most of God's comings into our life. He passes us like a ship in the night, and in the morning we are not even aware that He was close to us.

The pure of heart do not have to wait until after death to see God. If we practice a genuine and generous mortification of our selfish desires and intentions and strive to seek God in every event and in every thing, God will reward us here on earth by granting us the grace to see Him in each of our neighbors, in each passing event of the day, and in all the events of history. Seeing God in every person and every event, the pure of heart will be filled with the beginning of a happiness on earth that will be the foretaste of the eternal joys of heaven.

The Seventh Beatitude

"Blessed are peacemakers, for they shall be called the sons of God."

We might translate this beatitude: "Blessed are they who produce right relationships in every sphere of life, for they shall be truly God-like."

This beatitude is at the very heart of the purpose for which Jesus Christ came to earth. He came primarily to be a peacemaker. The purpose and vocation of Jesus was to reconcile the world to God, and to restore harmony among the people on earth who had become alienated from God and from one another. The human race had become estranged from God through sin. Not only was there alienation between God and the human race, but through our sinfulness there were also many forms of disagreement and hostility between different races, nations, groups and ages. The reconciliation of all these alienated parties was the major task that was assigned to Jesus when he came to earth.

A priest is a reconciler, or a mediator between God and man. A priest is anyone who is able to take two parties who have become alienated and succeed in restoring harmony between them. In this beatitude we are told that God wishes us to participate in the priestly work of reconciliation and peace-making. This is accomplished, basically, by the injection of the power and energy of love into an area where alienation has occurred.

We might think of Jesus Christ as pumping new love, God's love, into a situation where there was alienation and separation between the people and God, and between individuals and various groups. By the injection of fresh love into the situation, a reconciliation occurred, and a new state of affairs was created.

Peacemakers, by their contribution of love, are therefore able to create a new relationship that did not exist before. There is a danger that a human being will take credit for this new creation which has been brought into existence through peace-making. Because this is such a powerful force, we are sometimes tempted to imagine this power to be our own, and forget it is entirely the work of God. Realizing that we are only agents, and that it is God's love which we are using to bring about reconciliation, we must see ourselves merely as co-creators with God when we introduce this new element of love where it did not previously exist.

St. Augustine, and later St. Thomas Aquinas, defined peace as the tranquility of order. Peace is that state of being where everything is in its proper order, where God and the things of God are always put in the first place. Therefore, peace is the situation where truth, justice, freedom and love prevail. These are God's priorities and they must never be compromised in order to buy some temporary peace. It is never a question of peace at any price; some things are even more important than peace. This is the meaning of Jesus' words: "Do you think I have come to establish peace on earth? I assure you the contrary is true. I have come for division" (Luke 12:51).

The angels sang on Christmas Day that there would peace on earth to people of good will. Jesus came to bring us God's good will and to lead us to share this good will with others. Jesus' first salutation to his disciples after his resurrection was, "Peace (shalom) be with you. ... As the Father has sent me, so I send you" (John 20:21). Our duty as disciples of Christ is the same as that of the apostles, which was to bring God's love to the world and thereby to create peace on earth. This particular task of peace-making is probably the most important task that Christians have today because if we fail in our work of peace-making, mankind will destroy itself.

There are three areas where we must work to bring peace: within ourselves, with God and with our neighbor. Peace-making, therefore, must begin within ourselves with the excision from our hearts of everything that is alienated from God and makes war on God's will. If our own hearts are at peace with God, with ourselves and with our neighbor, then our very presence among other people will bring about an atmosphere of peace among them. It is only when we have created harmony, a tranquility of order, within ourselves -- that is, when we have established the right priorities, placing God and the doing of His will before our own will -- that we expect to have inner peace.

A part of inner peace is the serene acceptance of ourselves as we are. Inner peace is present when we are cognizant of our own worth, our loveableness, our God-likeness, our basic goodness despite the many things in ourselves which we do not like. We must not be afraid to face up to the full truth about ourselves. We must accept ourselves as we are, and not as we would like to be. We must be willing to look at the blind sides of our personality, the dark shadow, the unlived life which we keep repressing. We must be willing to admit even the worst about ourselves without losing hope, and trust in God's mercy and forgiveness. We must be able to love ourselves, as we are, in the same way that God loves us, no matter how much sin or evil or frailty may be found within us.

A major adjunct to finding peace within ourselves is to establish peace with God, which means to ask for forgiveness for our sins and to experience God's mercy. When we can come to the deep realization that God forgives us and loves us as we are, sins and all, we can accept that we are His children and He will take care of us.

Furthermore, to be at peace with God means to be at peace with these four attributes of God: His truth, His justice, His freedom and His love.

To be at peace with truth means we are not afraid of truth, but have an all-consuming desire for truth. Jesus says, "You shall know the truth and the truth shall make you free" (John 8:32). We must have such a tremendous love of truth that we are willing to pursue it at any price, regardless of the cost or consequences. It is better to be truthful than it is to be good. Why? Because you cannot be good until you have a basic foundation of truth and honesty. This is what is called *authenticity*.

Secondly, we must be in harmony with the concept and practice of justice. This means to be ready and willing to give what is due to all persons, never cheating or depriving others of what belongs to them, regardless of the cost or consequences to ourselves. Our love of justice must be such that whenever we see an injustice in the world or in our own conduct, we will leave no stone unturned to remedy that violation of rights. We will work to establish a situation of security and order so that no one's rights are violated. Since peace is defined as the tranquility of order, there can be no real peace until we establish justice.

Thirdly, if we are to be at peace with God, we must be at peace with freedom. This means to respect the freedom of others, never to use force, or manipulation, or threats to get others to do something that they don't want to do. We must be content to appeal to truth, justice and love to encourage them to make the right choice. Our love and respect for freedom should be so great that we are willing to die not only for our own freedom but also for the freedom of others.

Fourthly, if we are to be at peace with God, we must be on peaceful terms with love, and recognize the all-importance of love of God and love of neighbor. We must be willing to pay any price, including the sacrifice of our lives, in order to proceed in love and loving service to others.

If we are successful in finding peace within ourselves, and establishing the tranquility of right order within our own life; if we have been successful in bringing about a true peace between ourselves and God by overcoming whatever alienated us from God and things of God; if we have recognized the importance of truth, freedom, justice and love as operating principles in our life, then we are capable of becoming a good peacemaker here on earth. We are ready to help establish a right order and harmony among the different human groups and institutions: between blacks and white, Russians and Americans, Jews and Arabs, the people of Northern Ireland and those of Southern Ireland, rich and poor, etc. We will become successful peacemakers only when we have succeeded in creating peace within our own life, and are at peace with God.

Our efforts at peace-making should begin with the human relationships which are a part of our daily life, which means with the person to whom one might be married, one's children, parents, people with whom one works and the people with whom one daily associates. If we are to accomplish the task of the seventh beatitude, we should look around us to see where there is any alienation, where people are not working together peacefully and lovingly, and then ask ourselves, "How can I inject some new love into this disruptive situation and thereby bring about reconciliation?"

We cannot always expect to be successful. Jesus Christ himself was far from successful in his efforts at peace-making. He was not able to overcome the dislike that the Sadducees had for the Pharisees, nor the unfriendliness the Jews felt toward the Samaritans, nor the disaffection so many of the leaders of his own people had toward him. Yet he tried, and was willing to give his life to overcome these alienations and bring about reconciliation. That too is our task. We begin at home, or wherever we find ourselves, and start injecting new love into the situation, helping people to love one another because of our great love for them and for God.

We know that in his efforts at peace-making, Jesus refused to use violence. He respected the freedom of others and called them to peace, but he never tried to force peace upon them. This refusal to use violence is based on the conviction that every human being, as a creature of God, is basically good and capable of great love; that there is good in every person; that injustice, hatred and selfishness are against nature. No matter how thick the crust of faults may have become in a person, we must believe that there is a core of inner goodness in every person, and we try to appeal to that core through our love for that person, with the willingness to love even unto death. As Jesus said, "There is no greater love than this: to lay down one's life for one's friends" (John 15:13).

In some cases, we find that if we are willing to enter into an exchange of love with one who is filled with hatred, anger or selfishness, the injection of this love can often bring about a conversion, a reconciliation, a restoration of the tranquility of order.

If we are to be good peacemakers, we must be willing to tolerate the differences of attitude, opinion, temperament and worldviews of other people. Different people look at things in different ways. It is not always true that we are right and the other person is wrong, or that we are wrong and the other person is right. There are simply different ways of looking at the same reality, different worldviews. We must be willing to accept people as they are, and give ourselves entirely to another, accepting his particular way of looking at things, and try to help him with his own worldview to find his own peace. We do this by constantly injecting new love, accepting their freedom, avoiding violence, avoiding threats but remaining humble-minded in our own convictions, realizing that no matter how certain we are that our way is right, we could be mistaken. We don't know everything. We never know all of the facts.

It is always possible that those who disagree with us are nearer to the truth than we are. Therefore, we must be tolerant of others and their differences with us. We try to identify with others and see things from their point of view, to get in their skin, to walk in their shoes, to understand and sympathize with them. We must never take advantage of their weakness or of our own superior knowledge, skill, or strength, but always respect their human dignity and freedom, no matter how little they might respect ours. Our stance should be never to seek revenge, never to return evil for evil. St. Paul says, "Be not overcome by evil, but overcome evil with good" (Rom 12:21).

The area today where there is the greatest need of peace is international relations, particularly in the current situation that exists in the Middle East. Unless we are able to establish peace, harmony and order in this section of the world, sooner or later we can expect a raging war. Shortly before Carl G. Jung's death in 1961, he was asked at a workshop, "Is there any hope of preventing a nuclear war between the east and the west?" The response Jung gave is just as appropriate today as it was thirty-five years ago. Jung said, "Yes, there is one hope. The basic problem of alienation and hostility is that we project upon others our own negative shadow and they in turn project upon us their own rejected unconscious negative shadow. The only hope for peace is if enough individuals both in the east and in the west are willing to take back their projections and accept ownership for their own negative shadow, then it is just possible that the world will be able to squeeze through and prevent a nuclear holocaust."

Every one of us is able to make a contribution to world peace. It is not merely a question of expecting the world leaders to resolve the differences. Every individual is a peacemaker, even at the international level. Every one of us is capable of making a very positive contribution to world peace. This will happen if each one of us begins to accept ownership of our own negative shadow by discovering those particular evils, faults and dispositions that we are now projecting upon other people. If we accept ownership of them and work with them, trying to transpose the energy behind them into the energy of love, we can make a substantial contribution to world peace.

Another way we, as individuals, can contribute to world peace is to send out from our heart, waves of grace, love, mercy, forgiveness and peace to all the peoples of the world, and especially to world leaders. Through these vibrations of love and peace, we, in a positive way, will be making a substantial contribution to the establishment of world peace.

CHAPTER 5

MISSION OF CHRIST, MISSION OF CHURCH

Worldview of Christ & Church

We are all called to carry on the mission of Christ in today's world. This mission has many different aspects. None of us is expected to carry out all of these missions. We need to discern which of them we are being called to fulfill at the present time in our life. Our mission frequently changes in the course of a long life. We must be willing to accept whatever part of Christ's mission divine providence appoints to us. Frequently it is only after the fact that we discern which mission of Christ we have been fulfilling.

Jesus saw that his primary mission on earth was to convert the fallen evil powers in the world, and restore them to their original good purpose. The name given to this power over evil is *exorcism*. This power over evil was the greatest sign that the Kingdom of God had come into the world with the coming of Jesus. Jesus shared this power over evil with the Apostles and with the whole Christian movement which began after the Resurrection of Jesus. This Christian movement became the Christian Church. All baptized Christians share in this power over evil. The Sacraments of the Church are the main way that the Church uses to cast out evil spirits, and convert them to their original good purpose for which God created them. Jesus insisted that faith is the key to the reception of the powers of the Kingdom of God over evil powers. There are two sides to this faith. It involves a turning away from evil (*metanoia*) and a positive commitment of oneself to God in unconditional love. Jesus also insisted that there were certain evil spirits that could be cast out only by prayer and fasting (Matt 17:21).

In the Old Testament, God appointed three different groups of men to lead the Israelites and Jews on their journey of faith to the Kingdom of God. They were the priests, the prophets and the kings. In the New Testament, Jesus combines these three vocations in his own unique life on earth. Jesus is priest, prophet and king. In addition there are at least nine other aspects of the mission of Christ on earth besides that of priest, prophet and king. As disciples of Jesus we are called to share in one or more of these twelve aspects. We need then to study these twelve aspects of the mission of Christ and try to discern in which of these areas we are being called to follow Christ.

Twelve Aspects of the Mission of Christ

1. **PRIEST**: reconciler, peacemaker. A priest is called to bring about a reconciliation between two or more parties who have become alienated from each other. The main alienation is caused by sin, whereby we alienate ourselves from God. Jesus came to reconcile sinners who have become alienated from God. By Baptism every Christian shares in the priesthood of Jesus. Therefore, every Christian is called to work for the reconciliation of sinners to God. The priest is also called to bring about a reconciliation between alienated persons or communities upon earth. This will include reconciliation between ethnic groups, between different races, different nations, different sexes. The task of reconciliation is so widespread that every Christian should feel called to this ministry of priest, reconciler and peacemaker.

2. **PROPHET**: teacher, wisdom figure who is able to read the signs of the times and counsel and teach others the way to God and the doing of God's will. The public ministry of Jesus was carrying out his mission as a prophet. "Jesus

went throughout Galilee teaching in their synagogues, and proclaiming the good news of the Kingdom, and curing every disease and sickness" (Matt 4:23). "The crowds were astounded at his teaching, for he taught them as one having authority, and not as their scribes" (Matt 7:2829). On the night of his resurrection, Jesus gave the same mission of teaching to his disciples. Before his ascension, he commissioned the apostles, "Go therefore and make disciples of all nations ... teaching them to obey everything I have commanded you. And remember I am with you always to the end of time" (Matt 28:19-20). All of us share in this work of teaching the good news of Christ. Every day we need to discern how we can fulfill this ministry of prophet, by word and example.

3. **KING**: servant leader who gives an example of loving service to others and thus leads and encourages others to do likewise. Jesus rejected the roles of military leader and king. "The Son of Man came not to be served but to serve and give his life as a ransom for many" (Mark 10:45). At the Lord's Supper he washed the feet of his disciples and told them: "You call me Teacher and Lord, and you are right, for that is what I am. So if I, your Lord and Teacher, have washed your feet, you also ought to wash one another's feet" (John 13:13-14). All of us are called to be a humble servant-leader in our community.

4. Reveal to the world the true nature of God; tell people about God as *Abba*, Father, all-powerful, all-wise, all-good, all-loving, always faithful to his word. Jesus, in the Gospels, reveals many new aspects of God's nature that had not been previously revealed in the Old Testament. One of them is the love of enemies

and the way of non-violence. We need to study these new insights into the nature of God, and follow them rather than the out-dated teachings of the Old Testament. Then we teach others these new insights into the nature of God.

5. Announce the good news (Gospel) of the new Covenant which God wishes to make with the human race. It is called the Kingdom of God, the activity of God in the world for the sake of His chosen ones. Jesus proclaimed the Kingdom by word and by his actions. His actions were four-fold: teaching, exorcising evil spirits, healing of physical illness, and nature miracles. God is extremely generous in forgiving sin and sharing the blessings of heaven. The good news that Jesus announced is that God has freely chosen to expand the family circle of heaven to include all of us. We now have the ministry of spreading the good news of the Kingdom to the whole human race. We must tell people about the new Covenant of love Jesus announced.

6. Teach by example and word how to live a fully human life of wholeness and maturity, the life of unconditional love of God, neighbor, self and creation. This new teaching is best expressed in the Sermon on the Mount in Chapters 5, 6, 7 of Matthew's Gospel, and Chapters 6 and 11 of Luke's Gospel. The eight Beatitudes describe how Jesus lived a life of wholeness and maturity, and how we need to lead to follow his example.

7. Correct the mistakes of Mosaic law as it was being taught by Scribes. Over the centuries since Moses taught the Israelites in the desert, there had grown up a large number of interpretations of Mosaic law. Some of these traditions were good and useful, but others

were long outdated. Throughout the public ministry of Jesus, he attempted to correct the wrong interpretations of Mosaic law. This resulted in strong opposition from the Scribes and Pharisees. Their opposition was so great that they decided to put Jesus to death. Unfortunately many Christians today are still adhering to the fundamentalist interpretation of the Old Testament that the Jewish Scribes followed, and which Jesus condemned. One example of this is the emphasis on the externals of the Mosaic law to the neglect of the spirit of the law. Another example is the attitude of Jesus towards money and poverty. Many Christians are unwilling to accept Jesus' teaching on money.

8. Confront everyone with the paradoxes of the Gospel. Many of the parables in the Gospels confronted people with a whole new way of living. This did not make Jesus popular, but led ultimately to his death. If we wish to be a follower of Jesus, we must be ready and willing to follow the same path that Jesus followed. As G.K. Chesterton once wrote, "It is not that Christianity has failed, it has been tried, found difficult and abandoned."

9. Introduce the way of non-violence and love of enemies as the best way to conquer evil. "Be not overcome by evil, but overcome evil by good." This is the most dramatic of Jesus' teachings. It was an entirely new way to handle evil. Instead of killing the evil person, Jesus taught that we should go out in love for our enemies and confront them regarding their evil in a loving, non-violent way even though this might result in the loss of our life at the hands of the enemy. Gandhi and Martin Luther King, Jr. are examples, in the past century, who

taught and practiced this new way of loving, non-violent confrontation of evil.

10. Suffer the personal consequences of this confrontation of evil by a willingness to die on the cross, rather than change a single point of his teaching. The Christian martyrs have followed the example of Jesus. To be a true follower of Jesus we must be willing to die for our Christian faith.

11. By unlimited love (agapic love) we bring unlimited good out of these sufferings and persecutions (salvation of the world). Agapic love is characterized by consistently putting the needs of God and others ahead of our desires. This is the love Jesus showed throughout his life, and for which he became the savior of the world.

12. How to bear sufferings properly: this is the paradox of the cross, the Paschal Mystery. St. Paul says "I am now rejoicing in my sufferings for your sake, and in my flesh I am completing what is lacking in Christ's sufferings for the sake of his body, the church" (Col 1:24). Jesus, as the head of his Mystical Body, has completed his sufferings. It is now our task as members of this same Mystical Body to complete the full complement of sufferings needed for the salvation of the world.

Mission of the Church

Jesus Christ died before he finished his work of establishing the Kingdom of God on earth. He passed on this mission to the Apostles, and to the whole Christian movement. "As the Father has sent me, so I send you" (John 20:21). It is the mission of the Church to carry forward the work begun by Jesus. Therefore, the twelve aspects of the mission of Christ are also a description of the work of the Christian Church. In order to fulfill its God-given mission, the Church must endeavor to have an authentic worldview. At the present time, the Church is in the process of choosing between three worldviews. We have given the names of Ptolemaic, Copernican and Einsteinian to these worldviews. There are many sincere, intelligent members and leaders of the Church who adhere to each of these worldviews. There are elements of truth in each worldview. However, for the past century the leadership of the Church has slowly shifted from the Ptolemaic to Copernican, and from Copernican to the Einsteinian worldview. This shift of worldviews influences every aspect of Church structure and theology. On pages 122-124 is a chart showing how the different worldviews affect Church structures.

Pyramid Church Structure

During most of the two thousand years of Catholic Church history, we have operated under a pyramid structure at all three levels: parish, diocese, world. This has meant strict, authoritarian control of the whole by the man at the top of the pyramid, be it pastor, bishop, or pope. In the pyramid structure, the man at the top reserves the right to make final decisions in doctrine, administration, and methods of operation for programs in which the Church is involved. He can delegate work to subordinates, but assumes the final responsibility. In the pyramid structure, the pastor is answerable only to the bishop, the bishop only to the pope, and the pope only to God. This enables the leader to run a very tight ship, provided he is capable, able to remember and handle the myriad details of a large organization, able to make workable decisions, and is capable of following through the implementation of the decisions.

The degree of success of the pyramid structure depends primarily upon two factors: 1) leadership capability of the man at the top, 2) a large corps of hard-working assistants who are willing to live and operate under this type of structure. However, the pyramid structure breaks down or become ineffective if: a) the leader is weak, vacillating, unable to make good decisions, or allows subordinates to manipulate him for their own selfish purposes, b) the subordinates refuse to live and operate under an undemocratic, authoritarian system.

Beginning in the early Middle Ages, Church theologians attempted to prove that the pyramid structure was of divine origin, based on the New Testament and the words of Jesus in the Gospels, and therefore was the only possible structure for a Church established by Jesus Christ. Both the New Testament and Church history were interpreted from this point of view. Even false decretals (letters of the pope that formulate decisions in ecclesiastical law) were fabricated to give added credence to it. Church councils, papal decrees and theological arguments were directed to the preservation of the pyramid structure for the Church. However, during the past fifty years techniques of historical criticism have been perfected, and the scriptural and historical foundations of the pyramid structure for the Church have been more and more discredited. Today, few Catholic theologians would claim that the pyramid structure was divinely established by Christ.

The Ptolemaic Church

Until the Second Vatican Council, the leadership of the Catholic Church accepted the pyramid Church structure as the only valid Church structure. The most revolutionary event that occurred during the four years of Second Vatican Council was a shift by the vast majority of the Council members from the vertical, pyramid, Ptolemaic worldview to the horizontal, Copernican worldview. A loud minority of bishops still insisted on the old vertical, pyramid structure. As a result, the most important document of the Council, *Lumen Gentium*, is a schizophrenic document. It advocates both a vertical, pyramid, Ptolemaic worldview as well as a horizontal, Copernican worldview. Those who insist on maintaining the old Ptolemaic church structures can find

110

texts in this document to back up their claim. Similarly, those who advocate horizontal, Copernican church structures can find ample texts in the same document to back up their claim. In order to get almost unanimous agreement, the Council Fathers chose to go in this direction. Today, forty years after the close of the Council, we find Church leaders and members in both camps. We also find a minority of Church leaders and many Church members advocating a move to the Einsteinian, co-relational worldview as the direction the Church needs to go. Actually, there is truth and value in all three worldviews as applied to the Church. The Church is important (Ptolemaic model). The future coming of Christ is important (Copernican model). The Christian's work in today's world for justice, freedom, truth, and love (Einsteinian model) is also very important.

The symbol for the Ptolemaic Church is the rock of St. Peter—solid, immovable, unchangeable, everlasting. "Upon this rock I will build my Church and the gates of hell shall never prevail against it" (Mt 16:18). There are two dimensions to the Ptolemaic Church—past and present. The accent is upon the past, the long-standing, traditional way of teaching and doing everything relating to religion. According to the Ptolemaic worldview nothing substantial ever changes. Therefore it was sufficient for each new generation to know what former generations taught and then do exactly as they had done. For the Ptolemaic Church salvation is a thing of the past, a thing already accomplished by Jesus. We need only to make contact with Jesus through the Sacraments and we are saved. The problem arose when historical criticism was able to prove that many of the traditions we were following today originated in the early Middle Ages. We now know that the actual events of the Church of the first century were quite different from the Church of the Middle Ages.

Horizontal Church Structure

This form of structure is closest to the model of authority and administration used by modern political democracies such as our own national government. However, the horizontal model for the Church puts an arrow at the end of the line to indicate that the center of attention should be directed to the goal of the Kingdom of God which is beyond the present. This structural model sees the Church as a pilgrim people on a desert journey, similar to the Israelites, working their way to the promised land of the Kingdom of God.

The Protestant reformed Churches originated in Europe at the time that Copernicus and Galileo were propagating their heliocentric (sun-centered) worldview. It is more than a coincidence that the church structural model for the Reformation churches is similar to the Copernican worldview. Instead of a static, systematic, uniform, sacrament-oriented Church, the reformers proposed a more dynamic, Biblically-oriented church model. They saw the church as a community of believers who accepted Jesus Christ as their Lord and Savior. They denied the all-importance of structure, hierarchy and sacraments. The church no longer served a specific, irreplaceable function in the transmission of God's truth and grace. The emphasis was on a personal acceptance and faith in Jesus Christ. The future Kingdom of God, and the congregation of the saints in this Kingdom became more important than Pope, bishops, priests, or external church structures.

Only during the past forty years since the Vatican Council has the Copernican worldview affected any great change in the Roman Catholic Church. However, as early as 1936 Father Josef Jungmann in Germany was advocating such a change. He coined the term "*kerygmatic*" to describe a very Biblically-oriented theology. He suggested three dimensions to this kerygmatic theology: 1) to bring to life the sacred events of the past, especially the life, death and resurrection of Jesus through the symbols of the liturgy; 2) to celebrate God's call of the people of God to His Kingdom; 3) to anticipate the future events of the Second Coming of Christ upon earth. The Second Vatican Council adopted all three of these recommendations of Father Jungmann.

Pierre Teilhard de Chardin had also written extensively before the Council regarding the forward and upward movement of mankind toward a point of convergence with Christ and God, which he called the "Omega Point." He saw the Church as a continuation of the history of salvation whereby the people of God, the new Israel, progresses forward and upward toward that future point in history when Christ will establish his Kingdom upon earth.

The Copernican Church Model

Those who accept this model of Church structure make a distinction between the Church and the Kingdom of God. Those who accept the pyramid model identify the Church of today with the Kingdom of God. In the horizontal model the Kingdom of God has already come only for Jesus Christ. It is "not yet" for the rest of us—still out ahead of us at some unknown point in the future. If we accept the horizontal model, the Church becomes secondary to the Kingdom of God. The Church loses some of the importance it used to have in the minds of most Catholics. The important thing in life is no longer becoming a member of the Church, but rather preparing ourselves to become worthy citizens of the Kingdom of God. Membership in the Catholic Church is no longer considered necessary for salvation. According to this model, membership in the Church is not for everyone on earth, but only for those human beings who are willing to pay the price of discipleship of Christ—willing to carry on the same mission of Christ in today's world, including crucifixion on the cross. The horizontal model emphasizes that the Church is a very important means for the establishment of the Kingdom of God upon earth, but that it is only one of a number of means which God is using to establish His Kingdom of love, justice, truth and freedom.

According to this model the Church has three tasks: 1) To bring to life the life of Christ, also the total history of the people of God. The past events are so important that they need to be made present to us through the Sacred Mysteries; 2) To anticipate the future event of the Kingdom

concerning final matters and death and the Judgment etc

of God by making this future live for us today through the Sacraments (Eschatological dimension); 3) To celebrate God's call and choice of us and our adoption, here and now, into the family of God. (Baptism and Confirmation)

Those adopting this model are very biblically and liturgically oriented. The Gospels are not used as a polemical justification of church structures (pyramid model), but they are brought to life and made meaningful to the needs and problems of today's world. For the proponents of this model the emphasis is on the joyful acceptance of the call of Jesus to his Kingdom, and our generous response to all that is required of us as members of his Kingdom.

St. Peter is the patron saint of the Ptolemaic Church, while St. Paul is the patron saint of the Copernican Church. Following Pauline tradition, two of the most pronounced elements of the Copernican Church are its emphasis on the Church as the people of God, and the importance of the whole community of believers participating in the celebration of the liturgy.

Instead of the accent on the past as the Ptolemaic Church insisted, the accent is now placed on the future events of the history of salvation. The Church is no longer the center of history but simply one of the many agents working on earth for the future establishment of God's Kingdom. No longer is the Church considered absolutely and forever unchangeable, but rather it is an evolving organism which must change and adjust to the new conditions of each age, each nation, each culture. The horizontal line running through history from the past toward the future is the symbol that best describes the Copernican Church.

Co-Relational Church Structure

The co-relational is an added fourth dimension to the past, present and future dimensions of the horizontal model. Values and realities are seen to exist primarily in whatever relationships we have with others, rather than in some objective value and reality in themselves. For those who accept this model the only absolutes are relationships such as love, truth, justice and freedom. They are unwilling to admit that natures and substances are absolutely unchanging. This model sees everything on earth, including the Church, as part of an evolutionary process of growth and change from a less perfect to a more perfect stage. Those adopting this model claim that Church structures are temporary expedients, formulated by fallible human beings, to meet the needs of their time. As such everything in the structure of the Church is subject to change and growth as new needs and new situations arise in the course of history. The primary concern is not so much the kind of church structure that Jesus Christ established, or that was created by the Christians of the first and second centuries, but what is the structure that will best foster the establishment of good relationships of love, justice, truth and freedom among the people of today.

The adoption of the co-relational model for the Church requires us to reject the Grecian-Aristotelian concept of unchanging substances which most Christians have accepted as truth for the past two thousand years. We must not totally disregard all permanence and order, but we must re-situate the absolute in the transcendental principles of love, truth, justice and freedom. If this is admitted, we must then realize that these transcendental principles never exist in isolation, but only in relationships. Most people will agree with this once it is presented to them, but until we reflect upon it, we fail to realize what a tremendous revision of our customary assumptions is required with this new worldview.

If we admit the absolute value of these relationships of love, truth, justice and freedom, it will be readily seen that the place where the Church must be primarily involved is in the day-to-day existential relationships where these values can best be implemented. Those accepting the co-relationship model are interested not in the Church as such, nor in some future Kingdom of God upon earth, but in how we can best create, preserve, and increase love, truth, justice and freedom in the "here and now" on earth. The <u>Vatican II Document</u>, *The Church in the Modern World,* was written from this co-relational worldview and is the first official church document which endorses this model for church life. As yet, most of the leadership in the Church has not been willing to adopt this new model for Church structures. However, many theologians in recent years maintain that, for survival, the Church must adopt this model in every facet of its life.

Those accepting this model maintain that Jesus did not establish a Church, as such, and probably did not envision the establishment of a Church structure of the type which actually evolved. They claim that Jesus was a totally other-centered person, God in human flesh. Because he was totally other-centered, he saw himself primarily as a servant to the needs of the people of his time. Regardless of the afflictions (illness, hunger, ignorance, fear, death, possession of evil spirits), Jesus responded to the human needs of his day. Because he had the insight to see the total reality of mankind, he was not content merely to satisfy the needs of the present moment, but endeavored to fulfill the long-range, everlasting needs of people. Thus the call to the apostles and disciples to carry on his work after his death. The particular method and structure to fulfill this commission of Jesus had to be worked out from day to day during the early days after the Resurrection. Those who accept the co-relational model must also look beyond the superficial needs of today's world and attain the worldview of Christ regarding the total reality of the world in order to best serve the needs of humankind.

The Einsteinian Church

As applied to church structures, the co-relationship model means that we consider no person or institution as untouchable, sacrosanct or unchangeable. Because the world and mankind are constantly changing, it is necessary continually to update Church structures as well as other structures of society. The challenge for leaders and members of the Church today is to find the kind of structure and relationship that will enable us to do the best possible service to the world. Jesus maintained that his disciples would perform even greater works than he did. In the co-relationship, processive, evolutionary model, we can even improve on the methods of service which Jesus used. Life is capable of unlimited increase, growth and perfection.

According to Einstein's theory, the value of everything is found in the relationships each object has with everything else. Applying this to religion, the Church is no longer seen as something entirely apart from the rest of the world, and governed by special laws that apply only to itself. Everything in the universe, including the Church and religion, is seen to be constantly adjusting itself to all other realities. In the Ptolemaic Church, changelessness was considered a sign of validity. In the Einsteinian worldview changelessness is a sign of death and separation from reality. Therefore, as part of a constantly evolving and progressing world, the Church must be a dynamic, constantly moving organism. To run away from change is to run away from life. Church structures and even Church doctrines must be conceived as part of an evolving process toward an ever more perfect truth. In the Einsteinian model the only absolutes are transcendental principles such as truth, justice, freedom, love, peace and joy. These principles are permanent inasmuch as they are universally right and true. By the very fact that they are relationships which exist between living, growing persons, they too must continue to evolve and develop from the less perfect to the more perfect.

In the Ptolemaic Church, emphasis was on the past. In the Copernican Church the emphasis is on the future. In the Einsteinian Church the emphasis is on the present. God is not someone far away, but right here with us in every person we encounter, in everything we experience, in every event that occurs. Salvation is not something already attained, nor something that awaits us in the future. Rather salvation is found right here, today, in the proper fulfillment of our

nships with one another, and with the world around ne secular and the sacred are not two isolated and different worlds. For the Einsteinian, there is only one world, today's world, of which every event and every part is sacred and religious. The supernatural is no longer something contradictory to the natural, but rather the introduction of a new energy into our life which enables us to carry out our relationships more justly, freely, truthfully, lovingly, peacefully and joyfully. For a person who is oriented by the Einsteinian worldview, religion and the world are not separate entities, but two sides of the same reality.

Everything in the Church—sacraments, liturgy, hierarchy, parish structures—have value insofar as they help the members of the Church to carry out their mission of establishing, here on earth, a situation where truth, justice, freedom, love, peace and joy reign supreme. Just as Jesus was a totally other-centered person who addressed himself constantly to fulfilling the needs of the people among whom he lived, so we, his disciples, must see as our primary mission the ministering to the social and physical needs of all of mankind—the alleviation of hunger and poverty, of war and fear, of sickness and suffering, of injustice and violence. But this is not enough. Like Christ, we must also look beyond the temporary solution of today's human problems, and accept the challenge of trying to solve the long-range, everlasting needs of people—the problem of death, of life after death, of a final judgment and reckoning for all that we say, do or think.

If St. Peter is the patron saint of the Ptolemaic Church, and St. Paul the patron saint of the Copernican Church, then St. John, the beloved disciple, is the patron saint of the Einsteinian Church. The difference between the theology of St. Paul and that of St. John is that Paul constantly spoke and thought of the Kingdom of God as something to be achieved in the future with the second coming of Christ. For St. John, the death and resurrection of Jesus marked the beginning of the new Kingdom of God. Scripture scholars speak of the "realized eschatology" of St. John as compared with the future eschatology of St. Paul. For those who adopt the Einsteinian worldview to explain what is happening in the Church and in Christianity today, the place "where the action is" is not primarily in the past or in the future, but "right now" in all the daily relationships we have with one another, with the external world around us, and with the eternal reality we call God.

For the Ptolemaic Church, salvation was a thing of the past, a thing already accomplished by the death and resurrection of Jesus. We need only to make contact with Jesus through the Sacraments, and we were automatically saved. For the Copernican Church, salvation is still a future event, primarily or even exclusively dependent upon an event entirely beyond human control, the Second Coming of Christ. For the Einsteinian Church, salvation is the task of today's Christian in today's world. Either we get into the fray and establish a Kingdom of justice, truth, freedom, love, peace and joy, or it will never happen. The Second Coming of Christ is an event that takes place every time an individual Christian or the Christian Community opens itself to the Holy Spirit.

Church structures are important (Ptolemaic model). The future coming of Christ is important (Copernican model). The Christian's work in today's world for justice, peace, freedom, truth, love, joy, and fulfillment is also very important (Einsteinian model). All three models contain elements of truth. Any group of people working together, living together, worshipping together or learning together needs some kind of structure for efficiency. Structure is synonymous with order and the opposite of chaos. The high water mark of popularity for the Copernican Church was the period of the Second Vatican Council. Things which the kerygmatic, biblical, liturgical movements had been advocating for years finally became the official teaching of the Catholic Church. But this is not all that the Vatican Council did. It kept the door open to the Ptolemaic Church of previous centuries. It opened the door a tiny crack to the new, co-relational model of the Einsteinian worldview. The fullness of truth will probably be a combination of all three models, all three worldviews. It is the mission of today's Church and today's Christian to find a way to merge and include the truth that is present in every valid worldview, every valid Church model.

Three Worldviews of the Christian Church

PTOLEMAIC	COPERNICAN	EINSTEINIAN
Static, unchangeable universe	Dynamic, evolving, expanding universe	Converging universe – Omega point
Vertical, pyramid, hierarchical structure	Horizontal, collegial structure *(collegiality)*	Co-relational, experiential structure *Now we love + serve are*
Two-dimensional (past & present)	Three-dimensional (past, present, future)	Four-dimensional (relational) *on the way*
Church centered – church infallible	People of God centered – community	Person & world centered *How to help the world*
Individual salvation all-important	Salvation through community	Love & service to the world
Institutional church *serve in the Eucharist*	Church as sacrament, people of God *baptism*	Church as servant of people
Church is Kingdom of God on earth	Kingdom of God already in Christ, not yet in us	We already can begin to experience the Kingdom of God
Past oriented – present duplicates	Future oriented – second coming	Present world oriented
Unchangeable natural law	Evolving laws of nature	Only absolutes are transcendentals *love justice*
Scholastic, systematic method	Biblical, liturgical, kerygmatic	Eschatological – cosmogenesis
Fear of sin – angry God appeased	Mercy, forgiveness of loving God	Only heresy is failure to love *empathy in relation*
Goal: Life with God in heaven	Goal: Prepare for the Kingdom of God & second coming	Goal: Kingdom of God in present world

120

Triardion [handwritten]

Fr. Chet [handwritten]

PTOLEMAIC	COPERNICAN	EINSTEINIAN
Natural opposed to supernatural	All of nature is sacred	No distinction between nature and grace (The New Day) [handwritten]
Earth and man center of universe	Heliocentric (sun) universe	Christocentric universe (Omega Point)
Grecian-Mediterranean concepts	Western cultural concepts	World-wide concepts
Outside church no salvation	Outside Christ no salvation	Salvation open to all peoples
Salvation a thing of past (historical)	Salvation a thing of the future	Salvation is present, here & now
Unchanging, absolute truth attainable	Evolving truth	Only absolutes are relationships
St. Peter: rock of infallibility	St. Paul: good news of salvation	St. John: realized eschatology
Church: pure, sinless bride of Christ	A sinful church needs reformation	A world-wide, ecumenical church
Church structures formed by Jesus	Church structures need reformation	Church structures are human and open to change

Bring all religions together [handwritten]

Our task - How to bring all 3 together
without denying the value
of all 3. [handwritten]

CHAPTER 6

GOD'S PLAN FOR THE HUMAN RACE

Worldview of God

In the Gospels Jesus uses the image of the Kingdom of God to describe the plan of God for the human race. Another image can be used to describe God's plan— namely, to expand the family circle of heaven. We may think of the three persons of the Blessed Trinity as the original family circle of heaven. It is a circle of infinite, everlasting love. This original family circle of the Blessed Trinity could have remained intact for all eternity. However, God decided to expand this family circle to include both angels and human beings. It was an action motivated by pure, unselfish, unconditional love. To expand this family circle of heaven, there are at least seven steps.

The first step was the free decision on the part of the Blessed Trinity to include us as adopted daughters and sons of the heavenly Father/Mother. The second step was to create the physical universe where we could live and learn to love in the same way that the three persons of the Blessed Trinity live and love. Astronomers tell us that this second step occurred about fifteen billion years ago with the Big Bang.

The third step occurred about a million years ago with the creation of the first human beings on earth, human beings with the freedom to choose the life of love that is present in the family circle of heaven. The fourth step in God's plan took place just two thousand years ago in the little cottage of Nazareth, the home of the Blessed Virgin Mary. We call it the Incarnation of the Second Person of the Blessed Trinity in the womb of Mary. With that event God reached down into the body of Mary and chose to take a piece of human flesh and incorporate it into the human body of Jesus Christ.

The fifth step in God's plan takes place each time we celebrate the Sacrament of the Holy Eucharist. During the Eucharistic prayer God chooses to incorporate the bread and wine into the flesh and blood of the risen Lord Jesus. This is very similar to what occurred in the body of Mary at Nazareth. However, God is not especially interested in incorporating bread and wine into his body. He chose to use this particular method in order to incorporate us human beings into the mystical body of Jesus Christ. This occurs at Holy Communion when we receive the consecrated species of the sacrament into our body. Holy Communion is the sixth step in God's plan to expand the family circle of heaven.

Holy Communion is the eating of Christ's body and drinking of Christ's blood, but this sacramental act of eating and drinking is exactly opposite to our normal act of eating and drinking. In normal eating and drinking, we digest the food and drink into our body. In Holy Communion, the Risen Lord Jesus ingests or incorporates us into his sacred risen Body and Blood. The lesser is incorporated into the greater. In Holy Communion Jesus is the greater, we are the lesser.

God always respects our freedom and never forces Himself upon us. So the degree of our incorporation into Jesus Christ at Holy Communion is directly proportionate to the degree of our love for God and Jesus. If we go to Holy Communion with our hearts tightly closed to love, either love of God or love of our neighbor, nothing happens. If we receive Holy Communion with our hearts open just a wee bit in love of God and neighbor, Jesus will take that sliver of love and incorporate that into his Mystical Body. If we go to Holy Communion with our hearts wide open in love for God, for all other human beings, for ourselves and for all of creation, then Jesus will incorporate us completely into his Mystical Body.

There is a seventh step for expanding the family circle of heaven. It is what we do with the love and graces we receive in each Holy Communion. If we think of grace as divine energy that enables us to love as God loves, each Eucharist gives us the power to incorporate the whole human race into the body of Christ. Each Holy Communion creates new divine energy that we can use to take the whole human race another tiny step towards the Kingdom of God. Only God knows how many trillion of steps are needed to complete the family circle of heaven and bring forth God's Kingdom on earth.

Holy Communion does not automatically fulfill its purpose of expanding the family circle of heaven or creating the Kingdom of God on earth. It simply gives us a new supply of divine energy or grace that enables us to practice love in a more perfect way. Once we have received the Eucharist, we have much work to do in order to fulfill the purpose for which Jesus instituted this sacrament. We need to cooperate with God by our many new acts of unconditional love during our life on earth. By these acts of love we create a new energy of love that is everlasting. This new energy will remain alive on earth for thousands of years, long after we have passed on to join the family circle of heaven.

The Eucharist is not the only way to bring into existence new divine energy on earth. Each of the sacraments has this power to create new grace. We can also be sure that God's power to bring forth new divine energy of love is not limited to what we Christians are able to accomplish by our seven sacraments. God loves all human beings and desires us to be part of the family circle of heaven, and part of the Kingdom of God on earth. Therefore, we can be sure that every act of love by any human being on earth has sacramental value. By that we mean that every act of love takes the whole human race another tiny step towards the fulfillment of God's plan to expand the family circle of heaven and to achieve the Kingdom of God upon earth.

Five Bases of Prayer

In order to have a healthy relationship of love with God there are five areas where we need to touch base with God each day. They are gratitude, discernment, petition, intercessory prayer and review. All of them relate in some way to love. God is love, and since we are made in the image and likeness of God, love is the one word that best describes God's relationship to us and our relationship to God. We might also reverse the subject and predicate and say that Love is God. Therefore, whenever we have an experience of love, we are having an experience of God. Our life of love revolves around four areas: love of God, love of other human beings, love of ourselves, love of creation.

The first and most important base of prayer is GRATITUDE to God for the many gifts we have received from our God. Our first thought upon awakening each morning should be to thank God for the gift of another day of life, another day in which to practice the four ways of love: God, others, self and nature. Throughout the day we can lift our thoughts to God in loving gratitude for God's many gifts that enable us to carry on our daily life. In the evening we can thank God for the many graces we have received throughout the day. At the end of the day before we fall asleep we can close the day with feelings of deep gratitude to God for the many gifts we have received. Everything is a gift, every moment of the day is a gift from God, every event of the day is filled with God's love. Praise of God is another way to express our gratitude to God.

The second base of our daily prayer is DISCERNMENT. We need to take at least five or ten minutes each morning to look over our plans for the day, and try to discern how we can best express our love. We look at all four areas of love: God, others, self, the whole of creation. We ask ourselves, "How can I do a good job today of loving God, others, self, the world." This will form our Personal Growth Plan for the day. Each day we ask ourselves how best can we practice love in all four areas of our life. We open ourselves to the

Knowledge (How?)

Holy Spirit and ask for guidance in deciding how best to love. We use our common sense and intelligence in order to make as good a decision as possible. If we have a daily planner or appointment book, we look to see what we will be doing throughout the day, and the people we will be meeting. Then we ask ourselves how can we best show love in each encounter and event. Our plan should be to do the most good for the most people. If it helps to jog our memory, we might write down in our journal or appointment calendar our Personal Growth Plan of love each day.

Ask

The third base of prayer each day is to PETITION God for the needed grace to do a good job of the Personal Growth Plan of love we have decided to follow. Our Lord says, "Ask and you shall receive" (Matt 7:7). If we do not ask, we will not receive. Grace has a short shelf life. We need to ask for fresh grace each day in order to practice the needed love that is the foundation of our whole life. The purpose of our asking for grace from God is not to inform God of something He does not know. Rather the purpose of petitionary prayer is to remind ourselves of our need of God's help. Those who fail to petition God each day for grace are guilty of pride. Asking God for grace to practice love in all four areas of life will avoid pride, and heighten humility and authenticity.

The fourth base of prayer each day is INTERCESSION. God has seen fit to share with us some of His power. We have been given the privilege of being co-creators with God in bringing down from heaven to earth the divine energy we call grace. The word "grace" comes from the Latin word, "*gratia*," which means gift. God is exceedingly generous in sending down this divine energy of grace upon the world. We need to be equally generous in petitioning God to continue to send down this divine energy of grace upon the entire human race, the whole world and all of creation.

The fifth base of prayer is that of a REVIEW of the day before we fall asleep at night. We look back over the day and thank God for the many graces and opportunities God has given us to practice love that day. We also ask God to forgive us for any failures to practice love during the day. We do not have to belabor this examination of conscience. Two, three, or four minutes should be sufficient. We then ask God to protect us, and continue to bless us. With that we should be able to fall peacefully to sleep.

It is suggested that we incorporate these five bases of prayer into a Personal Growth Plan. See Appendix A for a description of such a Personal Growth Plan. It is recommended that we make a new plan each morning and that we limit our commitment to one day at a time. If we are faithful to such a growth plan each day, we will make much progress on our journey of faith and the fulfillment of God's plan for the human race. The daily repetition of these five steps of prayer will gradually reveal to us God's worldview and God's plan for the establishment of the Kingdom of God on earth. By our daily effort to practice love each day towards God, others, self, and creation we will thereby fulfill God's plan to expand the family circle of heaven to include all of us.

·

CHAPTER 7

Using the Bible in Prayer

Worldview of the Bible

Our relationship with God is primarily expressed in our prayer-life, and one of the best tools to be used in our prayer-life is the Bible. It is most beneficial to one's journey of faith to have a facility for using the Bible in prayer. We must understand clearly the difference between using the Bible in study and using the same Bible in prayer. Both prayer and study of the Bible are important aids on our journey of faith. The more we know about the Bible, its historical background, the different senses of meaning in the Scriptures, the various interpretations by the biblical scholars of its texts, the better use we can make of this tool in our spiritual life. But Scripture study is not prayer, although it is an excellent preparation for using the Bible in prayer. When used in prayer the words of the Bible become part of a dialogue between God and ourselves.

We must never forget that there is both a human author and a divine author of the words of the Bible. The human author in the Bible is capable of error; therefore, not everything in the Bible is to be taken as coming from God. For example, we do not have to accept as from God Paul's insistence that women have a covering on their head when in church, and not be allowed to speak in church. The Old Testament approves of polygamy and slavery. We do not have to accept these teachings as inspired by God. This of course raises some real and serious problems. How do we know which teachings of the Bible are from God, and which not from God? As Catholics we can rely on the magisterium of the church to interpret for us the teachings of the Bible. Since Protestants do not accept church authority over the teachings of the Bible, they are forced to rely on private interpretation of the Bible. Actually, Catholic Church authorities have only legislated on a few passages of the Bible, for example, that Jesus is the Son of God, and that the person of Jesus is divine. For most of the Bible, both Catholics and non-Catholics have to rely on their own private interpretation of the words of Sacred Scripture. We have to make use of our common sense to tell us which teachings of Bible are from God, and which from human authority and therefore subject to error. To help us make the right decision, we should pay careful attention to what reputable biblical scholars teach regarding difficult passages of the Bible.

Having admitted the presence of human authorship as well as divine authorship in the Sacred Scriptures, we can safely accept most of what we read in the Bible as inspired by the Holy Spirit. When we use the Bible as prayer, we go directly to the heart of a Scripture passage and ask ourselves what God is saying to us in this text. Prayer is primarily a dialogue between God and ourselves. Ordinarily, our first concern in prayer should be to listen to what God wishes to say to us. Only secondly do we respond to God's word. Prayer is not supposed to be a mere monologue where we do all the talking, and God merely listens and then reacts positively or negatively to our words. Prayer is primarily listening. Our first concern is to discern what God is saying to us. There will be exceptions to this, for example, in time of emergency when we cry out to God for help, or when we wish simply to praise and thank God for His blessings.

When we say that ordinarily we should let God initiate the prayer-conversation with Him, we are talking about those formal periods of prayer which we call *meditation*. If we wish to enjoy a vibrant, living, growing relationship of love with God on our journey of faith, we need to set aside a period of time each day in which we commune with God in prayer. We may call this our holy hour or sacred time in which God alone is the focus of our attention. A traditional name for this time of prayer is meditation. In this daily meditation period, it is proper that we let God do the first talking. God has many ways of speaking to us, but the primary way is by means of the Bible. We call it the word of God. We believe that the Holy Spirit was present to the biblical writers so that the words of the Bible are not only those of Paul or John or Matthew, but also the words of God Himself. If our prayer-meditation is primarily that of listening to God, then the Bible is the first and most important aid to this prayer time.

Exactly how do we use the words of the Bible in prayer? First of all, do not expect to be able to use every verse of the Bible in prayer. The Bible was written for an extremely wide variety of people and purposes and situations. Not everything in the Bible is meant for every person who happens to read it. We need to be selective, and look for those verses which seem to speak directly to us, and have a personal message from God to us. For the average person who uses the Bible in prayer, one is fortunate to be able to find even one-hundredth of the Bible as helpful to one's prayer needs. Therefore, by way of remote preparation for our meditation on the Bible, we need to read the whole Bible and look for those biblical verses or passages that seem to speak directly to us. We may call these our "Ah-Ha" verses. We should make a careful list of such verses because once we succeed in breaking open a biblical passage so that it speaks directly to our needs, we can go back to these same passages again and again the rest of our life, and find them equally meaningful. It is to be recommended that we make a repertoire of favorite Scripture texts, and refer to this list before beginning each meditation period. It is advisable to divide one's list of texts according to different topics and categories, for example, humility, charity, faith, trust, etc. On our journey of faith we will find that different spiritual needs arise from day to day. Depending upon the particular need for that day, choose a Scripture passage from one's list of "Ah-Ha" verses appropriate to one's need, and use this passage as the first part of our prayerful dialogue with God.

Not only is the Bible the primary source for discerning what God wishes to say to us during prayer, but it also gives many examples of divinely inspired responses that the biblical characters made to God in prayer. The 150 Psalms are examples of prayer responses to God that both Jews and Christians have been using ever since the Psalms were recorded. In addition, scattered throughout both the Old and New Testaments are canticles and other prayer responses which are appropriate for our use today. An example of this is the Magnificat of Mary which we can use to express our gratitude to God for His many favors (Lk 1:46-55).

It is often helpful to use a notebook or journal to write down what we think God is saying to us in a scripture passage, and then to write down the response we wish to make to God's word. For many people such writing helps to make the prayerful dialogue with God more real and meaningful. It is also something to which we can refer later in order to rekindle the spirit and fervor we first experienced when dialoguing with God. When we write down our dialogue, it forces us to slow down our thinking process to a walk, so that the dialogue makes sense and gives meaning to our prayer.

The Bible helps us to grasp both the tremendous and fascinating aspects of God's nature. The tremendousness of God is seen in His awesome majesty, His almighty power, His divine justice, His infinite truth, His final judgment. In contrast to this grandeur we have many fascinating aspects of God's personality, such as His infinite mercy, love, kindness, goodness, beauty and harmony. At first sight these two views of God seem to be contradictory and paradoxical. We find ourselves caught between a desire to run away from His overwhelming grandeur and an equally strong desire to run toward God and be engulfed in His infinite tenderness and love. Both aspects of God are equally true, so that anyone who emphasizes the one to the neglect of the other has a distorted image of God. The Bible clearly reveals both aspects, and by taking these Scripture texts to prayer and reflecting upon them we are able to keep a balanced view of God. One day we may emphasize one aspect, the next day the opposite.

Prayerful reflection upon the divinely inspired revelation of God in the Bible is a source of grace. Meditation on the Bible may be seen as an eighth sacrament. Some years ago Edward Schillebeeckx wrote a book entitled, *Christ the Sacrament of the Encounter with God*. We might expand this thought and say that the whole Bible is a sacrament of encounter with God. Each time we use a Biblical text during meditation, it becomes a source of new grace in our life. The time of prayer spent each day with the Sacred Scriptures becomes the means to purify and sanctify us. At each new encounter with God through prayerful reflection on the Bible, we experience new capabilities to understand, feel and know God. The Bible is like a gate into the city of God where we make contact with the reality of God, and begin to see the things of earth through God's eyes.

To prepare for one's daily meditation on the Bible, it is wise to select, beforehand, the particular Scripture passage. For example, if one normally prays early in the morning, one might try, the previous night, to leisurely read through a chapter or two of the Bible until a passage is found that seems to have a special meaning. The next morning, take those few chosen verses, and read them over several times, perhaps even memorize them. Try to imagine them as a personal message from God. What is God trying to tell me in these words? Having discerned some pertinent message from the words, one should then respond in whatever way seems appropriate.

Bruce Wilkinson has written a small best-seller book, *The Prayer of Jabez,* based on a biblical text in I Chronicles 4:10

> And Jabez called on the God of Israel saying,
> "Oh that you would bless me indeed,
> And enlarge my borders,
> That your hand would be with me,
> And that you would keep me from evil,

That I may not cause pain!"
SO GOD GRANTED HIM WHAT HE
REQUESTED.

Lectio Divina

During the fourth and fifth centuries of the Christian era, devout men and women in the deserts of Egypt, Palestine and Syria developed a particular method for using the Bible in prayer. The reputation for sanctity of these desert fathers and mothers spread through the whole Christian world. John Cassian, a priest from Rome, went to the East and spent several years learning this method of biblical prayer used by these hermits in the desert. Cassian then brought this method back to France and Italy and taught it to the religious communities of men and women. A century later, St. Benedict adopted this same method of biblical prayer for the religious communities of men and women he founded. Benedict gave it the name of Lectio Divina and built the whole Rule of St. Benedict around the four steps of Lectio Divina. Because the Benedictine Order is responsible for preserving this method of prayer in the Church down through the centuries, we sometimes call this prayer Benedictine prayer.

Lectio Divina, translated literally, means *"divine reading."* It refers specifically to the reading of the Bible as the first step of our prayer-relationship with God. The other three steps of Lectio Divina are *Meditatio*, *Oratio* and *Contemplatio*. Having read the appropriate Scripture passage, the second step of *Meditatio* consists of making a personal application of the words of the Bible to one's own life and situation. The third step of *Oratio* is the personal response we make to God's word. The fourth step of *Contemplatio* is simply resting quietly in the presence of God, and allowing our previous reflections to sink more deeply into our consciousness. A convenient way to express the four steps of Lectio Divina is to call them the four "Rs." They are Reading, Reflecting, Responding and Resting.

Once we have done the Reading, it is not necessary to follow the exact order of the three remaining "Rs," but during each prayer period we should try to touch base with each of the four "Rs."

Lectio Divina makes use of all four human functions of Sensing, Thinking, Feeling and Intuition. In the twelfth century Carthusian Prior Guigo II describes Lectio Divina as follows: "Reading, you should seek; meditating, you will find; praying, you shall call; and contemplating, the door will be opened to you." I prefer the definition of Lectio Divina by a Southern rural minister: "I reads myself full; I thinks myself clear; I prays myself hot; I lets myself cool."

Because it makes full use of all four human functions of Senses, Intellect, Feeling and Intuition, Lectio Divina is the basic foundation of all true prayer. In the book, *Prayer and Temperament*, we describe four specific ways to use Lectio Divina in prayer. The names given to these four forms of prayer are based on method of prayer used by four famous Christian saints: Augustine, Francis of Assisi, Thomas Aquinas and Ignatius Loyola. In all four prayer-styles, we first listen to what God has to say to us, then reflect upon God's word and make a personal application to our life. In the third step we use our heart and feelings to respond to God's word. Finally, in the fourth step we open our intuition to whatever God may wish to reveal to us.

Ignatian Prayer

Over the centuries Lectio Divina has been variously adapted to suit different needs, different temperaments and personalities. One of the most popular of such adaptations is the one developed by St. Ignatius of Loyola in his Spiritual Exercises. In the second step of personal reflection and meditation, Ignatius urges us to make use of our sensible imagination in order to project ourselves back into the actual Scripture scene and try to imagine ourselves a part of the scene. He calls this Composition of Place. The purpose of this exercise is to make the historical scene of the Bible become alive for the one meditating in order to draw some practical fruit for one's life today. Persons who are not accustomed to making use of their imagination often find it difficult or even impossible to project themselves back into Biblical times. The Ignatian method of using the Bible in prayer is not recommended for such persons. It is still possible for them to make use of the other parts of Ignatian prayer, especially the recommendation to draw some practical fruit from the Scripture text.

Prayer of the Liturgical Year

The Church makes use of a modified form of Ignatian prayer throughout the liturgical year. At Christmas we project ourselves back to the stable in Bethlehem and try to become a part of the scene when Jesus was born in Bethlehem. In other words, we use our imagination in order to make ourselves present at the first Christmas in order to draw some practical fruit for our spiritual life today. Similarly, during Holy Week, we follow Jesus in our imagination from Palm Sunday all the way to Calvary on Good Friday, and to the Resurrection on Easter Sunday. The homilies preached on these various Feast days attempt to draw some practical fruit to be learned by us, as a result of reflection on these Biblical scenes. In our meditations on these Liturgical Feasts we might make use of the four steps of Lectio Divina in order to make the original event come alive, so that we may dialogue with it and with God, and draw some practical fruit for our journey of faith.

Augustinian Prayer

The fathers of the Church, as well as the writers of the New Testament, frequently make use of a technique called "Transposition," in order to apply the previous passages of the Bible to their situation at a later time in history. One of their favorite ways of using transposition was to allegorize every word of the original text so that it fit the situation facing them on their journey of faith. By means of such allegorizing they were able to discern how God would want them to handle the problems of a later time. Matthew, Mark and Luke, in the Synoptic Gospels, make use of this technique of allegory to apply the teachings of Jesus to the problems facing the Christian community in the year 70 or 80 A.D. The writings of the ancient Church Fathers employ a similar method of interpreting the Sacred Scripture so that it applied to the needs of their time. St. Augustine, especially, made use of this method of transposition in his many commentaries on the Sacred Scriptures.

Many people today find this Augustinian method of transposition much more beneficial than the pure Ignatian method when making use of the Bible in prayer. For most people it is easier to forget the original historical events of the biblical passage and simply transpose the words of the Bible to our situation today. We imagine Jesus saying to us today the words he addressed to the apostles two thousand years ago. We imagine the prophets of the Old Testament speaking to us the messages they once addressed to Jews in Jerusalem or Babylonia. In this way, we make the Scriptures come alive and allow God to use the Bible to reveal His word and will to us. We usually do this transposition during the second step of Lectio Divina, the Meditatio or Reflection part. Then we respond in our own words to the living message of God's word.

Thomistic Prayer

During the age of rationalism, after the time of Descartes, spiritual writers tried to formalize the method of meditation in a way that appealed to the intellect. Until the middle of 20th century, this was the main method of prayer taught to seminarians and religious novitiates. In our book, *Prayer and Temperament*, we call this Thomistic Prayer, named after St. Thomas of Aquinas who was mainly responsible for the rationalist approach to Sacred Theology among Christians. Many intellectuals today still favor this method of walking around a Scripture passage in order to study it from every possible angle, then to draw some practical help for one's journey of faith. The danger of this method of prayer is that it may remain in the head as an intellectual conviction, and not involve the heart and feelings. If, however, during the third step of Lectio Divina, the feelings are involved, this method is another useful way to use the Bible in prayer. It is especially helpful when reflecting upon the various qualities of some virtue to be practiced, or the different aspects of some fault to be conquered. This method is especially to be recommended as an excellent way to prepare for the Sacrament of Penance.

Franciscan Prayer

Franciscan prayer is somewhat similar to Augustinian prayer. We try to discover a resemblance between a situation in our own life and a parallel situation in the Gospel or other parts of the Bible. We try to imagine how Jesus would act if he were present today. By a prayerful reflection upon comparable events in the life of Jesus, or of Paul or Moses or some other biblical character, we discover how to handle our present-day situation. Augustinian prayer uses the Intuitive function to transpose the biblical situation. Franciscan prayer uses the sensible imagination in order to discern how Jesus would act if he were here.

Centering Prayer

A popular method of using the Bible in prayer today is called *centering prayer*. It consists of using a word or phrase of the Bible that is very meaningful to us. We repeat this word or phrase over and over again, usually silently but it can be done aloud if we are alone. We focus our attention on the presence of God or Jesus at the very center of our being. This is why it is called Centering prayer. We then speak to this presence of God or Jesus, the particular Biblical word or phrase that we have chosen. In the delightful little book called, *The Way of a Pilgrim*, the author describes how the holy men of Russia sanctified themselves by repeating the Jesus prayer, thousands of times each day. The usual way the Jesus prayer is said is, "Lord Jesus Christ, have mercy on me." Another way of considering the Centering prayer is to think of it as a Christian mantra which one tries to connect with one's breathing. Ideally, such a mantra should consist of a prayer of seven syllables. We breathe in with the first three syllables, hold the breath for the fourth syllable, and breathe out with the last three syllables. This is a marvelous way to relax at night after turning out the light and lying down to sleep. Breathe slowly and gently, thinking of the Christian mantra one has chosen. "Anything, Lord, everything."

The Lord's Prayer

In the Lord's Prayer which Jesus gave to his disciples, we are given the model that we should follow in all of our prayers. The first half of the Lord's Prayer concerns God's needs. Most people are surprised to learn that God has certain needs. Because God shares the power of free choice with us, God needs our free cooperation in order to fulfill the purpose of his creation. Human freedom is necessary in order to love. In loving we must always be free not to love. Now that God has shared some of His power with us, He needs our free consent to His will. We need to hallow and respect God's name and person. God needs us to cooperate with Him in establishing His Kingdom of love upon earth. God needs us to use our freedom to carry out His will on earth as perfectly as it is done in heaven.

The second half of the Lord's Prayer is part of the model we need to follow whenever we pray. We never use the singular "me" or "my" but always the plural "us" and "our." Jesus teaches us in the Lord's Prayer to put the needs of others on the same level as our personal needs. We should want for others the same graces and blessings we desire for ourselves.

Most Christians fail to see the Lord's Prayer as a model for all their prayers to God. How often in your life have you prayed first for God's needs before praying for your own needs? How often have you simply prayed for your needs without much concern for the needs of God or of other human beings? Most people rattle off the words of the Our Father without concern for the basic teaching Jesus is giving us in this prayer. If we took to heart what Jesus is teaching us, our way of praying would be quite different from the way we now pray.

Non-Catholics add a closing doxology to the Lord's Prayer. This doxology was added to some of the ancient manuscripts of the Bible. We are quite certain these words did not come from Jesus but they are God's words, and so may be used if we choose.

Conclusion

The Bible needs to be studied in order to discern what God has revealed to us in these sacred books. The Bible has much to teach us about the nature of God, and the kind of relationship of love God wishes to have with us. The Bible also has much to teach us about our purpose in life, our destiny upon earth. It has much to teach us about how we should relate to our fellow human beings. So the Bible needs to be studied every day. Mere study, however, is not enough. We need to learn from the Bible the best way to pray and how to relate to God in prayer. In both the Old and New Testaments we have many examples of how holy men and women of the past have prayed and related to God. We can learn much from their example.

We call the Bible the "Word of God." The seventy-two books of the Bible give us the messages God spoke to the chosen people in the Old Testament, and to the followers of Jesus in the New Testament. Not all of these messages apply to our needs today. In prayer, especially Augustinian Prayer, we are able to transpose these ancient messages to our situation today. Through discernment we are able to recognize what God wishes to reveal to us.

Through daily Lectio Divina meditation on the Sacred Scriptures, we will gradually develop a Christian worldview that is appropriate to our needs today. Faithfulness to the five bases of prayer of our daily Personal Growth Plan will enable us to discern how best to live out our Christian worldview in today's world. Frequent, prayerful reflection on our "Ah-Ha" verses will have a sacramental value in enabling us to fulfill the particular destiny and purpose for which God created us. Once we have broken open a Scripture text so that it becomes alive and meaningful to us, it will become for us the living word of God the rest of our life.

CHAPTER 8

CELEBRATING COVENANT WITH EUCHARIST

Place of Eucharist in Worldview

Religion is mankind's search for God. The Incarnation is God's search for mankind. God and humankind, two opposites, meet in Jesus Christ. This meeting of God and humankind continues to occur today in the Church: "When there are two or three gathered in my name, there I am in the midst" (Matt 18:20). This encounter between God and ourselves in the church community reaches its peak in the Eucharistic banquet.

The Eucharist is the meeting place on the road of life where we encounter Jesus, the Risen Christ. Like the apostles who associated daily with Jesus of Nazareth we become so accustomed to the Eucharist that we do not realize or appreciate the wonderful gift it is. It should be the high point, the peak experience, of our union with the Risen Christ on earth. As a matter of fact, though, it usually is not. Why is this so? There are many reasons for the failure of the Eucharist to accomplish the purpose for which it is intended. Some people expect the Eucharist to carry the whole burden of their experience of God upon earth; but without many individual faith experiences during our intimate periods of personal prayer throughout the week, the Eucharist will usually be barren. Thus, the continued partnership of the seeming opposites—God, Ego and Self; private, liturgical and virtual (good works) prayer—aid in the continuing development of our psychological and spiritual life.

Just as we need to use all four psychological functions in our personal prayer life, it is also necessary to use sensing, intuiting, thinking and feeling in the Sunday worship service. The ceremonies, the music, the symbols of the liturgy will engage all four psychological functions and appeal to all four basic temperaments[1]. Since there will be representatives of all four of the basic temperaments in the congregation, a good homilist should make a special effort to address some part of the sermon to each of them. If one of them is consistently ignored in the material treated in the homily, that particular type will lose interest and may even stop attending the Eucharist.

As the Roman Catholic liturgy is now arranged, all four steps of *Lectio Divina* can be discerned. The Scripture readings allow us to use our senses to hear the Word of God (*Lectio*). With the homily, the thinking function is activated to reflect and meditate on the meaning of the Word of God and its application to us *(Meditatio).* The Collects and other prayers are intended to engage the feelings so that we are caught up in thanksgiving and wonder for all God has wrought (*Oratio*). In the six suggested periods of silence during Mass there is opportunity to use the intuitive function to experience *Contemplatio.* However, only when there is a sufficiently long period of silence after the homily and Holy Communion and only if the purpose of this silent period has been properly explained will the desire for a reverent silence for contemplation be fulfilled.

Through the readings of the four different gospels (and other books of the Bible), each of which reflects the attitude

---

[1] As far as we know, Hippocrates (450 B.C.) is the first person to speak of the human race as divided into four temperaments. Recently, David Kiersey in his book, Please Understand Me, assigns the four temperaments to the two psychological functions of Sensing and Intuition. The Sensing-Judging (SJ) temperament, the Sensing-Perceiving (SP) temperament, the Intuitive-Feeling (NF) temperament, and the Intuitive-Thinking (NT) temperament. For the sake of brevity, it is customary just to use the two letters to designate each of the four temperaments. In our book, Prayer and Temperament, we use the names of saints to designate each of the temperaments. They are Ignatian (SJ), Franciscan (SP), Augustinian (NF), and Thomistic (NT).

or particular temperament of the author, the Eucharist can speak to all four basic temperament types. With its emphasis on law and order, St. Matthew's Gospel will evoke a response from the SJ temperament; while St. Mark's Gospel with its dramatic descriptions of the events in Jesus' life will excite the interest of the SP temperament. Luke with his emphasis on personal relationships—love and compassion for the poor, women, sinners and outcasts—will please the NF temperament. The NT temperament is usually reached by St. John's Gospel with its depth of perception and the boldness of confrontation between Jesus and his enemies. The Epistles of Paul will draw both the NF and NT temperaments; those of James, the SJ. The Epistles of John and the Book of Revelation should appeal to the NT, NF, SJ and SP groups. The different books of the Old Testament will also draw different temperaments, as will the different Psalms which answer the need of different person..lities at different times in life.

Dimensions of the Mass

Because of the richness and variety of events in the life of Jesus, the Church very early divided these events over the course of the liturgical year so that we can celebrate each event in turn with the proper respect. The sweep and flow of the liturgical year from Advent and Christmas to Lent, Holy Week, Easter and Pentecost adds to our enjoyment, interest and fulfillment from participation in Sunday worship. This symbolic renewal or commemoration of the events of Jesus' life, death and resurrection appeals to everyone but especially to those of the SJ temperament. However, commemoration of these past events is only one dimension of the Eucharist. Each Mass also has dimensions of celebration, anticipation and contemplation.

The celebration of the sacrifice of the mystical body of Christ, now represented by the community of believers, appeals especially to the SP temperament. With the Epistle to the Colossians we can say, "We rejoice in the sufferings we endure for you. In my own flesh I will fill up what is lacking in the sufferings of Christ for the sake of his body, the Church" (Col 1:24). The sacrifice of Jesus of Nazareth was completed two thousand years ago on Calvary but the sacrifices of Christ's body, the Church, continue. The Mass is the opportunity for members of the Church to unite their sacrifices, prayers, works and sufferings with those of Jesus and thus add immensely to their value.

Anticipation of participation in the eschatological banquet in God's Kingdom which awaits us in the future is also part of the Mass. We might think of the Risen Christ coming down in each Eucharist to invest the bread and wine and incorporate them into his risen body. Jesus is not primarily interested in the bread and wine on the altar; he uses this method to reach out to us at Holy Communion and incorporate us into his resurrected body. He does not force this upon us but simply offers us this opportunity in each Eucharist and is ready to accept whatever part of our life we dedicate to him. If we are stingy and offer only a tiny portion, then only that part will become the Body of Christ. Whereas if we are generous and dedicate our whole life and being, then all that we freely give to the Lord is taken up into the Risen Body of Christ. This future dimension of the Eucharist appeals especially to the NF temperament.

The periods of silence in the Mass when we are asked to be open to the presence of God and Christ appeal especially to the NT as an opportunity to dwell on the messages but also to the NF who may thereby reach a more personal encounter with God. This dimension of contemplation, so often omitted or given short shrift in the normal Sunday parochial Mass, was the prevailing aspect in the pre-Vatican II Mass when the priest had his back to the congregation and the people were left to their own devices. Many of the more devout persons developed some wonderful habits of contemplative prayer during the old silent, non-participatory Masses; and they are the very people who have found the most difficulties in adjusting to the present day Mass with its emphasis on community participation. Actually, however, if the regulations of the new

Mass were followed properly, there would be ample time in each Eucharistic celebration for quiet prayer and contemplation. Altogether there are six different times when the action of the Mass stops for a period of silence. There is no regulation as to the length of each of these periods of silence. Unfortunately most celebrants and lectors limit them to just a few seconds. Many omit them altogether.

When the Eucharist is understood in all four of these dimensions: *commemoration*, *celebration*, *anticipation* and *contemplation*, it is quite evident that the four basic temperaments and the four psychological functions receive a sufficiency for prayer and reflection. The SJ (Ignatian) temperament will be happy with the dimension of commemoration which is such an important element of the Mass. The SP (Franciscan) temperament will rejoice in the celebration dimension of the liturgy as it is expressed in song, in praise, in gesture and action. The NF (Augustinian) temperament will find fulfillment in the future-oriented eschatological dimension of anticipation of the heavenly banquet. The NT (Thomistic) temperament will be satisfied if there is a well-ordered, well-thought-out homily, and if there are adequate periods of silence for contemplation.

Berakah — Thanksgiving — Eucharist

To understand the Mass we must go back not only to the Last Supper, but also to the *Berakah* or commemorative meals in which Jesus participated with his disciples. We now know that such meals were a frequent occurrence among the Jews at the time of Jesus. Ritually, as part of the main meal in a Jewish family, bread and wine were offered to God to express worship, gratitude, praise, sorrow, and petition. The one loaf of bread which was broken and distributed, and the one cup of wine which was shared, signified their unity with each other and with God. Scholars are of the opinion that Jesus partook of many Berakah meals during his public life.

The Jewish "Berakah" was the heart of Jewish piety at the time of Jesus. "Berakah," meaning "praise," or "bless," or "thanks," was the Hebrew word used by Jews as a response to every great deed of God, and to every revelation of God's power, presence and loving care. Translated "my whole self goes out to you" or "everything I have finds its meaning in you," it becomes the human response of love to each act of God's goodness. It includes praise, worship, adoration, love, thanksgiving, commitment and dedication.

The Jews ritualized Berakah, and gave expression to it in various ways in their daily living. Among all of these attempts to praise God, the Berakah meal stands out. For the ancient Jew, food was a sign of God's good pleasure and good will, a sign of the God who creates, nourishes, saves and shares his life with mankind. So, ancient Jewish people who gathered at a Berakah meal felt themselves plunged into divine life. Beginning with an experience of the bounty of nature and the inspired words of Scripture, the structure of the Berakah meal included the breaking of a loaf of bread and passing it around with a Berakah prayer of praise and thanks. At the conclusion of the meal, a cup of wine was mixed with water, and a very solemn thanksgiving prayer for all God's saving deeds was proclaimed by the host. Then the cup was passed, and all drank from it. This ritual expressed the communion of one's life with the life of God, and God sharing his life with his chosen ones.

The Jewish people believed that when they commemorated the marvelous deeds Yahweh accomplished for their ancestors, they made this same Yahweh really present to work similar marvelous deeds for them. This may be the real origin of the doctrine of the real presence. Just as we commemorate in the Eucharistic prayer the wonderful deeds of Jesus, we too believe that we make the same Jesus really and truly present to work similar marvelous deeds for us today.

The Berakah prayer consisted of four parts: a proclamation of God's great deeds of the past (our Liturgy of the Word), a hymn of praise (our Mass Preface), prayers of petition for the coming of God's Kingdom (our Prayer of the Faithful) and a short doxology of praise at the end. All of this was done in the context of a joyful fellowship meal. Making the Berakah meal into a covenant meal was the main contribution of Jesus to the ancient Jewish piety. The Berakah or fellowship meal of the Christians proclaimed the advent of God's Kingdom of salvation for sinners and outcasts. They also petitioned God to pour out his Spirit upon his people so that the Holy Spirit would continue the work of reconciliation begun by Jesus Christ. Early Christian communities continued the Berakah meal as part of their Jewish piety, but it became an anticipation of the eschatological banquet soon to be partaken in the Kingdom of God. At the end of the early Christian Eucharistic meal, they thanked God, especially for the presence of the Risen Christ among them, the greatest of all God's marvelous deeds.

Parallels between Passover and Eucharist

Since Scripture has placed the institution of the Eucharist in the events preceding the Passion, which historically took place during the Jewish Passover week, the first Christians very quickly saw the close connection between the Christian Eucharistic meal and the Jewish Passover meal. Just as the Jews commemorated and celebrated their deliverance from Egyptian slavery at the annual Passover meal, so Christians celebrated their deliverance from the slavery of past sins in the Eucharistic meal. Jesus became the new "Lamb of God" who was consumed in the Lord's Supper, and thus delivered Christians from the angel of death that threatened them because of their sinfulness. Just as Jews believed that deliverance from evil by their God Yahweh was available to them each time they commemorated the deliverance from Egyptian slavery, so Christians similarly believed that the Risen Christ was really and truly present to deliver them from the slavery of sin each time they commemorated Jesus' life, death and resurrection at the Eucharistic meal.

"Every time you eat this bread and drink this cup, you proclaim the death of the Lord until he comes … whoever eats the bread or drinks the cup of the Lord unworthily sins against the body and blood of the Lord … He who eats and drinks without recognizing the body, eats and drinks a judgment upon himself" (I Cor 11:26-29). "Is not the cup of blessing we bless a sharing in the blood of Christ? And is not the bread we break a sharing in the body of Christ?" (I Cor 10:16).

Although the Lord's Supper on Holy Thursday night is seen as the origin of the Christian Passover meal, other parallels with the Old Testament were drawn as Eucharistic theology developed. Jesus feeding the thousands of disciples during his public life was seen as another manifestation of God feeding his chosen people, the Christians, as Yahweh fed the Israelites with manna in the desert. The connection with the Eucharist was quickly drawn and we have the beautiful theological description in John 6 of the necessity of eating the body of Jesus, and drinking his blood. "I am the bread of life. Your ancestors ate manna in the desert, but they died. This is the bread that comes down from heaven. If anyone eats of this bread, he shall live forever. The bread that I will give is my flesh for the life of the world … If you do not eat the flesh of the Son of Man and drink his blood, you have no life in you … My flesh is real food and my blood is real drink" (John 6:48-55).

Development of the Christian Eucharist

After the resurrection, the presence of the Risen Christ among the community of believers was frequently experienced in the context of a meal. Luke's Gospel gives two such examples: the two disciples at Emmaus (Luke 24:13-35) who recognize the Risen Lord in the breaking of the bread, and later (Luke 24:36-43) in the Upper Room, "they (the disciples) give him a piece of cooked fish which he took and ate in their presence." John's Gospel gives us the beautiful and touching story of the Risen Jesus Christ feeding his disciples bread and fish on the shore of Lake

Galilee after a night of fishing (John 21:12-13). In the Acts of the Apostles Luke describes how the first communities of believers met in one another's homes for "the breaking of the bread" (Acts 2:42, 26). Scripture scholars point out that Luke is a very careful writer who would not have used the definite article "the" before "breaking of the bread unless he meant a very special "breaking of bread," namely, the Eucharistic celebration of the presence of the Risen Christ through participation in a sacred meal.

St. Paul (I Cor 11) and Mark, Matthew and Luke give us descriptions of how their particular Christian community celebrated the fellowship meal of the Eucharist. Evidently, in Corinth, the breaking and eating of the loaf of consecrated bread preceded the meal, while the passing and drinking from a common cup of consecrated wine followed it. In Mark's church, the Eucharist apparently was celebrated at the conclusion of a communion meal. Furthermore, the blessing was of God, not the bread, as we have now interpreted it. The words were words of administration rather than of consecration. In Mark, the drinking of the cup conveys the symbolic participation in the event of salvation history accomplished on Calvary. "This is my blood of the covenant" (Mark 14:24). A covenant was finalized in blood because it was apparent that the death of a victim had a finality about which made it irrevocable. Thus the New Covenant between God and us, effected by God's sending Jesus to live, die and rise from the dead for our salvation, is irrevocable. But, before a covenant is complete, the people must become participants. At Sinai this was achieved when Moses sprinkled the blood over the people. The covenant, accomplished by Christ's sacrifice, is completed when we receive Holy Communion. The Eucharist is thus an integral part of the once-and-for-all sacrifice of Calvary when Jesus presented and surrendered his life in obedience to the Father. However, merely eating the Eucharistic bread and drinking from the cup will not truly make us participants in the sacrifice of Jesus. This happens only when the external symbol of eating and drinking at Eucharist expresses a true, sincere, total commitment of our life even unto death to God, just as Jesus did by his acceptance of death upon the cross.

The New Testament sees the Eucharistic meal as an extension of three different events in the life of Jesus, and not just the one event of the Lord's Supper. (1) The Eucharist was a continuation of the meals which the Risen Christ had with his disciples after the resurrection, as well as those Jesus had with the disciples during his public ministry, especially the meal in the desert, half-way through his ministry (See John 6:26-29). (2) The Eucharist was a commemoration of the sealing of the new covenant between God and us through the sacrifice and death of Jesus. (3) All of these Eucharistic meals emphasize the eschatological aspect of the promise and assurance that the Lord will return at the end of time to set things right, once and for all. The Eucharist is meant to be a foretaste of the future messianic banquet, a symbol of the life we will enjoy with God forever in heaven. However, this future dimension of Eucharist was lost soon after the first century when Jesus disappointed his disciples by not returning as quickly as expected; and actually we have never recaptured this future, eschatological dimension of Eucharist, not even in the liturgical changes of Vatican II.

Lost Symbolism of the Eucharist

During the Middle Ages, Christians lost sight of the symbolism of the sacred meal. Their exaggerated reverence for the presence of Jesus in the Eucharist, coupled with magnified scrupulosity regarding their own sinfulness and consequent unworthiness, caused them to stop going to Holy Communion and partaking of the body and blood of Christ. Mass became a worship service to be performed by the clergy with the sinful people looking on at a distance. The banquet table around which the early Christians gathered for the eating and drinking of an eschatological meal was removed from the center of the church, and an altar of sacrifice was placed in a sanctuary at the back of the church nave. A Christian "Holy of Holies," introduced into the church, allowed only consecrated priests to enter while the sinful, unworthy laity became mere spectators from afar. Even the common language of the people was no longer used and instead a special language (Latin) known only to the clergy was adopted. People began to use the time at Mass for private prayer and devotion, and the Church lost sight of how the Eucharistic meal was celebrated by the first century Christians. Only in the last fifty years have scholars uncovered documents telling how early Christians celebrated the Eucharist, and a movement to restore the Mass to its original structure and practice began. The hardest thing for many Catholics to accept is the fact that the Church lost the original intent of the Eucharist for more than a thousand years. Instead, other purposes which were good in themselves, but not the original purpose of the Mass, were substituted.

For centuries, the Eucharist became more of a "thing" or an "object" to be worshipped rather than an event or action to be celebrated by the Christian community. The symbolism of a sacred meal was almost entirely forgotten and thus what had been a living, meaningful symbol became a dead symbol without meaning. Real bread was no longer used. Only rarely were ordinary Christians permitted to receive Holy Communion. Even then, only a small, thin wafer was placed on their tongue. The cup was denied them. Even the most vivid imagination had difficulty seeing the Eucharist as an earthly banquet which anticipated the heavenly banquet in union with Christ. What happened to the particles of bread and the spoonful of wine became more important than the experience of joyful celebration by the community of believers. The table fellowship of the first Christians was dropped in favor of a vertical worship of the Son of God hidden under the veil of bread. The horizontal dimension of a group of rejoicing, grateful Christians eating and drinking together around a common table was replaced by a silent, worshipping group of individuals looking at the host and chalice from afar.

In the way the Mass has been celebrated, and the way Holy Communion was distributed in the past and even today in many liturgies, it is next to impossible to experience the symbol of a community banquet such as the first Christians experienced in their Eucharistic meals. We would need to be seated around a banquet table and a substantial portion of the consecrated bread and wine would have to be consumed before we would be able to recapture the symbolism of a sacred, fellowship meal. In recent centuries concentration has been more on the things (species of bread and wine, especially species of bread) used in the Eucharistic liturgy rather than upon the symbolic act of gathering in fellowship with the community of believers and partaking of a community meal.

In the past, many Catholics believed the Eucharist, and all Sacraments, could magically accomplish results without any real participation on our parts. We felt that as long as we were present, and believed in the presence of Jesus in the Eucharist, this was sufficient to make the Sacrament active in our life. But we could not understand why our frequent Masses and Holy Communions, as well as our Confessions had so little effect upon our lives. We could see no real change or improvement in our life as a result of these sacraments. Because we had done these sacraments so long in this manner, we presumed they were the way Jesus intended them. Only through historical research into the early centuries of Christianity during this past century have we come to understand how different the original concept of Eucharist and sacrament was.

Recapturing Personal Meaning in the Eucharist

To make the Mass more meaningful for us today, we need to use it as the climax of our praise and gratitude to God for all his marvelous deeds, especially for the presence of Jesus among us, and for the good news (Gospel) of salvation and reconciliation. To be able to praise God we need to take time aside to contemplate his action in our life, and to become aware that He is the 'still point' around which all our life is focused.

To be meaningful, the Eucharistic externals must authentically represent the interior dispositions of the participants. The Mass is of no value to us unless it includes a sacrifice of our will and our whole being to God and God's will. We must have the same inner attitude as Jesus had during his life, and especially at his death on the cross. The rite of the Mass is symbolic, expressing in outward signs our personal commitment. Unless this commitment is real, the symbolic rite of the Eucharist is unreal or non-real. By going to Mass we commit ourselves to living a Christ-like life.

The Mass is meant to be our sacrifice, our opportunity to join our sacrifices to that of Jesus on the Cross. What, then, can we sacrifice in our life to bring it into accord with the life of Jesus? We can give up feeling sorry for ourselves; we can give up our anger, our impatience, our complaining, our criticisms of others, our rash judgments, our selfishness, pride, envy, jealousy, lust, sloth, gluttony, greed, unbelief. By getting rid of everything opposed to God, we can make room for the entrance of God and the Risen Christ into our lives. We will allow our whole self to be caught up in the person of God, just as Jesus allowed his whole life to be taken up into divinity. Thus the Eucharist will succeed in transforming and transfiguring us by the presence of God. We will then experience the fullness of God present on earth.

The Vatican II Document on the Liturgy speaks of five different ways by which the Risen Christ is present to us in each Eucharist: under the appearance of bread and wine; under the appearance of the human words of Sacred Scriptures; in the believing community; in the celebrant; in the music and other ceremonies and gestures of the celebration. However, none of these ways will have any meaning or value to us if we neglect to prepare ourselves for the Eucharist, and if we enter it without the readiness to make a blind act of faith and commitment to God and God's will. In other words, our Sunday Mass is not independent of what we do the rest of the week. Rather the Sunday Eucharist is where we bring to God the offering of our life, our prayers, works and sufferings of our whole life. If we have not been working for God and in loving service for our fellow human beings during the week, we will come to the Sunday Eucharist with empty hands. The principle is "nothing in, nothing out." If we bring no gift of ourselves to Mass, we can expect to take away little or nothing in the way of grace and gift from God.

It has been said that five elements contribute to a good Eucharistic celebration: the prayerfulness of the celebrant, the quality of the homily, the quality of the music, the experience of a community of believers, and adequate preparation. For the average Mass-goer many of these elements are out of one's hands. However, a good preparation is possible for everyone. This would mean spending an hour, or even two hours, prior to Mass attendance preparing oneself for a good celebration. Reflection on the Scripture readings, and an attempt to apply them to one's own circumstances are a must for a good Eucharistic celebration and experience. The Risen Christ comes down to our level in the Eucharist, but we must match this by a faith response that raises our whole life and being to God and His will. This is like completing the other half of a circle. The Risen Christ can be depended upon to do his part; the only uncertainty is whether we are ready and willing to do our part.

A good Eucharist involves not only a deepening of our covenant of faith with Christ, but an outpouring of the gifts and fruits of the Holy Spirit on those who have actively and properly participated. A good Eucharist follows the steps of every person's faith journey. In fact, the five steps experienced by everyone on a journey of faith are also part of the total Eucharist: (1) listening to the Word of God; (2) experiencing a conversion of faith, (3) entering into a covenant of faith with the Risen Lord; (4) celebrating this covenant of faith with a community of believers; and (5) receiving the Holy Spirit.

The Eucharist is the normal means for the sanctification of the Christian community. Eucharist is where we receive God's communication to us through the Scriptures, homily and prayer. It is where we should experience conversion and metanoia, where we make our faith commitment, where we renew our covenant of faith and celebrate it with the rest of the believing community. It is where we experience the consolations and power of the Holy Spirit to carry out our good resolutions. We need only to open ourselves as generously as possible, to the presence of God and the Risen Christ in the Eucharist.

The Eucharist as an Extension of Jesus' Incarnation and Resurrection

In the Eucharist we commemorate and celebrate the total sacrifice of the life of Jesus for the life of the world. It is not enough to remember and rejoice in the sacrifice of Jesus; we must add the sacrifice of our life to the sacrifice of Jesus. Through the eating of Jesus' body and drinking of his blood in Holy Communion we gain the needed grace and energy also to give our flesh for the life of the world. By Jesus' communing with the Father in prayer he received the strength to carry on his work of ministry. By our communing with Jesus in the Eucharist we receive the needed strength and grace to minister to the needs of other people. Then, in turn, by our communing with the people whom we meet each day and who depend upon us, we give them the needed strength, grace, encouragement and inspiration to carry out their duties to God and mankind. We thus return to the Father the gift of our lives through loving service to God dwelling in our fellow human beings. We are essential links in the whole chain which binds all creation to God, but we need the Eucharist to put us in contact with Jesus, just as Jesus needed the long nights of prayer to put him in contact with the Father. Other people need us in order to put them in contact with God and Jesus.

To understand the Mass in its totality we need to go back to the life and ministry of Jesus. The Kingdom of God was the heart of his message. By "Kingdom of God," Jesus meant the event by which God reveals his readiness and willingness to reconcile and forgive everyone, regardless of their past sins. This was the "good news" which Jesus proclaimed, and because of this, outcasts and sinners flocked to him. The reality of God's infinite love was the Kingdom event which Jesus came to earth to announce. This proclamation of universal reconciliation was expressed and ritualized by Jesus in his ministry of table fellowship. This table fellowship was a symbol, an outward sign, by which he expressed and spelled out universal redemption. To share a meal with people is to share one's life and make oneself equal to one's table-mates, and them equal to us. This ministry of table fellowship was unfolded by Jesus, in three stages: (1) throughout his public ministry in Berakah meals; (2) at the Last Supper with his disciples; (3) through his presence at the meals of the believing community after his resurrection. Our Mass today is a prolongation in history of this proclamation of the Kingdom of God and the ministry of Jesus through table fellowship of the Eucharist.

To participate properly in the Mass we must accept the announcement of Jesus regarding universal reconciliation. We must express this universality of redemption by opening our hearts, lives, actions and ministry to the whole world, to all human beings, even to our enemies, even to enemy nations. If we deny our love and loving service to anyone, we are guilty of the same mistake the Pharisees made when they rejected Jesus for his proclamation of universal salvation. Jesus committed this ministry of universal redemption to his church. "Feed my lambs, feed my sheep, take care of my flock" (John 21:15).

The Mass is more than a relinquishing of our life in sacrifice. It is also a feast, a banquet of love and joy, an anticipation of the heavenly banquet we will celebrate with the Risen Lord and the saints in heaven. It is a time to get together with friends and fellow-believers, and enjoy each other's company in the presence of God and the Risen Lord. It is a sacramental celebration of the presence of the Risen Lord in the community of believers. It is a rite of passage whereby we pass-over from a death to the things of this world to the life of God. It is a time when we celebrate the victimhood of Jesus and our own willingness to be a victim of love for the salvation of our fellow human beings.

In order to have a good liturgical celebration, we should join with all the others who are making an effort to make the Eucharist what it is supposed to be: a celebration and a sacrifice, a commemoration and an anticipation, an action and a contemplation. Using our thinking function to obtain a knowledge of the purpose of the Mass and of all the possible dimensions of the liturgy will enrich our commemoration. The feeling and intuitive dimensions of our personality enable us to handle comfortably our own emotions and feelings, as well as those of the congregation. We need to be well-rested, as free as possible of the distractions of this world, to experience with our senses the sacrifice and death of Jesus, and his and our own resurrection to a new life of grace. With personal effort, with the cooperation of our fellow worshippers and with the help of God's grace, our experience at Eucharist will be another in the series of resurrection experiences which began two thousand years ago on the first Easter Sunday.

CHAPTER 9

SACRAMENT OF PENANCE FOR ADULTS

Place of the Sacrament of Penance in Worldview

The Easter gift of the risen Lord Jesus to the Church: "Whose sins you forgive, they are forgiven." Many persons 60 or 70 years of age are still going to confession the way they were taught in the first grade. There is, however, an adult way of receiving the sacrament. There are no necessary words or formulas that need to be used. The more informal, the better. It is not necessary to tell how long it has been since your last confession. The act of contrition should be said before going to confession as part of the preparation for receiving the sacrament. The most important part of the sacrament is the resolution of amendment, which has to do with the future, the changes one proposes to make in the conduct of one's life. The Greek word for this is Metanoia, a change of direction in one's life. There is both a past dimension as well as a future dimension to the sacrament. Of the two, the future dimension is more important. However, "those who forget the past are doomed to commit the same mistakes as in the past."

In the old Baltimore Catechism there was a long laundry list of sins based on the Ten Commandments. I would recommend a more simple way to examine one's conscience in preparation for confession. Take the four relationships of love around which our life revolves. They are love of God, love of others, love of self, love of nature. Where have I failed to love God sufficiently? Where have I failed to love others sufficiently? Where have I failed to take proper care of myself? Where have I failed to show the proper respect for all the things of nature? What changes should I make in each of these four areas?

How often should one go to confession? In the old pre-Vatican II Church it was recommended that we go to confession before each Holy Communion, either once a week or once a month. However, if we go too often, there is danger that we will trivialize the sacrament. I would suggest that we try to go to confession about once every three months, at each change of the seasons. In this way we can connect the receiving of this sacrament with a Personal Growth Plan. As a minimum, I think everyone should go to confession at least once or twice a year.

When we go to confession, we not only make a covenant with the Lord to be more faithful to the four relationships of love. The Lord Jesus also makes a promise to us to give us all the grace and help we need to live up to the resolutions of amendment we have made. It is like receiving a blank checkbook drawn on the bank of heaven. We are able to draw upon this heavenly bank account for all the grace we need to grow in love of God, neighbor, self, and nature.

In the Sacrament of Penance, there is need to confess our wrongdoing of the past, as well as to express a resolution of amendment regarding the future. Both are important; but of the two, the future amendment is the more important. In the Gospels Jesus showed little concern for the misdeeds of the past. His only concern for the woman taken in adultery was, "Go, and from now on sin no more" (John 8:11). If we have done harm to anyone in the past, we are obliged to make restitution for that harm. The law of the Church is that one is only obliged to confess those serious (mortal) sins of the past which have not previously been confessed. The law of the Church also states that in case of serious doubt, one is not obliged to confess past sins.

The new regulations for the Sacrament of Penance recommend that one should go to the Sacrament, face to face, with the priest. However, it does state that confession behind a curtain should also be available for those who choose to go anonymously. It also recommends that the penitent bring a bible and read an appropriate passage, either of contrition, or in reference to what the penitent wants to discuss with the confessor. The new regulations recommend that the act of contrition be said by the penitent during preparation for the Sacrament and before going to confession.

There are no magic words that need to be said during confession. The more informal the whole event, the better. It is recommended that the person sit down facing the confessor and simply ask the priest for a blessing to begin the rite. It is not necessary to state how long since the last confession, but this is optional. After reading the Scripture passage, which is also optional, one should mention those sins and faults of the past for which one is especially sorry. Then, one should talk about the changes of direction in one's life which one hopes to make in the immediate future. At this point, it is recommended that the penitent ask the confessor for any suggestions to help him be faithful to the resolutions of amendment just mentioned. After listening to whatever advice the priest might wish to give, the penitent may bring the confession to a conclusion by asking the priest, "Father, please lay your hand on my head and ask God to forgive me." This laying on of hands is also optional. The confessor will assign some simple act of penance to help the penitent be faithful to the resolution of amendment.

In the past we have not given enough attention to the resolution of amendment regarding the future. Our concern has been almost exclusively on the confession of past sins. The frequent result was that we found ourselves repeating the same old sins over and over again, without any real improvement in our life. The old Baltimore catechism insisted that there be a resolution of amendment, but it was often neglected by both confessor and penitent. In preparing for this sacrament most of one's concern should be what changes one needs to make in order to experience a real conversion in one's life. It is suggested that one try to decide on a single change in the direction of one's life in each of the four relationships of love: love of God, others, self and nature.

To be faithful to one's resolutions of amendment, it is recommended that one develop a Personal Growth Plan. This plan should cover the four relationships of love around which our whole life revolves. We should never be satisfied with the present level of love in each of these four areas. All of our life we should strive to improve our love for God, neighbor, self and nature. Each time we go to confession we should choose one way that we will try to show a greater love for God, another human being, one's own spiritual and bodily health, and one's attitude towards God's creation. These are the resolutions of amendment we should mention to the confessor, and we should ask for suggestions to put them into practice in the days and weeks immediately ahead. Each morning it is suggested that we renew our Personal Growth Plan. See Appendix A for an example.

The Sacrament of Penance is one of the most beautiful gifts of the risen Lord Jesus to His Church. It is tragic that so many Catholics today fail to make use of this Sacrament. What are the reasons for this widespread neglect? I think the main reason is the lack of good adult education concerning the proper way for adults to receive the Sacrament. Old men and women are still going to confession the same way they did at age seven. Priests have not been instructed in this new, adult form of the Sacrament. Therefore, they fail to pass on this knowledge to their parishioners. The unhappy result is that most Catholics today go for many years without receiving this Sacrament.

There are also other reasons why this Sacrament is neglected today. There is the reluctance to admit that we have been guilty of wrongdoing. It is indeed humbling to have to disclose to another human being that we have done wrong. Confession, however, is good for the soul. The fifth step of Alcoholics Anonymous states, "We admit to God, ourselves and another human being the exact nature of our wrongs." Embarrassing as it may be, we need to admit our guilt to at least one other human being besides God and ourselves.

Another reason for the neglect of this Sacrament has already been stated above, namely, too much emphasis on confession of past sins, and not enough emphasis on resolution of amendment. A fourth reason is simply that many adults have forgotten the old formula for confession and are too embarrassed to admit this. This is why I have suggested that the more informal one is in confession, the better. There are no special, magic words that one needs to say. Jesus is waiting with open arms to receive us, regardless of the sins of the past. Jesus is not interested in our past. His only concern is the present and the future. All He asks is that we try to love as best we can: love God, love all our fellow human beings, love ourselves, love the whole of creation. If we ask for help from God to do a good job of all these loves, we can be sure that such help and grace will be present and available to us.

At the present time it is the custom of most parishes to celebrate a Communal Penance Service each year during Lent and again during Advent. I would like to suggest that parishes should schedule a Communal Penance Service four times a year, one each three months. Our human nature changes with each season of the year. It would be beneficial for making these changes if we had the opportunity to receive the Sacrament of Penance each three months.

It has been my experience that most people are able to be faithful to their resolutions of amendment for a period of about three months. New Year's resolutions almost always fail because twelve months is longer than most of us are able to persevere. Since resolution of amendment is the most important part of the Sacrament of Penance, it would be most helpful to our spiritual growth if we had the opportunity to receive this Sacrament every three months.

In the past, spiritual direction was frequently given at the same time one received the Sacrament of Penance. However, it is not convenient to receive spiritual direction during a Communal Penance Service. It would unduly lengthen the service for the whole congregation. Therefore, for those who wish to receive spiritual direction from their confessor, it is recommended that they make an appointment sometime during the week. When the spiritual director is a priest, it is quite appropriate to receive absolution at the end of the spiritual direction session.

CHAPTER 10

OPENNESS TO THE HOLY SPIRIT

Place of Baptism and Confirmation in Worldview

On the night of the Lord's Supper, Jesus promised to send us the Holy Spirit who would remain with us always. This Holy Spirit is the Spirit of Truth and Love, the Spirit of Wisdom and Discernment. It is the same Holy Spirit that descended upon Jesus at his baptism and that guided him in all his actions and words throughout his public life. We need to maintain a constant openness to this Holy Spirit throughout our life on earth. In order for this to happen we need to hold on loosely to everything in our life and all the things of this world. This is the opposite of holding on tightly, and being excessively attached and addicted to the things of this world. One way of expressing this openness to the Holy Spirit is to repeat, again and again, the prayer, "Anything, Lord, Everything." We need to be totally open to love and truth, always open to new ways of loving and serving God and neighbor.

Awakening our Sleeping Giant

Every baptized Christian has a sleeping giant within his soul. We might think of this sleeping giant as the Holy Spirit. As a result of our reception of the Sacraments of Baptism and Confirmation we have been given this Holy Spirit who will remain with us throughout our life. However, most of us fail to use the gifts of the Holy Spirit that now belong to us. Instead, we allow this immense gift of grace to remain idle, and thus it becomes a sleeping giant within our soul. How do we awaken this sleeping giant and make full use of the gifts of grace which belong to us as a result of Baptism and

Confirmation? We need to keep ourselves detached from everything except God and God's will. This is what it means to hold on loosely to the things of this world. We need to invite and ask the Holy Spirit to activate each of the gifts of the Holy Spirit. These gifts include both the general gifts which Isaiah mentions in Chapter eleven, as well as the special gifts which St. Paul lists in chapter twelve of both the first Epistle of Corinthians and Epistle to the Romans. Then we need to maintain a constant openness and friendly reception to each of these gifts. Each gift requires our cooperation. The gifts are free but in order to make full use of them we are called upon to use our free will to cooperate with them. Using the above little prayer, "Anything, Lord, Everything," is a good way to maintain a constant openness to the Holy Spirit.

We receive Baptism and Confirmation only once during our life on earth. The reason this is true is because these Sacraments give us permanent possession of the Holy Spirit. This Holy Spirit remains alive and ready to come to our assistance the moment we call upon it. Through these two Sacraments we are able to have an intimate relationship with the Holy Spirit similar to the relationship Jesus had with the Holy Spirit throughout his life on earth. The Gospels speak of Jesus being filled with the power of the Holy Spirit and thus full of the Spirit, being led by the Spirit in whatever Jesus said and did.

The Holy Spirit is always alert and ready to come to our assistance the moment we call upon Him/Her. We might think of the Holy Spirit as the feminine aspect of God's nature. The Hebrew word for Holy Spirit, *Ruah*, (breath) is feminine as well as the Greek word, *Sophia* (Wisdom as a person). We invite the Holy Spirit to come and take possession of our life. The Holy Spirit is very respectful of our freedom, and will never force an entrance into our life. But once invited, the Holy Spirit will make available to us the infinite power, wisdom, and love of God.

We need the help of the Holy Spirit in each step of the journey of faith. Openness to the Holy Spirit means openness to God's call, openness to a constant conversion (metanoia), commitment, covenant. It also means openness to all the consolations and fruits of the Holy Spirit. According to St. Paul these fruits are love, joy, peace, patience, kindness, generosity, faithfulness, gentleness, and self-control (Gal 5:22-23). It means openness to all the general gifts of the Holy Spirit. They are fear of the Lord, piety, counsel, fortitude, knowledge, understanding, and wisdom. It means openness to all the special, charismatic gifts of the Holy Spirit which we need in order to fulfill our divinely appointed mission on earth.

As a result of our reception of Baptism and Confirmation all of these gifts and blessings of the Holy Spirit are available to us. Unfortunately, most people allow this presence of the Holy Spirit to remain a sleeping giant in the inner depths of our soul. How then do we awaken this sleeping giant? The primary way to do this is to renew the six baptismal vows which we made or were made in our name by our parents and god-parents. Three of these vows are negative. They consist of our rejecting sin and the glamour of evil and refusing to be mastered by it. They consist also of our rejection of Satan, father of sin and prince of darkness. There are also three positive baptismal vows, whereby we pledge our faith to each of the three persons of the Blessed Trinity.

There is a very simple way to renew our baptismal vows and awaken the sleeping giant of the Holy Spirit in the depths of our soul. It is to use holy water to make the sign of the cross on our body. This is the purpose of the holy water font at the entrance of our churches. In order to purify our souls and prepare ourselves for the celebration of the Holy Eucharist, we renew our baptismal vows by this simple sign of the cross with holy water. Unfortunately, most Catholics are unaware of the symbolism of this sign of the cross with holy water. As a result, we allow the Holy Spirit to remain asleep within our souls. External actions, such as making the sign of the cross, have no value or meaning of themselves. They become true symbols of grace only when they express what is in our heart and mind. Otherwise, these external actions become mere superstitious signs.

Activating the Graces of Confirmation

For most Catholics, the Sacrament of Confirmation is even more dead than that of Baptism. So often, Confirmation has been received in grade school and then forgotten the rest of one's life. In recent years, Confirmation has been delayed until near the end of high school. This is some improvement over the past. However, since this is the sacrament of adulthood, it would be better if Confirmation were delayed until adulthood. A good time to receive this sacrament would be at the end of a three-day Cursillo weekend.

The purpose of Confirmation is to give the needed help of the Holy Spirit in order to carry on the work of evangelizing the human race for Jesus Christ. We need to have an adult understanding of our Christian faith and maturity to know how best to evangelize the world for Christ. This is no easy task, and we will need all the help we can get from the Holy Spirit. We need to awaken the sleeping giant of the Holy Spirit that is very much present in our soul, regardless of how much time has passed since receiving the Sacrament of Confirmation. We will do this by making a total dedication of our life to the work of evangelizing Christ. Each of us needs to discover the particular way God is calling us to evangelize. Having discerned our special ministry, we invite the Holy Spirit to come and take full possession of our life, and help us fulfill our ministry.

The Role of the Holy Spirit in God's Plan

The Holy Spirit has an essential role to play in carrying out God's plan for the human race. We may think of God's plan as the establishment of the Kingdom of God upon earth, or the expansion of the heavenly circle of divine love. Each of the persons of the Blessed Trinity has a part to play in fulfilling the plan of God for the human race. The Heavenly Father (Mother) is the one who conceives the divine plan. Jesus Christ is the one chosen to free (redeem) the human race from the control of the fallen evil powers. The Holy Spirit is the one chosen to apply the fruits of Christ's death and resurrection to each generation of human beings as it lives here on earth. We need to keep in constant contact with the Holy Spirit throughout our journey of faith. We must always be open to the reception of the graces and helps of the Holy Spirit. We need this assistance of the Holy Spirit at every step of the journey of faith. Without the help of the Holy Spirit, God's plans for the human race would never be fulfilled.

There is another way to help us realize the importance of the Holy Spirit in fulfilling God's plan for the human race. We might think of the two thousand years before the birth of Jesus as the age of God the Father. This would involve the gradual revelation of Yahweh (God) to the Chosen People from the time of Abraham to the birth of Jesus. The past two thousand years may be seen as the age of Jesus Christ. We have gradually come to realize the tremendous gift of salvation and redemption Jesus Christ has accomplished for us. Now, as we enter the third Millennium, we may think of this new age of the human race as the age of the Holy Spirit. Perhaps, for the next two thousand years, we will experience a fuller revelation of Holy Spirit.

In this new age of the Holy Spirit, it behooves us to get to know all we can about this third Divine Person. We can be open to new knowledge and even new revelation regarding the role of the Holy Spirit in our sanctification. We can eliminate all obstacles to the free flow of grace from the Holy Spirit into our soul and our whole life. Since the Holy Spirit always respects our freedom, every day we should invite the Holy Spirit to come and take possession of our life. We invite the Holy Spirit to bestow upon us each of the gifts and fruits which the Holy Scriptures have revealed. A good way to keep open the lines of communication between the

Holy Spirit and ourselves is to pray the Divine Office prayer to the Holy Spirit every morning.

> Breathe on me, breath of God,
> Fill me with life anew,
> That I may love the things you love,
> And do what you would do.
>
> Breathe on me, breath of God,
> Until my heart is pure,
> Until with you I have one will,
> To live and to endure.
>
> Breath on me, breath of God,
> My soul with grace refine,
> Until this earthly part of me
> Glows with your fire divine.
>
> Breath on me, breath of God,
> So I shall never die,
> But live with you the perfect life
> In your eternity.

CHAPTER 11

LITTLE WAY OF SPIRITUAL CHILDHOOD

Worldview of the Saints

In the busyness of today's life we become so fragmented that sometimes even to think about sanctity, much less practice it, seems to be beyond our capabilities. Yet, within all of us lies the dream or hope of being better than we are, and of someday reaching and touching Goodness (God). Our past training has afforded us opportunities to hear and read about saints; but our present life says to our pragmatic self that sainthood is beyond our reach. However, if we, in our present maturity, will go back and dwell on the way of a saint, perhaps we may perceive how "the way" can be incorporated into our life, and be encouraged to embark on this road once again. For most of us ordinary people, our sanctity will not be heralded by glorious deeds; it will come through every day living.

Some of my counselees have thought St. Therese of Lisieux, the Little Flower, an insipid young girl. However, after reading her autobiography and some of the commentaries on her life, (particularly Ida F. Goerres, *The Hidden Face*), new insights regarding adaptation of "the little way" into their life came abounding. Our object, then, is to share some of the aspirations of St. Therese so that our own desires will be enkindled anew. Called the greatest saint of modern times by St. Pius X, the appropriateness of her doctrine by the ordinary person is still evident today. In 1997, John Paul II declared St. Therese to be a Doctor of the Church, thus giving Church approval to her teaching of the Little Way. The teachings in her autobiography, *The Story of a Soul*, first published over a hundred years ago, have encouraged countless persons to become saints.

With the following words, St. Therese introduces us to the doctrine of Spiritual Childhood: "I have always wanted to be a saint. But when I compare myself to the saints, there is between them and me the same difference that exists between a mountain whose summit is lost in the clouds and the obscure grain of sand trampled underfoot by the passer-by. Instead of becoming discouraged, I said to myself: 'God cannot inspire unrealizable desires. I can, then, in spite of my littleness, aspire to holiness. ... I want to seek out a means of going to heaven by a little way, a way very straight, very short, totally new. ... I want to find an elevator which would raise me to Jesus, for I am too small to climb the rough stairway of perfection.' I searched, then, the Scriptures for some sign of this elevator, the object of my desires. I read these words coming from the mouth of Eternal Wisdom. 'Whoever is a *"little one*," let him come to me' (Proverbs 9:4). I felt that I had found what I was looking for. But wanting to know, my God, what you would do to the very little one who answered your call, I continued my search and this is what I discovered: 'As one whom a mother caresses, so will I comfort you' (Is 66:12). The elevator which must raise me to heaven is your arms, O Jesus. For this I had no need to grow up, but rather I had to remain little and become so more and more."

"Sometimes when I read books in which perfection is put before us with the goal obstructed by a thousand obstacles, my poor little head is quickly tired. I close the learned treatise, which wearies my brain and dries up my heart, and I turn to the Sacred Scriptures. Then all becomes clear and light. A single word opens out infinite vistas, perfection appears easy and I see that it is enough to acknowledge our nothingness and like children surrender ourselves into the arms of God. Leaving to great and lofty minds the beautiful books which I cannot understand, still less put into practice, I rejoice in my littleness, because only little children and those who are like them shall be admitted to the heavenly banquet."

"Sanctity does not consist in those spiritual exercises or achievements. It consists in a disposition of the heart which allows us to remain small and humble in the arms of God, knowing our weakness and trusting to the point of rashness in his fatherly goodness."

St. Therese was wont to speak of God as "God, our Papa." She tells us how she ceaselessly pored over the Gospels "to discover in them the character of God." She plumbed the depths of the mystery of God's relation as father to us, a father overflowing with love and mercy. She came to understand the supreme desire of the Heart of God to communicate his love to us, to pardon us when we fall, and to make us forever a part of his divine family. But the doctrine of divine Fatherhood illuminated Therese's whole spiritual life, inspiring her with the most daring confidences to become a saint. Thus her spirituality incorporates the essence of Jesus' teachings as expressed by St. Paul: "You have been adopted into the very family circle of God and you can say with a full heart, 'Abba, Father'. The Spirit himself endorses our inward conviction that we really are the children of God. Think what that means. If we are his children we share his treasures, and all that Christ claims as his will come to us as well" (Rom 8:12-17).

The Little Way

Only during the final weeks of her life did St. Therese begin to use the phrase, "The Little Way," to describe her doctrine of Spiritual Childhood. To call her teaching a "Little Way" is to emphasize its adaptability for use by average people. Traditionally, sanctity has been considered as possible only for great and heroic souls who performed miracles or other remarkable feats. St. Therese insists that none of these are necessary to reach sanctity. This does not mean that sanctity is easy, or that tepid, selfish, or careless souls are automatically assured of perfection. Rather, holiness can be found in doing the most ordinary and simple tasks with extraordinary love and confidence in God. For Therese, being child-like is the opposite of being childish.

Littleness refers to one's attitude toward one's self. One recognizes one's helplessness apart from God. "What have you that you have not received?" asks St. Paul (I Cor 4:7).

St. Therese was fond of saying that "humility is truth." She knew, instinctively, that pride is the greatest obstacle to holiness because it is a dishonest and false attribution of good to oneself and thus a stealing of credit from God, the source of all goodness. Thus, the Little Way makes humility the foundation for the whole structure of perfection. For Therese, being a little child was simply another way of expressing what other spiritual writers call *spiritual poverty*. "To remain little means to recognize one's nothingness, to expect everything from God, and not to worry too much about one's faults." It is living the first Beatitude, "Blessed are the poor in Spirit." She realized that the strength of a small child to charm an elder is in its utter helplessness. The weaker and more helpless, the more eagerly do we hasten to a child's aid. She was convinced that God also treated little ones in this same fashion. "Because I was little and weak, Jesus stooped down to me and tenderly instructed me in the secrets of His love."

Consequences of Littleness

As a consequence of this sense of littleness there grows a dependence upon God's providence from day to day, and even from moment to moment. St. Therese wrote, "Many a time I have noticed that Jesus will not give me provision for the future. He sustains me from moment to moment with nourishment that is ever new. I find it in me without knowing how it is there. I believe quite simply that it is Jesus himself, hidden in the depths of my heart, who acts in me in a mysterious manner and inspires me with all he wills me to do at the moment." Thus a little soul practices spiritual poverty, and at the same time enjoys the blessing of the first beatitude, "For theirs is the Kingdom of God." God does not give his graces in advance but only at the moment when they are needed.

A second result is the joyful acceptance of one's frequent falls. Being little, one can expect to fall many times. Children often fall, but they are too small to hurt themselves seriously. "When I happen to fall into some fault, I rise again immediately without any of that anger that comes from wounded pride in the case of complicated souls."

Therese did not always experience such a joyful acceptance of her faults. For years she struggled with scruples. For a number of years after she entered the Carmel convent she was filled with anxiety concerning her indeliberate faults. She was observed during the annual retreat, after being told how easy it was to fall into mortal sin, as being pale and exhausted, neither eating nor sleeping very well. However, in 1891, Father Alexis, a Capuchin Missionary, assured her in confession that her faults did not grieve the good God since they were not deliberate. From then on she could rejoice in her falls since they served to remind her of her littleness and her total dependence upon God. After the example of Therese, we should rejoice in our non-deliberate falls which give no offense to God but serve to remind us of our littleness. "The more one humbly recognizes that one is weak and miserable, the more God lowers himself to us to lavish his gifts upon us."

A third aspect of Therese's littleness may seem strange to us today. It was her desire to be ignored and forgotten by everyone. Therese saw this as a necessary consequence of being spiritually a little child. "I wish to be forgotten not only by others but also by myself, so as no longer to have any desire except to love the good God. I desire to be unknown to all creatures. I never longed for human glory. Contempt from others had formerly some attraction for my heart, but when I saw that this was still too good for me, I conceived an ardent desire to be forgotten." This indeed is a sign of genuine humility.

Therese took as her name in religious life, "Sister Therese of the Child Jesus and the Holy Face." The "Child Jesus" portion referred to her desire to become a little child in God's arms. The "Holy Face" portion referred to the despised, humiliated face of Jesus in the Passion. She explains: "Those words of Isaiah, 'There is no beauty in him, nor comeliness. His look was, as it were, hidden and despised' became the substance of all my piety. I too desired to be without beauty, without comeliness, alone to tread the winepress, unknown to creatures. I wished that my face, like that of Jesus, be hidden from all eyes, that no one on earth would recognize me. I thirsted to be forgotten."

Simplicity and Authenticity

Akin to humility in the doctrine of Spiritual Childhood is simplicity. The life of a simple soul goes like a straight line to God, and doing God's will. This simplicity is expressed in the Beatitude, "Blessed are the pure of heart." Jesus says of this simplicity, "If your eye is single, then your whole body will be filled with light" (Mt 6:22). Therese says: "For simple souls there must be no complicated ways or procedures, no overtaxing of the mind, nothing to distract one from the one occupation of love and obedience to God's will." Such simplicity will manifest itself especially in one's prayers when we simply tell God whatever is on our mind and in our heart, knowing well that he will understand. There will be no pretense, no attempt to appear different from our real self.

Simplicity means accepting ourselves as we are, and allowing everyone to know us as we truly are. We glory in the truth, appearing outwardly as within, without duplicity or insecurity. There is no artificiality, dishonesty or pretense. Depth psychologists insist that the mark of authenticity is the very first and most essential task for attaining maturity. Scripture scholars and theologians tell us that simplicity or authenticity is the natural quality in childhood which is behind Jesus' words in the Gospel, "Unless you turn back and become as little children, you cannot enter the Kingdom of God" (Mt 18:1-3). Therese remarks, "It is well that the Kingdom of heaven contains many mansions, for if there were none other than those of which the description and way seem incomprehensible to me, I should never be able to enter therein."

In the process of Therese's canonization, the witnesses who had known her testified again and again concerning her simplicity. "With her, everything was simple and natural." "She acted in so simple a manner that her life seemed quite ordinary." "The heroic character of her virtues was unnoticed by most of the sisters." The greatest saint of modern times was looked upon by some of the nuns in her convent as not even being a good religious. This is certainly the height of simplicity and self-effacement. Her life was so much like that of all the others that her daily companions did not suspect any heroic greatness in her.

Unlimited Confidence in God

An unlimited confidence in God is another characteristic mark of spiritual childhood. "We obtain from the good God quite as much as we hope for." God proportions his goodness to accord with the degree of our confidence in him, and takes great delight in showering his greatest favors upon the most weak and helpless, provided that we entrust ourselves completely to him and have good will." Near the end of her life, Therese prayed, "O Jesus, could I but tell all little souls of your ineffable condescension. I feel that if it were possible to find one more weak than mine, you would take delight in showering upon her greater favors still, provided that she abandoned herself with entire confidence to your infinite mercy." She was convinced that if souls felt what she herself felt, no one would despair of reaching the summit of the mount of love. The fact that she saw herself so imperfect after many years as a religious did not in any way take away her daring confidence to become a saint. She tells us that she does not count on her own merits but on the power of him who, being virtue and holiness itself, would clothe her with his infinite merits and make her a saint." "The good God has always come to my assistance. He has helped me and led me by the hand from my earliest years. I count on him."

Therese assures us that "never can we have too much confidence in the good God." Her confidence was based not only upon God's goodness, love and mercy, but in a special way upon God's justice. "It is because he is just that the good God is compassionate and full of gentleness, slow to punish and abounding in mercy. For he knows our frailty, he remembers that we are but dust." "What a joy to think that our Lord is just, that he takes into account our weakness and knows so well the frailty of our nature. What then need I fear? Will not the God of infinite justice who deigns to pardon so mercifully the sins of the prodigal son, be also just to me who am always with him?" "Justice takes account of good intention, and gives to virtue its reward. It is because he is just that he is compassionate and merciful, long-suffering and plenteous in mercy. I cannot understand souls who are afraid of so tender a friend."

"It is not because I have been shielded from mortal sin that I raise my heart to God in trust and love. I feel that even if I had on my conscience all the crimes one could commit, I should lose nothing of my confidence. Broken-hearted with contrition, I would go and throw myself into the arms of my Savior. I know that the Prodigal Son is dear to him. I have heard his words to Mary Magdalene, to the adulteress, to the Samaritan woman. No one could frighten me, for I know what to believe concerning his mercy and his love. I know that in one moment all that multitude of sins would disappear like a drop of water cast into a flaming furnace." As to our daily faults, she tells us that instead of running away from our heavenly Father, we need only to throw ourselves into his arms and implore his forgiveness. When we act thus, "he thrills with joy. He says to his angels what the father of the prodigal son said to his servants: 'Put a ring on his finger and let us rejoice.'" Whatever the fault, when thrown into the furnace of divine love with filial confidence, "it is immediately consumed forever."

For a number of years, Therese was besieged with a deep spiritual darkness, dryness in prayers and temptations against faith. If she had merely trusted her feelings, she would have been convinced that she had been abandoned by God. When questioned as to her mode of acting in these hours of darkness, she replied, "I turn to the good God, to all the saints, and I thank them just the same. I think they wish to see to what point I shall carry my trust. But not in vain have the words of Job sunk into my heart: 'Though he should kill me, yet I will trust in him.'" "He will weary sooner of making me wait than I shall of waiting." She reasoned that God was hiding himself in order to make himself longed for and sought after all the more. "My sufferings may reach the furthest limits, but I am sure that he will never abandon me."

Commenting on the parable of the laborers in the vineyard who labored but a single hour and received a full day's pay, Therese said: "You see that if we abandon ourselves, if we place our confidence in the good God, exerting our own feeble efforts and placing all our hope in his mercy, we shall be rewarded and paid as much as the greatest saints." "We must say to the good God, 'I know well I shall never be worthy of that for which I hope, but I stretch out my hands to you like a little beggar and I am confident that you will grant all I ask, because you are so good.'" Therese instructed her novices, "Hold fast your confidence. It is impossible for the good God not to respond to it, for he measures his gifts by our hope in him."

Immense Desires

Along with humility, Therese insists that the "Little Way" must also include bold confidence. "I feel always the daring confidence that one day I shall become a great saint. I am not trusting on my own merits, for I have none, but I trust in him who is virtue and holiness itself." "Our dreams and our desires for perfection are not fancies since Jesus himself has commanded us to realize them, saying 'Be you perfect as your heavenly Father is perfect.'" "Little children have a right to be daring with their parents. My excuse is my title of child. Children do not reflect on the import of their words. Nevertheless, if their parents are possessed of immense treasures, they do not hesitate about gratifying the desires of the little ones whom they cherish more than themselves."

God is infinite, in riches, in greatness, in power, in goodness, in mercy, in love. He can give forever without exhausting his bountiful treasures. His glory is to be able to give without measure, his joy to please his children on earth who come to him with loving trust. Even the most immense desires in relation to ourselves are exceedingly small in relation to what God hopes for us. Guided by this kind of thinking, Therese formed immense desires and having formed them, she dared to articulate them in the simplicity of her confidence in God. "Immense are the desires that I feel with my heart, and with confidence I call upon you to come and take possession of my soul."

"To be your spouse, to be a Carmelite, to be a mother of souls, should not this suffice me? Yet it is not so. I feel the vocation of the warrior, the priest, the apostle, the doctor, the martyr. I feel the need and the desire of carrying out the most heroic deeds for you, O Jesus. I want to die on the field of battle in defense of the Church. I would like to enlighten souls as did the prophets and doctors. I have the vocation of the apostle. I would like to travel over the whole earth to preach the Gospel on all five continents, simultaneously, and even to the most remote isles. I would be a missionary, not for a few years only, but from the beginning of creation until the consummation of the ages, but above all, I would shed my blood for you, even to the very last drop. O my Jesus, what is your answer to all my follies? Is there a soul more little, more powerless than mine? Nevertheless, because of my weakness, it has pleased you, O Lord, to grant my little childish desires and you desire, today, to grant other desires that are greater than the universe."

Experiencing these immense desires, Therese tells us that they became a veritable martyrdom until she found Chapters 12 and 13 of First Corinthians. "I read that all cannot be apostles, prophets, doctors, etc. Without becoming discouraged, I continued my reading, and this sentence consoled me: 'Yet strive after the better gifts and I point out to you a yet more excellent way.' The apostle explains how all the most perfect gifts are nothing without love, that Charity is the way that leads most surely to God. I finally had rest. Charity gave me the key to my vocation. I understood that if the Church had a body composed of different members, the most necessary and most noble of all could not be lacking to it. So I understood that the Church had a heart and that this heart was burning with love. I understood that it was love alone that made the Church's members act. I understood that love comprised all vocations, that love was everything, that it embraced all times and places. Then in the excess of my delirious joy, I cried out: ***my vocation is love***.'"

"In times past, victims pure and spotless were the only ones accepted by God. To satisfy divine justice perfect victims were necessary, but the law of love has succeeded the law of fear and love has chosen me as a holocaust, me, a weak and imperfect creature. In order that love be fully satisfied, it is necessary that it lower itself to nothingness and transform this nothingness into fire. O Jesus, I know that love is repaid by love alone. I am the smallest of creatures, I know my misery and my feebleness, but I know also how much noble and generous hearts loved to do good. I beg you then, O blessed inhabitants of heaven, I beg you to adopt me as your child. To you alone will be the glory which you will make me merit, but deign to answer my prayer. It is bold, I know, however, I dare to ask you to obtain for me your twofold spirit."

"O my Jesus, I love you. I love the Church, my mother. I recall that 'the smallest act of pure love is of more value to her than all other works together.' I beg you to cast your divine glance upon a great number of little souls. I beg you to choose a legion of little victims worthy of your love."

CHAPTER 12

LAW OF POLARITY: BALANCE OF OPPOSITES

Need of Balance in Worldview

Balance between opposite poles of truth runs as a constant theme throughout the whole of authentic Christianity. This balance is the opposite of extremism or fanaticism which takes only one aspect of truth and exaggerates it while other opposing aspects are ignored or denied. Heresy results by emphasizing a particular insight of truth while denying another equally true aspect of divine revelation. Both poles are partially true, but neither is absolutely true. St. Thomas Aquinas says that virtue stands in the middle between two opposing extremes.

Many Christians find satisfaction in accusing those who disagree with them of being fanatics, but fail to recognize the seeds of fanaticism in their own stubbornly held position. All of us, in one way or another, at one time in our life or another, are fanatical about something. This seems to be the lot of human existence and a part of the "original sin" we have inherited from our ancestors. We are somewhat like drunken drivers who are never able to keep a straight line but wander from one side to another. It behooves us to recognize and accept ownership for our own particular brand of extremism.

Total truth results only when we succeed in bringing about a merger between these opposite poles of truth. When opposites are brought together in a balanced tension, this union of opposites is creative of new understanding and new energy.

This balanced tension does not involve the negation of either pole of truth, but rather the maintenance of the full truth of each side. This naturally causes stress, and requires great effort to maintain. By this very union of opposites, new energy is created and released into the world. Two examples would be the creation of new life through union of opposite sexes, and release of electrical energy by union of opposite poles. This challenge of having to exist in tension with an opposite pole of reality can bring out the best in everyone. Without this challenge, most people would take the easy road of mediocrity and lukewarmness.

Because of the tension that a balance demands, with the constant struggle necessary to maintain it, countless Christians have sought to eliminate certain of their problems by denying one or the other opposing pole. This only gives a temporary relief; the problem does not go away, but simply erupts at some later date.

Christianity is based upon a conjunction of opposites: namely, the divine versus the human nature of Jesus Christ. The more we seek the perfection that makes us Christ-like, the harder we must strive to bring all our energies or powers into a balance. Our lifetime will be spent bringing into balance all the opposites within our nature. The opposites should maintain their individuality and at the same time be in conjunction with each other.

Some examples of these counterparts which we will discuss in this chapter are: the three commandments of love, the awesome and fascinating aspects of God, nature and grace, this life and life-after-death, meekness and mercy, self-development and self-renunciation, attachment and detachment, fulfillment and diminishment, spiritual childhood and spiritual maturity, consciousness and unconscious, femininity and masculinity, perceiving and judging functions, action and contemplation, change and status quo.

The centrist position between opposite poles is very difficult to maintain, and a high tension capacity is required to establish a union of opposites. Those who are unable to stand stress, or have a low tolerance of tension are unable to maintain a good balance. The more self-disciplined one is and the stronger one's will power, the more ability one has to maintain this tension. Maintenance of balance will necessitate self-denial or sacrifice and may cause pain, suffering, struggle and hard work. Those who have failed to learn how to handle these negative experiences will find it nearly impossible to maintain the balanced tension needed for creation of new energy and growth.

Attaining and maintaining balance between opposite poles of truth and reality is the one path to wholeness, maturity, sanctity, success and happiness. Hence there is a need to develop a high tension capacity through self-discipline, sacrifice and self-denial. Those who have led a comfortable life, especially during teen-age and early adult years, usually lack the discipline to maintain this balanced tension throughout their adult life.

Activity and passivity, development and curtailment, possession and renunciation, life and death are phases of our journey of faith towards wholeness. The third chapter of Ecclesiastes expresses this very well, "There is an appointed time for everything, and a time for every affair under the heavens. A time to be born and a time to die; a time to plant and a time to uproot the plant. A time to kill and a time to heal, a time to tear down and a time to build. A time to weep and a time to laugh; a time to mourn and a time to dance. A time to scatter stones and a time to gather them; a time to embrace and a time to be far from embrac es. A time to seek and a time to lose; a time to keep and a time to cast away. A time to rend and a time to sew; a time to be silent and a time to speak. A time to love and a time to hate; a time of war and a time of peace."

Balance Among the Three Commandments of Love

When Jesus was asked, "Which commandment of the law is the greatest?" he stated, "The whole law is based on two commandments: the love of God and the love of neighbor" (Mt 22:34-40, Deut 6:4). Actually, a third commandment of love is concealed in the second commandment: "to love your neighbor as you love yourself." Jesus may not have thought it necessary to command us to love ourselves, but because many people have such low self-esteem, they need to be reminded that we have an obligation to show a proper loving care for ourselves.

Our life revolves around these three commandments of love. A proper balance must be maintained between the obligations of love toward God, neighbor and self. If we are to follow Jesus' example, we are to practice unconditional love toward God and neighbor.

We might define unconditional love as the love which consistently puts the needs of the other ahead of our own desires. This is the kind of love God has for us. God consistently puts our needs ahead of his desires. God would have liked very much to establish his Kingdom on earth during the lifetime of Jesus two thousand years ago. However, to have done this, God would have had to take away human freedom. In order to be human we need to be free to accept God's Kingdom or reject it. So for these past two thousand years, God has been forced to delay his desire to establish his Kingdom on earth in order to respect our need for human freedom.

In the eleventh chapter of Luke's Gospel, the disciples asked Jesus to teach them how to pray. In response, Jesus taught them the Lord's Prayer, and teaches us something about unconditional love. If we concentrate simply on the words of the Lord's Prayer, we overlook a very important message that Jesus is trying to teach us.

In the Lord's Prayer there are eight petitions. The first four petitions express God's needs. Only in the second half of the prayer are we to express our needs. Jesus is teaching us that when we pray, our first concern should be God's requirements, and that we should always put our needs and desires secondly to those of God. This, then, is an example of unconditional love.

The commandment to love God with our whole mind, whole strength, and whole heart also urges a loving concern for our neighbor and our own well-being. Jesus makes it very clear that it is impossible to have a sincere love for God if we are in some way neglecting to love our neighbor. "As often as you did it for one of my least brothers, you did it for me. ... As long as you neglected to do it to one of these least ones, you neglected to do it to me" (Mt 25:40, 45). "This is how all will know you are my disciples: your love for one another" (Jn 13:35). "If you bring your gift to the altar and there recall that your brother has anything against you, leave your gift at the altar. Go first to be reconciled with your brother, and then come and offer your gift" (Mt 5:23-24).

It is interesting to note that in the Gospels of Matthew, Mark and Luke, for every reference to "love of God" there are three references to "love of neighbor." John's Gospel balances this by having three references to "love of God" for each reference to "love of neighbor." In his first Epistle, St. John asserts, "If anyone says, 'My love is fixed on God,' yet hates his brother, he is a liar. One who has no love for the brother he has seen cannot love the God he has not seen. The commandment we have from him is this: whoever loves God must also love his brother" (I Jn 4:20-21).

In order to maintain the proper balance between the three commandments of love, we must also give attention to our own personal needs. We need to take proper care of our bodily health, as well as our psychological and spiritual health. Our body is the instrument we need in order to carry out our duties and responsibilities of love toward God and neighbor. It is the only body we have, so to neglect the proper care of ourselves is contrary to this great commandment of love.

Lest we become scrupulous about giving proper care to our own needs, it is good to remember that there is a vast difference between selfishness and self-love. Selfishness is when we go to extremes in loving ourselves, and neglect the proper balance of all three relationships of love. Proper self-love obliterates our fear and conceit so that we can extend ourselves to others.

Balance Between the Awesome
and the Fascinating Aspects of God

transcending the universe, time, etc

There are two aspects of God which must be kept in balanced tension. They are the infinite awesomeness of God as contrasted with the attractive closeness of God. This balance is brought out in the three aspects of God which we honor in the Blessed Trinity. We think of the First Person of the Trinity as expressing the infinite *transcendence* of God. The Third Person of the Trinity expresses the *immanent closeness* of God. The Second Person of the Trinity expresses the *transparency* of God. It is through the revelation of the Second Person in the Incarnation of Jesus that all three aspects of God become transparent.

The Lord's Prayer beautifully contrasts these two aspects of God. First, we express our closeness to God by addressing God as "Our Father." Then, immediately we express the infinite greatness of God, "Hallowed be thy Name." God, our creator, is infinitely greater than we are, yet He allows us to call him Father, giving us a special closeness to Him. The transcendence of God evokes from us a proper humility in all our contacts with God. We must never forget the infinite distance that separates God the creator from us creatures. At the same time, the intimate closeness of God Who is always available to us allows us to have unlimited trust and confidence in God. These two aspects of God seem contradictory, yet it is only by maintaining a constant tension between these two sides of God that we are able to have a healthy, honest relationship with God. Some days our prayer should be centered on God's awesome transcendence. Other days our prayer should be centered on his availability, his immanence.

In other words, we need a good balance between the two gifts of the Holy Spirit which we call Piety and Fear of the Lord. Fear of the Lord refers to an attitude of reverence

Reverence for God or devout fulfillment of religious obligations

(piety/ saintly)

and respect for God, and a realization of the vast distance
which separates us as creatures from the infinite God. Piety
refers to the realization of the closeness and intimacy which
God wishes to have with us. Jesus teaches us to pray by
calling God "*Abba*" or "Daddy," and tells us that when we
pray we can also call God "Abba" or "Daddy" or "Father."
Piety emphasizes the immanence or closeness of our union
with God. Fear of the Lord emphasizes the transcendence
or infinity of God. We need both piety and fear of the Lord,
and every day we try to maintain this balance. *Not thinking of ourselves but thinking of ourselves less but thinking of ourselves already less*

Furthermore, our spiritual life is structured upon the two
basic virtues of humility and trust. Humility reminds us of the
infinite distance which separates us as creatures from God
the creator. Trust reminds us of the loving kindness and
concern which this infinite God has for each of us. In the
four Gospels there are at least 58 references recommending
us to have unlimited trust in God. Frequently this is *trust*
translated as having faith in God. Almost always when
Jesus and the Gospel writers speak of the necessity of faith,
they are referring to trust. At the same time, our confidence
in God must never allow us to forget who we are as finite
creatures, and who God is as the infinite creator. As Jesus
told Saint Catherine of Siena, "I am who am, you are who
are not."

We express this tension between the awesomeness
and the closeness of God by two aspects of prayer: listening
and speaking. Many people think of prayer only as speaking
to God. Actually prayer should primarily be listening to God
speak to us, and only then should we feel free to speak to
God. There will be emergencies in our life when it is quite
proper to initiate our contact with God by calling upon Him
for help. But, in our normal daily contact with God through
prayer, the proper respect and reverence for God is shown
by first trying to discern what God is saying to us. Only in the
second half of our prayer should we respond to God's word
by speaking to God.

A good way to practice listening to God is to begin each
prayer period with the reading or the remembering of some

appropriate text of Sacred Scripture. The Bible is "The Word of God." We should have our favorite passages of Scripture which reveal God's will to us. In reading the Bible we find "Ah-Ha" verses which seem to have a message from God for us. After reflecting upon them for a while, we respond to God in whatever way seems appropriate. Thus, all of prayer is a balanced tension between listening to God's word, and then making a response to God.

Balance Between Nature and Grace

Another area of our life that requires a balance between opposite poles of reality is the relationship between nature and grace. There are various ways of expressing this tension: natural vs. supernatural, human effort vs. divine grace, secular vs. sacred, time vs. eternity, this life vs. next life after death.

Many people claim that this opposition between nature and grace, secular and sacred, natural and supernatural is an artificial distinction. They claim there is no purely secular, natural area of life. This seems to be a valid insight which needs to be kept in mind. Actually, what is being said is that these two poles of truth are not really opposed to one another but should work together as a team. Even the most worldly and secular aspects of our life are sacred because they are created by God, and are a part of God's plan for the whole of creation.

Both body and soul are important. God's grace is present in every aspect of human nature. Unless we take reasonable care of our body, we will be without the energy needed to fulfill our duties and responsibilities towards others. Of course, we also need to develop the life of our soul so that we can have the fullness of filial love towards others. To neglect to take reasonable care of our body is just as sinful as to neglect our soul.

 St. Ignatius of Loyola is supposed to have said that "we should work as though everything depended on ourselves, and pray as though everything depended on God." This is an attempt to express the necessary balanced tension between our prayer-life and our actions. We cannot simply sit back and depend upon God's grace to take care of all our needs. At the same time, we must never imagine that whether or not we make a success of our life is solely up to us.

God has given us intelligence and common sense, and we are expected to use all our natural gifts in carrying out our duties of love toward God, neighbor and self. At the same time, we believe that we need special grace or help from God over and beyond our best natural efforts. Prayer and action, grace and nature, are ways of expressing the need to maintain a good balance between our dependence on God and our dependence upon our own efforts.

When we speak of reason, we are referring to the knowledge which the intellect is able to attain through the natural talents and gifts of our human nature. When we speak of faith, we refer to all the new knowledge about the mysteries of God and creation which come to us through divine revelation. Both are important, both are needed. There is no contradiction between faith and reason. Whenever there seems to be such a contradiction, we need to investigate further until we understand the problem. At times, the answer will be in the way that divine revelation has been presented in interpretation, for example, using Greek categories of thought which are no longer valid. At other times, the problem will be with the rational hypothesis which reason uses to describe reality. Both reason and faith need to be reformed and updated periodically in order to better express the truth.

Knowledge is the gift of the Holy Spirit that gives us good insights into the working of divine providence in the events of this earthly life. *Understanding* is the gift which enables us to penetrate the mysteries of God as they have been revealed to us. We need both of these gifts in order to live a full life of faith. To keep alive the virtue of hope we need to be able to see the hand of God's loving care at work in our life and the lives of others. To hold on to our faith, we need Understanding which helps us to delve deeper and deeper into the truth of God's mysteries.

All three theological virtues—faith, hope, love—are necessary, and attention needs to be given to each of them. There are three aspects of faith: conviction, confidence and commitment. If all three of these aspects are fulfilled, they will include hope regarding the future and practice of charity in the present. Our convictions regarding God's revelation will naturally lead to complete trust and confidence in God regarding hope for the future, the forgiveness of past sins and the needed help of divine grace to fulfill our duties of love toward God and neighbor.

We need a certain amount of self-confidence in order to live. This has to be balanced with a tremendous trust and confidence in God. These do not contradict each other but work together as a team. Thus nature and grace are necessary partners leading us to wholeness and balance.

Balance Between This Life and Life After Death

Many people give all or almost all of their attention to their present life, and have little or no concern for life after death. It is also possible to be so concerned about life after death that one neglects to assume one's responsibilities in the here and now. We need a balanced tension between leading a full life on earth, and preparing ourselves for the life of eternity which begins after death. Actually, there is a simple way to manage this. It is to live a life totally dominated by love. It is primarily by love that we best prepare ourselves for the life with God after death.

Many people who have had after-death experiences relate that, at the moment of death, they met a figure of light, often described as the Risen Lord Jesus. They state that this figure of light asked them two questions: "How have you grown in wisdom?" and "What good have you done with your life on earth?"

190

Growing in wisdom and practicing agapic love would seem to be the two main tasks we need to accomplish while here on earth in order to prepare ourselves for the life hereafter. To grow in wisdom and love involves our two main spiritual faculties: our intellect and our will. We often describe these two faculties as the head and the heart, not meaning the physical organs of our body, but rather the faculties to know and to love. Wisdom and love are the two attributes we most need to live a full life on earth and, it would seem, to enjoy eternity with God.

Throughout our life we need to keep a balanced tension between our efforts to grow in wisdom and our efforts to grow in love. God has implanted in our nature a curiosity to know more and more about reality: both the reality of God and all the realities of the created universe. At the same time there is an intense longing in our nature to be loved and to love. Adequate attention needs to be given to both of these drives for wisdom and love. It is gratifying to know that when we grow in love and wisdom we are not only fulfilling our mission on earth but also preparing ourselves for our mission in heaven after death.

Past, present and future are important, and need to be considered in making the decisions of life. We should learn from both our own past and the past experience of others. We also need to use our intelligence to assess the prospects for the future. However, most of our attention should be given to the present moment, the present time.

Abraham Maslow made a study of 500 successful persons in history to determine the key to their success. His conclusion was that all of them were primarily concerned about the present. According to his calculations, we should spend eight-ninths of our time and energy with the present, and only one-ninth in consideration of the past and the future. This is also the teaching of Jesus in the Sermon on the Mount. "Enough, then, of worrying about tomorrow. Let tomorrow take care of itself. Today has troubles enough of its own" (Mt 6:34).

rigorous self-denial

Now is the time

The Paschal Mystery of death and resurrection runs through the whole of life. The cross is the symbol of the asceticism required to rise above our nature and reach participation in the higher nature of God. To participate in this divine life we must die to some of our present ways and rise to a more Christ-like way of life. Rather than clinging to our present situation, we must empty ourselves, sacrifice the old and allow the new to be born. By sacrificing the externals of life, we allow the more important inner powers to take root and grow. Over and over again, we must disengage ourselves and go beyond to something higher. Each time our egotism suffers a defeat, we experience pain, but this pain becomes a loving fire which completes our union with God.

To put our faith in the Paschal Mystery of death and resurrection as the ultimate solution to the problems of life means to accept the presence of unresolved tragedy. To live the Paschal Mystery means an acceptance of suffering and death which are not resolved in this life but only in some mysterious way in the life beyond the grave. We don't really know what the New Testament means by resurrection, since it is a life different from all our present experiences. Once we put our faith in this promised resurrection, we are able to live with the possibility of incompleteness, rather than assured success, as the end of earthly life.

As Christians we have been promised constant help through the Holy Spirit. One of the gifts of the Holy Spirit is Wisdom; and through the Gift of Wisdom, we are able to put everything in our life in the proper perspective, giving the right priorities to everything and everyone. Sanctity, holiness, wholeness, maturity and balance are some of the effects of the working of Wisdom in our life.

"Lord of mercy ... grant me Wisdom ... to help me and to toil with me and teach me what is pleasing to you" (Wis 9:l, 4, 10).

Balance Between Self-Development and Renunciation

In his book *The Divine Milieu*, Teilhard de Chardin explains the particular tension between self-development and renunciation. Part One of *The Divine Milieu* treats **the divinization of our activities.** We sanctify all our activities by doing them purely for God, and in accord with God's will. Each of us exists for God, and whatever we do to help ourselves and others lead a full life is done for God, and thus is divinized.

Through us matter is transformed into spirit. We take the energy of the food we eat and the air we breathe, and transform this physical energy into the dispersal of the spiritual energy of love, truth, goodness, beauty and justice. Each time we use our human energy in an act of loving kindness to build understanding and unity, we become creators of new spiritual energy in the world.

Creation continues by our actions. Every act of love is a step toward the establishment of the Kingdom of God on earth. Thus we are in the process of creating the new earth, the new Jerusalem, the new Kingdom of God. We have the power to harness for God all the energies of love. Our task is to divinize the world, and we do this through our activities.

In Part Two of *The Divine Milieu* we find the concern to be with *the passivities of growth* and *the passivities of diminishment* which form the other half of our existence. That which we *endure*, as opposed to that which we *do*, also needs to be divinized.

The *passivities of growth* are those forces to which we are subject: our dependence on others, on nature, on the condition of our health, on the weather and on the countless circumstances beyond our control. These passivities greatly limit our freedom. It seems life controls us much more than we control it, and we are free only in a small radius of our life.

Besides the passivities of growth there are the *passivities of diminishment*: experiences of death, failure and frustration over which we have no control. There are the *external passivities* such as ill fortune, barriers and obstacles, negative experiences, accidents, bacteria, viruses. There are also the *internal passivities* of diminishment: our own sins, limitations, defects, weaknesses, disease, old age, illness, death.

We can find God in each and all of these events, provided that we try to love God, others and ourselves as best we can. Even the diminishment of death can become a communion of love with God and God's will. By the power of Christ's resurrection we are able to transform into love and life all of our diminishments. With Christ's example, we learn to develop, to the fullest possible extent, our powers of love. We detach ourselves from everything that hinders our ability to love. Beyond that we practice total resignation of our will to God's will.

The whole web of chance is a part of God's providence. Through these seemingly chance events God is at work leading us to the Kingdom. We must never miss an opportunity to appreciate the passive diminishments which Divine Providence puts in our path by accepting them peacefully knowing that "for those who love God, all things work together for good" (Rom 8:28).

Self-development is an obligation to which all of us are called. We can be certain that God had a definite mission for each of us on earth when we were created. In order to fulfill this mission we need to develop as fully as possible our potential for love, goodness, truth and justice. To strengthen our own resoluteness in fulfilling this mission we have to practice renunciation and self-denial.

In order to fully develop our potential for good and for love, we may need to renounce or reject many possible directions that we could go with our life. Every day we are faced with choices as to how to spend our time and energy. Each time we choose one particular path, we must, of necessity, reject other possible ways. It is impossible for us to fulfill all of our desires, dreams, hopes and ambitions. Therefore, as this will involve the sacrifice of many very attractive alternatives, self-denial and sacrifice become essential elements of our life. Only by the restraint of self-denial are we able to keep our human nature balanced and open to the diverse experiences needed for wholeness and maturity.

Development and renunciation—self-expression and self-denial—are not mutually exclusive, but are part of the general rhythm of growth from a lower to higher level of maturity. They are like the breathing-in and breathing-out of our body, two components of a healthy, developing life but subject to an infinite number of subtle variations. The exact blending calls for spiritual tact and wisdom which constantly needs to be improved. Since self-discipline will increase our tension capacity, we need to practice personal self-denial.

We frequently need to sacrifice bodily and worldly gratification to make room for the life of agapic love to grow within us. We should accept with gratitude whatever pleasures and joys God's providence gives us, but not linger too long in the enjoyment of them. Our task is to strive to bring our whole life into subjection to the higher law of the universe which is Love and God's will. Only by restraint can we keep our human nature balanced and open to the diverse experiences needed for wholeness and maturity.

There is more than a spiritual value to self-denial. Our mental and psychological health demands it. People who live only for the satisfaction of their selfish and bodily desires are disowned not only by the rest of mankind for their debauchery, but are also rejected by their own inner self. They find themselves plagued by fear, ugly moods, frustration and irritability. They are closed in upon themselves and become blind to the needs of others. Those who choose self-indulgence and the most comfortable life bring their growth in wholeness to a halt, and gradually regress to an infantile way of life.

The earlier we come to an understanding of the value of detachment and self-denial, the more quickly we will progress towards wholeness. Ideally, we should learn self-discipline during the first twenty-five years of life. If we fail to work on self-control of our conscious faculties during youth, the onus of accomplishing this all-important task will be thrust upon us later in life. After the age of twenty-five, we face other tasks of maturity and those who had life too easy in their youth will be burdened with psychological maladjustments during adulthood. However, it is never too late to begin the program of self-discipline to bring about the needed integration of inner faculties and attain a balance in our nature.

One interesting tension between these opposite poles of development and diminishment is that between feasting and fasting. We need to feast and enjoy the pleasures of life just as Jesus did during his life on earth. We also need to fast and abstain from the pleasures of our bodily appetites. A good way to know whether you have a good balance in your life between feasting and fasting is by comparing the number of times you have over-indulged in feasting with the number of times in your life you have gone to extremes in fasting too much. If we are honest, we will have to admit that we are still a long way from having a balance between feasting and fasting, between self-denial and over-indulgence of our bodily appetites.

Balance Between Fulfillment and Diminishment

A truly balanced life will have both fulfillment and diminishment. Unless we achieve fulfillment in the realization of at least some of our goals and objectives, we will become discouraged, bitter and pessimistic. On the other hand, a person who never experiences failure will lose sight of his creatureliness, and will rapidly assume the posture of a god.

For many people there is no need to look for opportunities to practice diminishment. Divine providence

196

provides them with physical, material, or spiritual losses. If we accept these uninvited crosses with patience and Christian love, they will help us establish the right priorities in our life to reach the desired goal of wholeness. However, if accepted with resentment, these adversities will hinder, not advance, our progress toward maturity. We need to realize that there are other things in life more important than the avoidance of pain and loss.

To find where we need to diminish our egotistic self, we attempt to discover the things to which we are excessively attached, those things about which we would be upset if they were suddenly removed from our life. Examples of possible excessive attachments are: alcohol, tobacco, coffee, drugs, sex, soft drinks, clothes, TV, golf, football, etc. We need to study our habits and discern the things upon which we spend our time, money and energy. How concerned would we be if one or the other of these enjoyments were denied us? A good way to find the answer is to deny ourselves the enjoyment of one of these things for a period of time—for example, during the six weeks of Lent—and see how we react.

Balance Between Spiritual Childhood and Spiritual Maturity

In the Gospel, Jesus recommends child-likeness, but not childishness. We are taught to have a child-like trust in God Who is our heavenly parent. At the same time we are urged to become spiritually mature disciples of Jesus Christ.

St. Therese of Lisieux is the spiritual writer who has best described the qualities of spiritual childhood. Besides a blind trust and confidence in God, a spiritual child of God has great simplicity and humility, and is keenly aware of her weakness and helplessness apart from God. Openness, simplicity and authenticity are qualities that make a small child very attractive. St. Therese also mentions two other qualities which are essential to spiritual childhood: great love and immense, even bold, desires. These qualities allowed

St. Therese to become one of the greatest saints of all time, despite the fact that her life was very ordinary.

St. Paul speaks of spiritual maturity at least twice in his Epistles. "Form that perfect man who is Christ come to full stature. Let us be children no longer. ... Rather let us grow to the full maturity of Christ, the head" (Eph 4:13-15). "All of us who are spiritually mature must have this attitude. ... It is important that we continue on our course no matter what stage we have reached" (Phil 3:15-16).

Carl Jung suggests four qualities of a fully mature person: (1) Authenticity, (2) Significance, (3) Transparency and (4) Solidarity. Authenticity involves full self-knowledge and is concerned with a proper attitude toward one's self. Significance is knowing our true significance (that is, importance and value) in God's overall plan for creation and the human race. Transparency is the freedom from artifice, which allows one to enter into relationships of love and friendship with other individuals. Solidarity is the realization of our oneness with all of humanity. We are all brothers and sisters, regardless of race, color, nationality or religion.

In the above four steps toward maturity, note that the first two revolve around self and God. The third step, Transparency, concerns our relationship with other individuals, while the fourth step, Solidarity, encompasses our relationship with the various communities or groups of people to whom we belong. We need to keep a good balance between our relationships with individuals and also with the different groups of people to which we belong. Both are important. Both are part of the second commandment of love of neighbor. We need some intimate relationships of love with individuals, but we also have certain social responsibilities toward each of the institutions or communities to which we belong.

Balance Between Consciousness and the Unconscious

There are two sides to every human being. In addition to all those things of which we are consciously aware, there is a deeper side of human personality that is called the unconscious. The center of our conscious life is the ego; the center of the unconscious is called "the self" by Carl Jung. It might also be called the "person" or "center of our personality." It is that point of our personality where we make our closest contact with God and the Holy Spirit. *(the unconscious)*

(dreams)

Jung claims that everything in the unconscious seeks and desires to become conscious. The task of the conscious ego is to make journeys into the unconscious, and bring up to the level of consciousness the truths and insights which are seeking to become conscious. One ordinary way this occurs is through an understanding and interpretation of our night dreams, for the voice which speaks to us in dreams is the voice of the unconscious. A second way to initiate a dialogue between the conscious and the unconscious is through prayer when we open ourselves to the Holy Spirit. A third way is to get in touch with one's positive and negative shadow by any of the ways that modern depth psychology suggests, for instance, by studying the projections of our shadow upon others and accepting ownership for this part of ourselves.

Balance Between Femininity and Masculinity

A mature woman or man will have a beautiful balance of personality between feminine traits and masculine traits. Carl Jung gave the name "anima" to the feminine traits needed by a mature man and "animus" to the needed masculine traits of a mature woman. It is natural that the average man spends most of the energies of youth developing masculine traits, while the average woman spends most of her energies of youth developing feminine qualities. Only during the second half of life does a man or woman succeed in establishing this balance between anima and animus. For both men and women, the goal of maturity is to develop both feminine and masculine traits to balance one's personality. Only thus can anyone hope to attain maturity.

There is much discussion today as to the true identity of masculine and feminine traits of personality, and a reluctance to accept the traditional characteristics of women and men as defined in the patriarchal society of the past. There is justification for such reluctance. However, regardless of how one may define anima and animus today, almost everyone will admit that there is a definite psychological difference, as well as physical difference, between men and women. The law of polarity simply states that to attain full maturity, both men and women need to develop both one's anima and one's animus.

Balance Between Perceiving and Judging Functions

Carl Jung revolutionized the intellectual world with his publication of *Psychological Types* in 1921. Katharine Briggs and her daughter, Isabel Briggs Myers, found an English translation of this work in the Library of Congress in 1923. This was the beginning of forty years of research that resulted in the publication of the Myers-Briggs Type Indicator, often referred to as the MBTI.

Following the insights of Jung, the two women developed an excellent psychological tool for determining how balanced one is between the perceiving functions of sensing and intuition as well as the judging functions of thinking and feeling. As far as we know, Carl Jung was the first to describe how each of these functions may be either extraverted or introverted. The Myers-Briggs team added a fourth pair of preferences of those who emphasize the judging functions (J personality) and those who favor the perceiving functions (P personality).

Persons who work with personality type and temperament have learned that it is not psychologically healthy to be exactly balanced between these opposite poles of introversion and extraversion, sensing and intuition, thinking and feeling, judging and perceiving. Such persons are fence-sitters who fail to take and maintain a definite position. On the other hand, it is not psychologically healthy to be totally unbalanced on either side of the four pairs of preferences. It is good to have a strong preference for one side or the other of the four pairs, but still maintain an openness to the opposite side when the circumstances of life require it. This will be true when the preference scores for each of the four MBTI letters are between 7 and 25. Those who have scores over 30 should make a special effort to develop the opposite side of their preference. Strong sensors should develop more intuition. Strong thinkers should develop more feeling, etc.

Balance Between Action and Contemplation

All of us need to find a good balance between the "Martha and Mary" sides of our life. One way of stating this is to say that our life needs a good balance between work and leisure. "All work and no play makes Jack a dull boy." We Americans frequently have an energy neurosis. We imagine that we have to be constantly active.

Our inner self tells us that *being* is more important than *doing*. We need some of both, but our doing should be the overflow of our being. This will happen only if we are able to make good use of our leisure time. Such good use does not simply mean another form of activity.

Real leisure requires us to be quiet and open to the spiritual side of our personality, open to love and being loved, open to God's presence in our life, open to our inner being. For super-active people, such quiet time will seem to be a waste of time. In order to have a good balance between action and being quiet, we need to be at peace with such an apparent waste of time. Ordinarily, God reveals himself to us very gently while we are reflecting, and we will recognize God's presence only if we are quiet. Psalm 46 tells us "Be still and know that I am God."

Of the two, being is more important than doing. Our doing should be the normal way of expressing our being. "What you are speaks so loud I cannot hear what you say." The older we get the more important being becomes. As our physical and mental faculties weaken, we no longer are able to do all the things we did when younger. If we have failed to understand and appreciate the importance of being, old age will be really miserable. Whereas, if we sufficiently value being in the precious present, we can look forward to old age and retirement with great peace and joy.

For most people, action will dominate the first half of life; while for mature women and men, reflection and contemplation will pervade the years of retirement and old age. In contemplation God does most of the work, while we try to be passive cooperators with God's graces. However, we need contemplation all through our life, not just when we are too old to be active. If our prayer-life is enriched by using *Lectio Divina,* we will have found the benefits of Contemplation or Resting in the Lord which is located in the fourth step of the practice of *Lectio Divina*.

Balance Between Change and Status Quo

There should be a place in our life for both change and permanence. If we are to attain full maturity, we must be constantly open to change in almost every aspect of our life. The Greek philosopher, Heraclitus, stands apart from other great minds of the ancient world because he insisted that perfection requires a readiness to change and grow. All the other Greek philosophers declared that to be perfect, a thing must be changeless. This has resulted in the traditional Christian concept of the changelessness of God. Certainly there is an unchanging permanence to God, but once we attribute love to God, we must admit some sort of change in God, depending upon whether we resist or cooperate with

God's love for us. God's attitude toward us changes depending upon how well we respond to God's gifts of love.

In order to become fully mature, we must be constantly open to growth and change. Change and adjustment will be required of us as long as we are alive. If we are afraid of change, we will never become the whole person God wants us to be. Each day we should ask ourselves what changes God might be asking of us.

At the same time, we must have a healthy respect for the status quo. While remaining always open to change, we should respect the status quo. If we keep jumping around and lack any permanence, we will never become the balanced person we were meant to be. We should not be too quick to make a change at the first suggestion that comes to mind. In case of doubt, we stay with the status quo. We should change only when there is proof of a need to change.

Both the old and the new are important. To neglect the wisdom of the past is the height of foolishness. It is equally foolish for us to refuse the deposit of truth in new insights which are presented to us.

Another way of stating this balance between old and new is the need for a balance between conservative and liberal points of view. Persons who are able to maintain such a balance belong to what is called the "centrist position." All of us would like to think that we are in such a centrist position, but in order to maintain this balance there is need of a constant new adjustment between the old and the new. Not only are we constantly discovering additional insights into the knowledge and wisdom of the past, but we are also gaining greater knowledge as we move forward. A balanced person will keep alert to these new discoveries regarding the knowledge of the past and the new insights of the present.

If God were speaking, how or what would He say? (handwritten)

Balance Between Counsel and Fortitude

Throughout this chapter we have discussed the pairs of the Gifts of the Holy Spirit. The three pairs of gifts and Wisdom are balancing spiritual powers which the Holy Spirit makes available to us. We need to understand them and keep them in good balance. When we consider counsel and fortitude we see how both attributes work to bring us to new grace.

Counsel reveals to us God's will regarding our actions and our speech. Fortitude refers to the needed courage to carry out what Counsel has shown us to be God's will. Our faith-life requires both these gifts.

faster! pointing (handwritten)

We need to have the courage to risk the loss of a present good in order to obtain what we judge to be a greater good. This courage needs to be modified by prudence and common sense. We will undoubtedly make many mistakes on both sides of this balance. At times we will find ourselves being too prudent, at other times too bold. We need to learn from our mistakes so that we can strike a good balance between the two.

Balance Between Freedom and Submission

In order to live a full life, we need the freedom to choose the way we will live it. However, our freedom will be limited to the extent that our freedom does not nullify the rights of others. The mistake of the pro-choice people in our society today is that they imagine that a woman's freedom is unlimited, to the extent that it is right for her to destroy the life of the innocent human being who lives within her womb. Our exercise of freedom must be balanced with a due submission to the rights of God and every other human being. Our obligations of justice must always modify our use of human freedom.

The basic reason for practicing self-discipline is to experience the fullness of freedom needed in order to

God's will is the highest will of the universe. (handwritten)

practice love. Only free persons are capable of love, since love means to make a free choice of giving oneself to this or that person, or to this or that mission or direction. In order to develop our full potential for love we need to experience freedom and detachment from the enemies of love: egotism or pride, excessive love of pleasure and greed. These are the three basic slaveries which prevent our attainment of maturity and wholeness. We may think of them as the three "Ps": Power, Pleasure and Possessions.

All of these are creations of God, and therefore meritorious as long as they are compliant with God's will. The problem is that they are so attractive that we have a tendency to idolize them and make a god of them. Only by humble submission and transformation of these basic instincts do we obtain the freedom to love God, our neighbor and ourselves properly.

During the forty days in the desert, Jesus found himself seriously tempted by these same three "Ps." To overcome them, Jesus had to submit his desires to a will higher than his own human will.

In the first temptation, Jesus felt inclined to use his divine powers for his own personal pleasure, namely to change stones into bread and indulge his appetite. Intuitively, Jesus knew that these special powers were never to be used for his own personal advantage. To do so would have been the beginning of an enslavement to the desires and cravings of the body. The way to freedom and the way to love required his submission to the higher will of God. Only by our submission to God's laws do we escape slavery to bodily pleasure.

The second temptation of Jesus was regarding his attitude toward earthly possessions. Satan tells him, "All the kingdoms of earth will I bestow on you if you will prostrate yourself in submission to me." Jesus was given a choice of submissions: either to God or to Satan. If he misused his divine powers in service of greed and worldly possessions, he would become a slave to Satan, the prince of this world.

Only by sacrificing worldly power and submitting to God's plan of salvation did Jesus obtain the freedom necessary to show his love for God and others.

The third temptation was the suggestion to misuse his divine powers by taking things into his own hands rather than submitting humbly to God's plan. To show off his power by floating down out of the sky into the temple courtyard was a temptation to pride and egotism. The alternative to this display was to take the way of the cross. The temptation was to take a short-cut to glory rather than the way of rejection, failure, dishonor, suffering, insult, agony and death. Satan urged him, "You have the power, why not cast yourself down from the pinnacle of the temple? Why not gain the easy acclaim of the crowd in the temple square below? Compel them to recognize you as king. Show off your power." This was a temptation to pride, pure and simple. <u>Pride is submitting ourselves to the instinct of self-love, and allowing it to reign over our duty to love God and neighbor.</u>

Balance Between Meekness and Mercy

Meekness to God is what mercy is to our neighbor. A meek person is one who is totally open to God and God's will. A merciful person is one who is open to the needs of others. Together, these two virtues beautifully fulfill the two commandments of love of God and love of neighbor. A meek person is so attuned to God that the least desire of God's will is immediately perceived. A merciful person is so attuned to the needs of others that their least need is recognized, and efforts are made to fulfill it. With both meekness and mercy one's life is no longer centered in one's selfish needs, but is centered in what is most pleasing to God and what will do the most good for others. In proper balance, an appropriate and loving care for one's needs is not precluded in order to serve others.

Justice means giving to others what is due to them. Mercy is the perfection of the virtue of charity which is willing to go beyond our duties of justice toward others. However, the practice of mercy must not contradict justice but simply go beyond it. All of us are obliged to show justice toward God, neighbor and ourselves. Charity invites us to go beyond fulfilling our obligations of justice. This is the meaning of the new commandment which Jesus gave his disciples, "I give you a new commandment, love one another as I have loved you" (Jn 13:34). We need only to study the Gospels to see what is meant by mercy. Jesus showed great mercy, especially to all the outcasts of society of his day: sinners, tax collectors, Samaritans, women, children, the poor.

CHAPTER 13

SEVEN TRUTHS LEADING TO LIFE

Necessary Aspects of our Worldview

In her book, *Anatomy of the Spirit*, Caroline Myss speaks of seven truths that are essential to our spiritual well-being and to our physical and psychological health. These seven fundamental principles are as follows:

1. All is one
2. Honor one another
3. Honor oneself
4. Love is a divine power
5. Surrender personal will to divine will
6. Seek only the truth
7. Live in the present moment.

She connects these seven truths with the seven Christian sacraments, the seven Chakras of the Buddhist-Hindu tradition, and the ten Sefirot of the Tree of Life of the Jewish mystical tradition. If we wish to be whole, balanced persons, it is necessary that we strive to live out each of these seven truths. If we fail to resolve any one of these truths, we will suffer the consequence of physical illness, as well as psychological neuroses and spiritual aridity.

All is One

At the Last Supper Jesus prayed, "I pray that they all may be one as you, Father, are in me and I in you … so that they may be one as we are one. I in them and you in me, so that they may be brought to perfection as one" (John 17:20-23).

SEVEN TRUTHS LEADING TO LIFE

All of God's creation is united by countless cords. This unity is especially present in the members of the human race, but it is also present in all creation. What we do has an effect, for better or worse, on every other human being in the world, as well as on all the other beings of the universe. We can influence for good or evil every other reality in existence. The answer to Cain's question is "Yes, we are our brother's keeper."

We need to acknowledge this unity throughout our life. Religious ecumenism, inter-racial justice and ecological health are some of the important ways we can make our contribution to the unity of the world. Racism, sexism and selfish nationalism are all serious sins against this unity. St. Paul, in the third chapter of Ephesians, writes of God's plan to unite Jews and Gentiles, a plan which recalls the mystery of Christ. "The Gentiles are coheirs, members of the same body, copartners in the promise in Christ Jesus." (Eph 3:6). This unity is not limited to Gentiles and Jews, but embraces the human race and all creation.

Others need us and we need them. "No man is an island." We are equally dependent upon God and upon one another. This is the solidarity which Carl Jung insists is necessary in order to be a whole, balanced, integrated person. Each morning we need to ask ourselves what we can do today to foster this unity in our family, our neighborhood, our parish community, our country, the whole human race.

Honor One Another

There is a divine spark in each of God's creatures. We need to honor that spark of divinity in every person and every creature we encounter. In the Gospels, Jesus insists that the second commandment of love of neighbor is like the first commandment of love of God. He insists that he will consider as done personally to him what we do, or fail to do, to our neighbor. Every human being, every creature has a piece of the dignity of God, the creator. God leaves the mark of divinity on every one of his creatures. Therefore, we need to honor, reverence, respect, encourage, love and help this divine dignity to manifest itself and grow each day. We must not despise or look down on any one of God's creatures. Many people today have a low self-image, low self-esteem. By our showing honor, respect, reverence and love for the divine spark present in others we help them to grow in self-esteem. By our affirmation of their dignity we help them to develop a healthy self-image. By acknowledging dignity in others we affirm dignity in ourselves.

We will never bring about the unity for which Jesus prayed unless we honor and respect the dignity of one another. One of the ways to do this is to affirm every person we meet, finding something in their life or conduct which we can praise and compliment. As St. Francis de Sales writes, "You can catch more flies with a spoonful of honey than a barrelful of vinegar."

Honor Oneself

We must show proper self-respect for our own divinely-given dignity. Besides the two commandments of love of God and neighbor, there is a third, hidden commandment to show a proper love for oneself. "You shall love your neighbor **as you love yourself**." Many students of human nature claim that most people only develop about 20% of their potential for good. This means that we make the same mistake as the servant whom Jesus condemned for burying his talent. "You wicked, lazy servant … Take the talent from him, and give it to the one with ten. For to everyone who has, more will be given, but from the one who has not, even what he has will be taken away" (Matt 25:26-29).

We must honor and respect the talents and abilities which God has given us, and make the most of them. It is not pride to recognize our gifts as long as we are keenly aware that all our blessings are gifts from God. We must work hard to develop as fully as possible our potential for good. Sinful pride is present when we steal credit from God and attribute our blessings to our own efforts. It is not wrong to show honor and love for oneself as long as we realize everything we possess is a gift of God. This is the virtue of humility and truth.

Love is a Divine Power

God is love, and when we love we are making use of a divine power present within us. We thus participate in the power of God which is infinite. "Nothing is impossible with God" (Lk 1:37). Since God has unlimited power, when we love we have available to us this infinite power of God. When we love we are more God-like than anything else we might do. By loving we become more and more like God, more and more divine. This love includes mercy, compassion, forgiveness, almsgiving and every possible way by which we assist and help others.

Since God is love, every experience we have of love, either receiving it from others or giving it to others, is a religious, divine experience. Even the atheist who claims not to believe in God is actually experiencing God every time he/she gives or receives authentic love. This authentic love means to put the needs of others consistently ahead of our selfish desires. It means not to have a personal agenda of trying to benefit oneself while engaged in loving others. We become God-like and closest to God each time we have an experience of authentic love.

Surrender Personal Will to Divine Will

Divine will for us is the destiny which God chose for us when we were created. We need to practice a constant openness to the Holy Spirit and to our intuitive function in order to discern God's will and destiny. This will change from day to day, so we need to spend time each morning discerning God's will for that day. Jesus tells us in the Sermon on the Mount, "Seek first God's reign over you and his way of holiness and all these other things will be given without the asking" (Matt 6:33). The beatitude of meekness is the disposition to keep ourselves always open to God's will and the endeavor to bring our will into conformity with God's will as it is revealed to us.

At the end of the thirty days of the Spiritual Exercises of St. Ignatius Loyola, we are given the Oblation of love which very beautifully expresses this surrender of personal will to divine will: "Take into your hands, my entire liberty. Receive my memory, understanding and entire will. All that I have you have given to me. I give it back to you to be disposed of according to your good pleasure. Give me only your love and your grace. With these I am content and desire nothing more." Another way of expressing this surrender to God is to say, "Anything, Lord, everything." It is helpful to connect this 7-syllable prayer with one's breathing. Breathe in on the first three syllables, hold one's breathe on the fourth syllable and breathe out with the last three syllables. Using this prayer in this way is very relaxing and is a wonderful way to fall asleep at night after you turn out the lights.

Seek Only the Truth

"You shall know the truth, and the truth will set you free" (John 8:32). We must have a great love of the truth. We must love truth even more than we love goodness, since honesty is a higher value than goodness. Putting it another way, it is not possible to be dishonest and good. We need to seek the truth about God, ourselves and others. We will come to a knowledge of the truth primarily through Jesus Christ. St. John's Gospel speaks of Jesus, the second person of the Trinity, as the word of God (Greek - *Logos*). This Word of God or *Logos* is the truth of God. "I am the way and the truth and the life. No one comes to the Father, except through me. If you know me, you will also know my Father" (Jn 14:6-7).

God is truth, and so when we find truth, we find God. A search for the truth is a search for God. Teilhard de Chardin asserts that our research for truth has value equal to our search for God's love. Hence, scientists in today's world who are engaged in research are striving to live out this sixth step to wholeness in life, "seek only the truth."

We must hunger and thirst for the truth at all levels. This means to seek the truth about ourselves, about God, about others, about the world and the whole of reality. The pursuit of truth about ourselves is what Carl Jung calls *authenticity*. "To thy own self be true," Shakespeare says in Hamlet. Our search for self-knowledge is a part of the virtue of humility. We seek to know both our strengths and our limitations, our virtues as well as our vices. This search for truth about oneself means the willingness to face up to our helplessness apart from God, our total dependence upon God, our nothingness apart from God. It is the realization that everything we have is a gift of God.

We need also to seek the truth about God who is a truly unique being and an infinite mystery. We probably only know, at present, about 1% of the total truth about God. But our research into the mysteries of God and nature gradually reveals more and more of the truth about God. This is a task that never ends since God is infinite. An important and necessary part of seeking the truth about God is to discern the particular destiny God chose for each of us when we were created and conceived in our mother's womb. This destiny is gradually revealed to us each day of our life as we seek to discern God's will for us. This search for God's truth about our divine destiny should be a part of our prayer each morning of our life.

We need also each day to seek the truth about others, to help them discern their God-given destiny. Part of this truth about others is the realization that everyone is fragile, everyone is carrying a burden, everyone is in need of our help. The truth about others includes an appreciation of their value and goodness as well as a realization of their limitations.

Finally, the search for truth includes all the efforts of research into the truth about the whole physical universe as well as all reality, spiritual as well as physical.

Live in the Present Moment

The past is history. The future is mystery. The only part of time over which we have some control is the present. We call it present because each moment of our life is God's gift to us. The best way to make amends for our past failures is to know and do God's will at the present. The best way to prepare for the future is to do God's will as best we can in the present moment. Jesus tells us, "Do not be concerned about tomorrow. Tomorrow will have troubles enough of its own. Sufficient for the day is the trouble thereof" (Mt 6:34). God gives us the grace to handle the problems only of the present moment and present day. We need then to ask each morning for the grace to face and handle the problems of that day. We will best prepare for the future by doing God's will as perfectly as possible today.

Many physical and spiritual ailments result from our failure to live in the present moment. Much chronic depression results from continuing to live in the past and failing to forgive both ourselves and others of past mistakes. We must be humble enough to admit our mistakes and compassionate enough to forgive those who did us harm in the past. Furthermore, much anxiety and lack of security regarding the future will bring about chronic exhaustion and other physical ailments. In order to overcome this anxiety we must endeavor to grow in trust of God every day.

In the Gospels Jesus speaks constantly of the need of faith. By faith Jesus means a trust in God's infinite mercy and loving kindness. This is a grace of God that will be given to us if we ask for it.

Conclusion

There is a certain order to the pursuit of these seven truths. Both the Christian and Hindu-Buddhist traditions follow the order suggested here. However, the Jewish mystical tradition of the tree of life reverses the order. Different persons will be attracted to any one of the seven truths. They should follow whatever order seems appropriate to their needs. Pick out the truth that you most need at present, or the one to which you are especially attracted. Follow this truth for a while, perhaps a whole year, then go on to one of the other truths. The important thing to keep in mind is that all seven truths are important and necessary for a whole, mature, complete, balanced life. The order in which we pursue them is optional as long as we make sure to get around to the pursuit of all of them in the not too distant future.

The seven truths are in accord with the belief of all the world's religions. Even atheists and agnostics are able to buy into all seven truths as long as we use the generic terms of life, love and truth. This should present no problems for Christians or members of non-Christian religions since we see God as being absolute truth, love and life. As Christians, we see God as the complete personification of love, truth, beauty, goodness and life. This divine Love, Truth and Life is a real person who is conscious, free and present to us and to the whole of creation. For Christians, the three persons of the Blessed Trinity express these three aspects of God: First person represents Life, second person represents Truth, and third person represents Love. A good way to remember this is to think of God as expressing the totality of the three "Ls"—Life, Love, Light (Truth).

It is interesting to read about the experiences of persons who have been clinically dead, but then revived. Many of them speak of meeting a figure of light (for Christians, perhaps the risen Lord Jesus). This figure of light often asks how the person has grown in wisdom and love. It would seem that the standard by which our life on earth will be judged will be the three "Ls"— Life, Love, Light. In other words, our life will be a success or failure, depending upon how well we have carried out the pursuit of the seven truths of life.

CHAPTER 14

DREAMS AND THEIR SIGNIFICANCE

A Way to Discern God's Will in our Worldview

Each of us has close at hand a wise guide and counselor who communicates with us every night, showing us the way our life should go, warning us of a wrong turn we have made or are in danger of making, encouraging us in what we are now doing. We will call this inner guide our "Dream Ego." Ego is the Latin word for "I."

In addition to our conscious Ego, the "I" which directs our conscious thoughts, words, actions and decisions, there is also an unconscious "I," or inner self, which also directs us. Sometimes the unconscious "I" speaks to us while we are awake in visions, inspirations, insights, intuitions; but it is primarily during our sleeping hours that the inner self or "Dream Ego" communicates with us. During sleep our conscious ego is dormant, and so does not drown out the messages which the inner self wishes to share with us. During prayer and meditation, as well as in methods developed in psychotherapy, it is possible to quiet the conscious ego sufficiently to discern the messages of the inner self. But, in this chapter we will confine our remarks to the messages which our inner self or Dream Ego gives us while we dream.

What about those who claim they never dream, or at least never remember their dreams? It has been scientifically proven (for example, in experiments at Duke University) that everyone dreams every night. The problem is that one's memory has not been trained to recall these dreams upon awakening. So-called "non-dreamers" can do several things to jog their memory into recalling the images of their dreams.

One recommended method is to keep a pad of paper and a pen by one's bedside, and write down all of the dream images that can be recalled, even the most insignificant, immediately upon awakening. By honoring our dreams thusly, we institute a process that usually starts a better recall of one's dreams. One needs to want to remember one's dreams. If the desire to have and remember dreams is strong enough, our unconscious self usually obliges. Some people are afraid of their dreams because they had bad experiences with nightmares in childhood, and so have suppressed the memory of them in adult life. Others are so preoccupied with the things of the physical world that they have no room in their life for non-physical areas of reality.

If you really want to remember your dreams, you might set your alarm clock for three hours after you go to bed and then reset it for every hour and a half thereafter. Usually the most vivid dreams occur at intervals of every ninety minutes. After a few weeks of such a regime, you will probably train yourself to awaken naturally as soon as an important dream occurs.

Not all dreams have the same value. There are big dreams, medium-sized dreams and little dreams. The little dreams frequently are just a rehash of the events of the previous day or a continuation of the thoughts that one had just before falling asleep. If the dream approximates the same mood and attitude, the same level of emotion that the similar conscious activities did, one can usually dismiss the dream as having no special message. On the other hand, even these little dreams are imparting something important. They are telling us that our conscious life of the previous day was on target, and that we simply need to continue in the same direction that we were going yesterday. This, of course, is a marvelous help in guiding our life. The Dream Ego is confirming and approving what the Conscious Ego is doing. To have this double assurance from both the

Conscious Ego and the Dream Ego is peaceful and satisfying.

The medium-sized dreams are much more vivid and concerned with something quite different from our conscious activities of the previous day. Usually they have an unexpected twist or turn of events that causes us some surprise when we awaken and remember them. After a medium-sized dream, we usually ask ourselves, "I wonder why I dreamed **that** last night?" Almost always there is puzzlement and an unanswered question requiring further study and deciphering. Very often, the medium-sized dream breaks off abruptly or before any resolution, so that more work needs to be done consciously to resolve the dream, bring it to completion and thus discern the message of the Dream Ego.

Finally, there are the big dreams which, for most people, occur only a few times in life. Whenever a big dream occurs, the dreamer knows very clearly that it is an important dream, and that it has a very important message, if only one can interpret it. Most people who are not trained in dream interpretation will be tempted to take the dream literally, and seek its meaning in the same way as one might an experience of conscious life. However, this is probably the most serious mistake in interpreting.

Understanding the Language of Dreams

The language of dreams is the language of symbols, the same language which poetry, art, music and drama employ to tell a message. Therefore, we should seldom take the language of a dream literally.

If we dream that someone dies, this is not foretelling that this person has died or is going to die shortly. Rather, some sort of symbolic death is to occur shortly or has occurred in the dreamer's life. For example, the end of some particular struggle in one's life and the beginning of a new era could be the reference. Death in dreams never means a mere end, but it means the end of something old so that something new can be born. The Paschal Mystery of life, death, resurrection or rebirth is relived over and over again in the world of the unconscious with which dreams are concerned. There is never a death without a resurrection or rebirth. Something old dies, and gives way to something new.

In his writings, Carl G. Jung speaks at length of dream archetypes, by which he means primordial images of all those different relationships which occupy one's life, and by which we progress toward maturity and wholeness. One of the best ways to understand and interpret the meaning of one's dreams is to think of the different relationships that the dream sequence might be pointing to or expressing. Some of these possible relationships would be with mother, father, spouse, child, church, country, law and order, power, love, truth, peace, violence, success or failure, priest, king, enemy, friend, brother, sister, God, Jesus, judge, savior, trickster, clown, hero or heroine.

Dream life is interested in our worldly life, but only insofar as the transcendental and everlasting values are concerned. Dreams are primarily expressions of the inner life of the spirit, that part of life which will last forever. The inner world from which our dreams speak to us has a different set of values from the materialistic, rationalistic, pleasure-loving culture in which we live much of our conscious life. Those values are love, truth, goodness, beauty, hatred, forgiveness or lack of forgiveness. Probably one reason many people today repress the memories of their dreams is because the significations to which our dreams call our attention are the same values as religion and religious faith emphasize. Therefore, it is recommended that we approach the interpretation of our dreams in a reverent, prayerful way.

Putting Dreams in Their Proper Perspective

For those who remember many dreams from their sleeping hours, working with just one dream each week is recommended. We have other tasks in life besides trying to interpret our dreams. Choose the particular dream that was most vivid, most surprising, the most unusual or different from what was happening in your conscious life. Try to use a medium-sized dream, one which you intuitively feel has a message for you, or one which arouses your curiosity. "I wonder why I dreamed that!"

The dream you use does not have to be a recent dream. It might have occurred at some time in the past, perhaps even a long time ago, but you have never tried to work it through to a satisfactory conclusion. The fact that you still remember it might mean that it has some importance to your life.

Resolve to spend an hour dialoguing with the different characters in the dream. Do this in the presence of God, in a prayerful way, asking God's enlightenment and guidance as you go along. In fact, this hour of working with your dream could easily be your hour of formal prayer and meditation for that day. Approach the dream with an openness and desire to discern God's will, and with a willingness to change the direction of your life if the dream seems to point that way. This means that you must be open and ready to give up something which your heart is presently set on doing. Frequently, the purpose and message of a dream is to point out an alternate choice to the path we are presently taking. Almost without exception, this new way will be an improvement over the conscious way we have chosen or were about to choose.

Jung insisted that dreams never lie. Only the conscious ego is capable of deceit and lying. The Dream Ego, or the Inner Self, is absolutely trustworthy, provided only that we understand the special genre of language used by our Unconscious Self. St. Paul has written that the Holy Spirit of God dwells within the inner being of each one of us. The

Holy Spirit uses numerous ways to speak to us, but dreams are one of the best ways to learn what God is saying to us from day to day.

Although dreams are a way by which God communicates with us, they are not the only way; for some people a dream can be the most important way. Dreams are a valuable way for all of us to discern God's will. By connecting the work of interpreting our dreams with prayer-time, we can make our dreams an encounter with God.

Dreams and dream interpretations are not the most important things in our life. Living and working at the three relationships of love with God, with our neighbor and with our inner self are life's most important tasks. In the third relationship, between our conscious ego and our inner self, dreams can especially help us because dreams are the normal, ordinary way that our inner self communicates with our conscious self. God also reveals messages from the inner, spiritual, transcendental areas of reality through prayer, intuition, inspiration and insights. If we fail to understand the language of our dreams, then the unconscious inner self will seek other ways to communicate its message. The Holy Spirit uses many ways to speak to us, but dreams are one of the best. It is exceedingly foolish to neglect the dream communications which God is constantly using to reveal His will in our regard.

Subjective Interpretation of Dreams

Most dreams have more than one meaning. "Of the two levels of interpretation of dreams, subjective and objective, the more important is the subjective. The subjective interpretation is almost always the level at which we should begin any attempt to discern the meaning of a dream. To interpret a dream subjectively, think of every character in the dream as representing a particular part of one's own personality. We are each a complex being that reacts in different ways to different persons in different situations. The persons in the dream may symbolize the different ways we react to different situations. They will represent not only actual traits of character we presently manifest but also all of the possible ways we might respond to a given situation. For example, if there is violence in the dream, the Dream Ego may be telling us that we have a streak of violence in us and that we could easily act or react in that way. The dream may be telling us that we need to become aware of the potential for violence lurking beneath the level of our consciousness, and that we need to accept ownership for this particular hidden trait and do what is necessary to transform its energy into something more positive.

When subjectively interpreting a dream, take each person, as well as each situation presented in the dream, and try to discern what the person or situation might symbolize to you. Does it symbolize violence, love, hate, forgiveness, revenge, compassion, gentleness, severity, cruelty, injustice, justice, envy, jealousy, lust, greed, sloth, anger, etc? Go down the list of all the possible traits of character, both good and bad, that each character or each event in the dream might represent. Whenever something instantly clicks, you will say, "Yes, that makes sense." Then, try to discover where this trait fits into your life or at least where you can envision yourself acting in a similar way. If it is something good, the dream may be telling you to develop it more consciously. If it is something evil, the dream may be telling you to be on guard against this trait erupting, and do what is necessary to sublimate its energy into something positive and good.

The purpose of the subjective interpretation of our dream is to help to know ourselves better and to make contact with our unconscious shadow, which is the part of us that we have repressed, or of which we are not consciously aware. Each one of us is capable of unlimited good and unlimited evil. Most of us tap less than 20% of our potential in the course of our life. Interpretation of our dreams will make us consciously aware of this vast, untapped potential for good, and also warn us of our great potential for evil. When the elements of our unconscious shadow are brought to our attention by a dream, we can take this as a sign that this or that aspect of our personality is ready to erupt into conscious life. The dream is telling us to give serious consideration to these new insights into our character and personality, and to direct them properly.

Dialoguing With Dream Characters

A most effective method for interpreting dreams is to dialogue with each of the characters in the dream. Writing the dialogue in your journal is very helpful. The best way to begin is to carry on an imaginary conversation between your conscious ego ("I") and the "I" in your dream (Dream Ego) which are two different aspects of one's personality. The Dream Ego knows a lot more about our inner feelings and reactions than our Conscious Ego. There is, however, a very friendly relationship between the Conscious and Dream Egos, and our Conscious Ego can learn a lot about the meaning of the dream by simply asking questions of the Dream Ego. "What does this or that character or situation in the dream mean?" One asks this question of the Dream Ego, and then simply writes down the first answer that arises. The answers that come forth are often amazing. Frequently, the conversation with the Dream Ego is sufficient to uncover the basic meaning of the dream. To illustrate how this conversation might be conducted, I will give you an example of such an exchange after a rather unusual dream of mine. The persons in the dream are close friends but will be given fictitious names. First, the dream itself:

> I dreamed that I was at the home of some friends. Let us call them Joe and Mary Smith. It was Sunday morning, and we were all getting ready to go to the parish church for Mass. I was leaving in my car, and the Smiths were to follow in their car with their family. But, as I watched the actions of Joe Smith, I sensed that he was planning to commit suicide with his whole family by carbon monoxide poisoning after I left! I confronted him with my intuition. He agreed that this was what he had

planned and was amazed that I had been so perceptive. When I questioned him about why he was contemplating this, he said that so many things were going wrong, the world was getting so bad, and he could not cope with it. Therefore, he had decided that the only thing to do was for the whole family to commit suicide. I began to talk to Joe, telling him that, if he thought things were bad now, we had not seen the worst, that the whole economy would soon collapse. I then tried to help him see things from God's point of view, and encouraged him to trust in God rather than in the world or in himself. As I spoke, I realized that if the family was to survive, a spiritual conversion changing their attitude and whole life was required.

I was busy the next day and did not have time to work on the dream until two days later. As Carl G. Jung advises not to dialogue in our dream interpretation with people who are still alive, the following dialogue between my conscious Ego **(I)** and my Dream Ego **(DE)** was undertaken.

(I) Dream Ego, why did you have the dream about Joe Smith and his family committing suicide?

(DE) This was primarily for your benefit, not for Joe Smith's. The purpose of the dream was to let you know that God wants you to stop worrying about the future, about things in the world, about the condition of church leadership, about peace and war, about the future of the country and of the human race.

You must trust the future to God. Joe Smith is an example of someone who is over-anxious about future possibilities. The dream was telling you not to follow the example of Joe Smith since this could lead ultimately to despair and even suicide. Rather you must blindly and totally trust the future of the church, world, country and yourself to God.

(I) Did the dream have any message for the Smiths?

(DE) Yes, the very same message as for you; but the dream was primarily for your sake. Joe Smith was used in the dream because he is someone with whom you are familiar, who is a prime example of a person who is over-anxious and over-concerned about many things.

(I) Thank you, Dream Ego, for the message. Is there anything more you want to tell me about how to trust more?

(DE) No, you yourself have enough knowledge, experience and common sense to know what to do. You have been preaching this trust to others for many years. Now, you yourself must strive to practice it to a more heroic degree than you have been doing.

One can dialogue with everyone in a dream; but as suggested earlier, one should use caution in dialoguing with living persons who appear in a dream.

For example, one can call the dream characters "Dream Joe" or "Dream Mary" to distinguish them from the persons in real life. From his observations of synchronicity, Jung adopted the opinion that we are able to influence, either for better or for worse, the lives of living persons when we bring them vividly into our imagination. If this is true, we can easily see how praying for others and thinking of others in a loving, merciful, forgiving way can be helpful. Our prayers and thoughts help these persons to live up to the high hopes we have for them. Whereas, if we have low or evil expectations of them, we could add our influence to making them worse than they would otherwise be.

Dialoguing with Animals and Nightmare Characters

My experience in working with my own dreams and those of others in counseling has been that if we approach each dream figure in a loving and friendly way, invariably that image turns into a friend and helper, no matter how frightening, dangerous, or threatening it appeared in the dream.

For example, when we dream that some animal or person is chasing us, threatening to kill us or hurt us, dialoguing with such characters later in active imagination is safe and sure. I have never seen it fail to work. The key is to force yourself to act in a friendly way toward the animal or threatening enemy. In the dialogue with the dream characters, instead of running away, one imagines oneself turning to approach the animal or enemy without fear and conversing with it.

If it is an animal, you may attempt to feed it. Even if it refuses your first offer of food, keep offering different kinds of food until it finally accepts food from you. If it is a human being, show love, friendliness, mercy, compassion, forgiveness. This method of approach is a marvelous way to counteract the fear and fright that sometimes results from what we call bad dreams or nightmares. Observing some of the cautions which will be given later, you might try it yourself if you are ever plagued by a nightmare or threatening situation in a dream.

After establishing some sort of friendly relationship with the animal or person, you then ask several very important questions in a friendly way. The first is, "What is your name?" You insist that the animal or person answer your question. If some name that has no meaning to you is given, you then ask, "Do you have another name?" You keep asking until the animal or person gives you a name that has some meaning, or makes sense to you. For example, it may answer, "Fear is my name," or "Envy," or "Greed," or some symbol, the meaning of which you are able to understand. Once you know the name of your adversary, it no longer has any power to hurt you, but instead, you now have power over it.

Then you ask the dream character (animal or person), "What do you want?' or "What can I do for you?" By treating the dream figure with respect the presumption is that it wants to be helpful and not harmful. Another question you can ask is, "What do you want me to do?" Still another question is, "What do you have to give me?"

You act on the assumption that there is some positive good that the dream and the dream figure have to offer you. You can safely presume that everyone and everything in the dream is your friend, and is ready and willing to aid you. It may have been chasing you because, for some reason, you have been blind to the help that it wants to give. Now by your questions you try to discern the grace or favor the dream and the dream character is trying to reveal. When you approach the frightening figures of a dream in this open, trusting, friendly fashion invariably you will find that they respond in a positive way to your love and trust. Usually they become transformed from something ugly and fearful into something friendly and good. They then become your companions on your journey of life, there to help rather than harm you.

One big caution needs mentioning in regard to nightmares and other terribly frightening dreams. The first time you enter into dialogue with these nightmare characters it is advisable to have a trusted friend present to help you with dialogue, perhaps by suggesting questions. If the dialogue is attempted alone, the feelings aroused may be so powerful and overwhelming that you will not be able to handle them.

A nightmare usually results when we have repressed something unpleasant for a long time. During this period of repression, our emotions have been building up below the level of consciousness. In the dream, and then in the dialogue later with the dream figures, these powerful feelings are suddenly released. At such times we need a steady friend by our side to help us cope with these released feelings or energies. With a trusted friend to assist us, we can allay the full brunt of the feelings aroused by the dream. For a moment, we may imagine ourselves in danger of being swept away by the tremendous surge of emotion engendered by the dream; but aided by the friend who is with us, we will survive the experience and come out of it a stronger, wiser and better person.

When working with dreams, we must never forget that we are dealing with symbols which in most instances are not being taken literally. Therefore, when working with the interpretation of a dream, no harm will actually come to us when we consciously allow an animal to tear our Dream Ego to pieces or an enemy dream figure to shoot, stab, or kill us. We are doing this in the area of imagination where everything is possible. For instance, if someone dies in a dream, one can simply fantasize that the person is brought back to life; or if injured, miraculously healed. If and when this happens during a dream or the ensuing interpretation of a dream, almost invariably one will experience some sort of a rebirth or resurrection to a new and higher level of life. This is just one more example of the truth and value of the Paschal Mystery which Jesus historically experienced in his life through death and resurrection, and in which we can participate through the liturgy, or dreams, or other ways.

One very important point to remember in working with a nightmare or frightening dream is never to end the work of interpretation on a negative or evil note. Instead we should make sure to find some way to end the dream in a positive, constructive, loving, helpful way. We must always make sure that the outcome of every dream interpretation is morally good. Again, this can be done by using one's imagination. However, as stated earlier, in the case of a dream filled with strong emotions, one should have a friend to help us bring the dream to a happy, satisfactory conclusion. A general principle always to be followed is: NEVER, NEVER, NEVER end dream work on a "down-beat" of negativity or evil. ALWAYS, ALWAYS, ALWAYS close on an "up-beat" of love, with a constructive, positive attitude toward life, God, the future, one's self and others.

The Meaning of Different Images in Dreams

In discussing dreams, one frequently hears "What does it mean when we dream about a snake ... a horse ... sex ... etc.?" You can buy dream books at the corner drugstore which pretend to give an answer to such questions. My recommendation is that you throw away such books for they are useless in dream interpretation. Carl Jung insisted that the interpretation of dream images depends upon the particular background and experience of the dreamer. Therefore, his question to the dreamer always was "What does the snake ... the horse ... etc. mean to **you**?"

For different persons the same image will have quite different, even contradictory, meanings. So the way to discern the meaning of different images in a dream is to make a long list of the possible meanings that each important image might have. Then go down the list slowly until you come across a meaning that seems to "ring a bell," that clicks with something within you. This will usually be the symbolic meaning of that particular image for you.

According to Jung, there are certain basic images, which have a similar meaning for everyone, which come out of what he has called the Collective Unconscious or Objective Unconscious. He discovered these universal meanings through a study of ancient mythology, fairy tales and alchemy.

Some examples of these common or collective meanings follow. Dreaming of crossing a stream or body of water usually indicates some change in one's life, for example, a change in one's attitude or disposition toward God, self, others, or the change to a higher level of maturity and wholeness. Crossing a body of water is always a positive and hopeful symbol. A large body of water in a dream, especially if one is in the water, usually refers to the world of the unconscious in which we are always immersed.

A dream of finding a jewel or an egg is a symbol of receiving some new insight or wisdom. Dreaming of someone or something chasing one usually means that we are running away from facing up to something important. Dreams of being naked in a public place or before others usually mean that we are over-anxious and worried that some aspect of our life or personality may be exposed and known by others. As one becomes more familiar with dream symbols, one's intuitive faculties are honed and sharpened so that one is quick to discern the meaning of different dream images.

Objective Interpretation of Dreams

The subjective interpretation of dreams, where every character and every situation in the dream represents some aspect of the personality of the dreamer, should almost always be the primary way to work through one's dreams. The sub-personalities to which our conscious ego has not given enough attention make their presence and message known during the night when the conscious ego is asleep and helpless to prevent the repressed areas from expression. Therefore, these sub-personalities need to be considered when we interpret the meaning of the dream; otherwise we will miss some very important messages from God and our unconscious.

However, there are other levels of dream interpretation which are more objective. Precognitive dreams and those which deal with our relationships with others fall into this category. There are also prophetic dreams when God occasionally uses the dream to bring some message to others.

PRECOGNITIVE DREAMS: On rare occasions, certain persons receive what are called precognitive dreams. In such a dream the dreamer clearly foresees some future event either in their own life or in the life of another.

Persons who have precognitive dreams can be called psychics or mediums because they have a highly developed intuitive faculty. When such dreams occur, the guidance of a mature balanced other party should be sought. The danger is that the psychic will be inclined to imagine that many ordinary dreams, whenever they are quite vivid, are precognitive.

There is also the danger of reading more than it contains into a particularly vivid dream. The dream may simply indicate one of the several possible routes the future may take unless something is done consciously to change it. In no way do precognitive dreams take away human freedom to change the future or indicate that we live in a purely deterministic world.

As to the reality and truth of the existence of precognitive dreams, I have no doubt whatsoever. I know personally a person who saw in a dream an accident which actually occurred some weeks later and in which a friend lost a leg, exactly as it was portrayed in the dream. In no way was the dreamer personally involved in the accident but saw clearly what was going to happen to the friend.

PROPHETIC DREAMS: Occasionally some persons are given a dream which has a message for others, either individuals or a group, such as a community, a nation, or even the whole human race. Like precognitive dreams, psychic persons with a highly developed intuition are the ones most likely to receive a prophetic dream. Again, like precognitive dreams, prophetic dreams should be submitted for discernment to a second party or to a community before any action regarding the dream is taken. Self-deception with ensuing harm to many people is always a danger with the interpretation of such a dream. However, the fact that such dreams do occur cannot be denied.

Both the Old and New Testaments of the Bible contain many examples of prophetic dreams, and the age of prophecy is far from over. We have with us, today, prophets who are given the wisdom and insight to read the signs of the times, and point out the wrong directions which we are taking and the right direction we should go. Dreams are not the only way that prophets receive their messages from God, but they are surely one of the ways that God speaks.

RELATIONSHIP DREAMS: Another type of objective dream interpretation is to see the dream as giving some insight or direction to the dreamer's relationships with other persons, possibly regarding the attitudes which others might have toward the dreamer.

Such dreams are more frequent than either precognitive or prophetic dreams. In fact, after trying to discern the subjective interpretation of a dream, it is recommended that one take a fresh look at the dream from the objective point of view. Is it pointing to our relationships with others or our attitudes to others? For example, the dream may point out to us that we have a lopsided attitude toward a certain person or a situation. Until a dream brings this to our attention, we may be totally blind or unaware of this faulty attitude in ourselves. The dream will in some way make us conscious of the attitude that needs to be changed, or of the right attitude which we need to strive to develop.

Let me give you an example of a dream which clearly pointed out to me the need to make a change of attitude in my life. The dream, my Christmas gift from the unconscious, came to me on a Christmas morning.

I dreamed that another priest wanted me to join him in a team ministry to some rural counties near Richmond. The two of us went to Bishop Sullivan to talk about it. I told the Bishop that I was willing to give it a try. However, Bishop Sullivan said that he wasn't much in favor of it because it was more important for me in my retirement to get closer to Jesus Christ; whereas, if I joined the other priest in the team ministry, I would find myself involved in active ministry. Developing an intimacy with Jesus was the primary purpose or goal to be pursued in retirement.

Completing Unfinished Dreams

Dreams frequently end before the action of the dream has been resolved. The dream suddenly stops in the middle of an event, and we awaken wondering what might have happened if the dream had continued its course. Jung suggested that the experience of the unfinished dream usually indicated some inner road block was preventing one from carrying out one's God-given destiny. Therefore, it is especially important to try to work through such unfinished dreams to discern what is holding back our development. Through dream dialogue, either with a trusted friend or on the pages of one's journal, we can usually work through an unfinished dream and bring it to completion.

The recommended approach is to relax with some non-vocal instrumental music, preferably some quiet, peaceful classical rendition, keeping our eyes closed throughout the exercise. If we use a journal, we will need to open our eyes to write down the images. After listening for ten or fifteen minutes to the music, try to put yourself back into the unfinished dream, and relive it as vividly as possible. Use the present, rather than past tense to describe the dream. "I am doing this or that in the dream." When one gets to the point where the dream suddenly ended, try to imagine what might come next, accepting whatever image or word that pops into the mind. Then follow, as spontaneously as possible, whatever direction one's fantasy or imagination leads. We must be careful not to ask ourselves why this or that image suddenly came into our head. Rather, let the imagination wander as it wishes until one feels the dream has reached some sort of conclusion. Only then, either alone or with the help of a friend, should we dialogue with the different events or characters in the dream, and with its imaginary conclusion to discern its meaning.

Using Commonsense in Interpreting Our Dreams

In working with dreams, one must never renounce one's conscious faculties of intelligence, experience and commonsense. The results of one's efforts at dream interpretation should always be submitted to the tribunal of our commonsense to judge the validity of the conclusion. To blindly follow the suggestions that come to one in a dream or in the use of imagination in interpreting a dream is never advisable. God has given us an intellect and a deposit of wisdom which we are expected to use in making decisions regarding the conduct of our life. Dreams are only one of a number of ways to discern God's will. A wise person does not neglect other ways, but endeavors to use all the help available.

Sometimes dreams give us a message so clear and self-evident that we do not need any dialoguing to interpret the meaning. The Christmas dream given above is an example of a dream with a very clear message. The Holy Spirit used the image of Bishop Sullivan to remind me very clearly that my primary purpose in retirement is not the active ministry of my earlier days,.but is growth in intimacy with the Lord. I knew this theoretically but needed to be reminded of it more forcefully. The dream was the particular method God used to bring this truth home to my consciousness.

Regardless of the nature of our dreams, we must always approach the meaning of each dream with the assumption that the dream is our friend, always there to help us and never to harm us. Dreams come to us from the area of our inner being which is closer to the eternal wisdom of God than our conscious intellect is. However, there never will be a contradiction between authentic commonsense and the wisdom of the dream-world. This is true of even the most frightful nightmare.

The Dream Ego knows so much more than the conscious Ego. Our wiser Inner Self gives us dreams to help us lead a better, wiser and happier life. Therefore, it is extremely short-sighted for us to ignore the messages which our inner self sends us each night in dreams.

Sometimes the meaning of the dream is so obtuse, or the feelings and emotions elicited by the dream so strong and over-powering, that we do not get a clear message the first time we try to interpret it. In such instances, we may be required to rework a dream several times to resolve the meaning. If we are still unable to discern the real import of the dream, then we should go to someone who is more experienced in working with dreams, or to someone who has a highly developed intuitive faculty. Very often we need the help of others to know the right direction to go with our lives. Frequently, others need our help to enable them to know the truth about themselves. "No man (or woman) is an island."

CHAPTER 15

HEALING MINISTRY

Correcting Our Worldview When It Goes Astray

In today's world there is much that needs to be healed. It is a wounded world. The evil in today's world originates from one or more of these four causes: 1) our own sins, faults and failures; 2) the sins, faults and failures of other human beings, both living and dead; 3) the fact that we live in a very imperfect world which is gradually evolving towards wholeness; 4) Satan or cosmic evil which originates from somewhere outside this world. God could directly heal these evils and occasionally He does, without any human mediator. However, in most instances, it is clearly the plan of God to use human instruments to do the work of healing.

There are four basic kinds of sickness: 1) Sickness of the spirit caused by our own personal sins; 2) Psychological sickness and problems, for example anxiety, depression and complexes frequently caused by the emotional hurts of our earlier life; 3) Physical sickness of our bodies caused by disease or accidents; 4) Oppression or possession by evil spirits. There are also four basic kinds of healing for these four types of illness. 1) Repentance and forgiveness of personal sin; 2) Healing of memories or inner healing for emotional problems; 3) Healing of bodies for physical sickness; 4) Deliverance or exorcism from demonic oppression.

All of us have some capability to be a healer in all four areas, for example, by means of prayer, faith, hope and love. Usually, God has given each of us a special ability to heal in one or two of these areas. As St. Paul says, "There are different gifts but the same Spirit; there are different ministries but the same Lord; there are different works but the same God who accomplishes all of them. To each person the manifestation of the Spirit is given for the common good" (I Cor 12:4-7). One of our tasks is to discern which particular kind of healing we have been given as a special talent or ability. Secondly, having discerned where God is calling us to be a healer, what can we do to develop as highly as possible this special gift of healing to which God has called us?

Some of the virtues that will help us to be a good healer are: faith, hope, charity, humility, courage, wisdom, discernment, prudence, perseverance, patience, compassion, gentleness, balance, meekness and non-judgmental mercy. All of us can do something to heal the world of evil. We have been born to serve, to minister to the needs of others, to heal, to help others carry their burdens. Our ability as a healer depends on how spiritually and psychologically healthy we are. It also depends on our willingness to forgive, a non-judgmental attitude towards others rather than a negative attitude. "Your attitude must be that of Christ" (Phil 2:5). What do I have to change in my present attitude towards others in order to bring it into accord with the attitude of Jesus Christ?

Four Methods of Healing

Forgiveness of Sins. This is not limited to the Sacrament of Penance. All of us share in this power to forgive. We pray for this power each time we say the Lord's Prayer. By baptism we share in the priesthood of Christ. We have the power to bless and the power to curse, the power to forgive and the power to retain the sins of others. We should make use of this power by sending out a constant stream of loving forgiveness to all the sinners of the world. We do this when we show a positive, non-judgmental, loving attitude towards others instead of a negative one.

Healing of Memories. We usually need the help of another in order to experience the inner healing of memories. All of us have some ability to help others heal past bad memories. It means to be a good listener, and show unconditional acceptance and love for the person who relives a traumatic experience of the past. One way to do this is to bring Jesus into the scene and to experience the love Jesus shows both to the victim of abuse and to the abuser. We need to look at every situation and person from the same point of view that Jesus, our Savior, views them.

Healing Bodies. Physical healing is often the most dramatic kind of healing because it goes beyond the ordinary laws of bodily healing. Some persons have this power much more than others, but all of us have some healing power. We should be very generous in using this power. It can be done by prayer, by sending the healing graces of God into the sick body. Agnes Sanford recommends that we pray for the physical healing "in accordance with God's will," not "if it be God's will." If physical healing does not occur, in no way should we accuse the sick person of lacking faith. Frequently, there will be a time-delay between the prayer for healing and the actual experience of healing. Whenever possible, the healer should use one's hand to touch the head of the sick person or the afflicted bodily member. It is recommended that healing be carried out by a whole group of persons, each one touching the body of the sick person or touching those who are closest to the sick person. We call this the "laying on of hands."

Deliverance from Demonic Oppression. Formal exorcism should be done only by a delegate of the bishop. All of us can pray for deliverance from demonic oppression. By baptism each of us shares in the power of Jesus over evil spirits, and we should not be afraid to use this power to command the evil spirit to leave a human being. Rather than drive evil spirits into hell, it is better to turn them over to Jesus to do as he sees fit.

Areas that May Need Healing

1. Forgiveness of those who have hurt or offended us in the past, both living and deceased persons. We identify those towards whom we feel resentment, anger, bitterness, a negative attitude or a judgmental attitude. Even if we have forgiven them in the past, we may need to forgive them "seventy times seven."

2. Take a look at our heritage, our childhood, our relationships with parents, siblings, fellow students. Where do we find ourselves acting or reacting in the same negative way our parents or childhood associates acted? What needs to be healed, changed, forgiven, resolved?

3. In the area of justice is there anyone we have treated unjustly in the past, unfairly, dishonestly or uncharitably for which we need to make amends?

4. Is there anyone whom we dislike intensely or even mildly, that we go out of our way to avoid, or we find it hard to love as Jesus commands us to love?

5. Is there anyone whom I frequently have negative thoughts, judgments or words? Who are the persons about whom I negatively gossip? What am I doing to recognize my secret faults, my negative shadow?

6. What am I doing in a positive way to show love to each member of my family, for each of those with whom I work or associate in the course of each day? Am I spending sufficient quality time with my spouse? Children? Parents? Relatives? Friends?

7. What changes should I make in order to be of more loving service to others? How much money or possessions have I shared with the have-nots of the world during the past year?

8. Do I have a good self-image? Is it too high or too low? What do I dislike in my present personality that I would like to change? How self-disciplined am I? What do I need to do in order to gain better control of my addictions, desires, passions or indulgences?

9. Do I keep too tight a rein on my feelings? Am I able to express them freely and naturally with proper respect for feelings of others? Am I frequently depressed or discouraged? How do I handle loneliness, sexuality, anger, confrontations, opposition, stress, compliments?
10. How much time and energy do I give to intellectual development of my mind and growth in wisdom? What serious books have I read in the past year?
11. Do I take good care of my bodily health? Is there something I should do about bodily care that I have been putting off and neglecting? What about my eating habits? Too much of the wrong food? Do I drink too much? Do I take sufficient physical exercise each day? Do I get enough sleep? Is there a good balance of work and leisure in my life?

Healing of Memories

Healing of memories is closely connected to forgiveness of sins, either our own sins or the sins of others who have abused and hurt us. Many times we need a mediator between God and ourselves before we are able to experience the healing of memories. Sometimes one is so wounded that one is unable to forgive oneself. We need the word of another human being to convince us that God has forgiven us. Sometimes our unconscious needs to hear the words of forgiveness and absolution spoken aloud by another person. The Sacrament of Penance is one method for healing of memories, but forgiveness and healing are not limited to the Sacrament of Penance. All of us can be a mediator of healing and forgiveness.

To be a healer of memories we need to be a good listener, concentrate on the other person and project upon that person the perfect love of God. Laying on of hands is a good way to confer the energy of our love upon another person. We pray that the healing love of Christ may come into their life, their soul, their heart, their mind, their memory.

Our most basic need is to know that we are loved. The purpose of healing of memories is to take the negative experiences of the past, and heal the wounds caused by them through an outpouring of the love of God. Sometimes this can happen directly without the mediation of another. Frequently the wounds are so deep that another person is needed to mediate that love of God into the consciousness of the person who has been injured. We ask Jesus to fill the vacant spaces left by the bad memories with the gift of his great love for us.

We need to make full use of our imagination in order for this healing of memories to be effective. We imagine Jesus accompanying us each step of our journey back into the past. We put our hand in the hand of Jesus, and let him lead us. We try to imagine how Jesus would act towards the person who has hurt us. Then we try to show a similar love and forgiveness of that person. In the healing of memories we can begin with the present and work back gradually, year by year, to our childhood and infancy and even to the time we spent in the womb of our mother. Another way is to begin from the moment of our birth, and imagine Jesus holding us in his arms and caressing us. Then gradually work our way to the present time, taking time to pray and reflect upon each year of our life, trying to recall any memories that we can from each period.

The basic purpose of healing of memories is to experience the love and forgiveness of God not only for ourselves, but for all those who may have hurt or abused us in the past. If we are unable to show forgiveness ourselves, we imagine Jesus forgiving them. Healing of memories is a process, rather than a single event. It usually happens gradually. Often we need to repeat the process again and again, before we succeed in completely forgiving those who have hurt us, and thus experiencing a full healing of our soul, mind, spirit, heart and memory.

Healing the Family Tree

Dr. Kenneth McAll has written an important book called *Healing the Family Tree*. He has had phenomenal success as a healer in all four areas of healing: physical healing, healing of memories, repentance of sins and deliverance from Satanic powers. He considers the Eucharist the most powerful method of healing for all four kinds of illness. He claims that much of the illness in the world today is due to the negative influence of our ancestors. This is a modern extension of the Christian teaching on Original Sin. He is convinced that one of the most important ministries of healing is the healing of the family tree.

We not only inherit evil tendencies and wounds from the sins of our ancestors, we also inherit all the good and virtuous habits which they developed during their lifetime. We find ourselves pulled in two opposite directions by the genes we inherit from our family tree. Some of us are pulled more strongly by our negative genes, some more strongly by our positive genes. We need to take whatever we have inherited from our ancestors, and do all in our power to heal the wounds we find in our personality, regardless of whether we ourselves are to blame by our personal sins, or whether the origin is outside of our present life. We should take the positive tendencies we have inherited, and develop them as highly as possible, so that we can pass on to the next generation a better inheritance.

Both the Sacrament of Eucharist and the Sacrament of Penance heal the wounds caused by our own sins, and are a healing remedy of the family tree. When we talk about Sacraments we are speaking of those special graces that result from the life, death and resurrection of Jesus Christ. God's mercy and healing is not limited to the Christian Sacraments but is available to all sincere persons, both Christian and non-Christian. We have many natural ways of healing, such as medicine, surgery, counseling, healing of memories, therapy, etc. God expects us to make use of every available method of healing.

We make use of the Sacraments, especially the Eucharist. Why, then, do we not experience more healing than we feel now? Why is there still so much evil in the world, so many wounds unhealed? In Mark 5:25-34 we are told that many persons pressed upon Jesus, yet only one woman was healed. Jesus told her, "Daughter it is your faith that has cured you." So it would seem that it is our lack of faith that makes our Eucharist so barren of healing miracles.

Agnes Sanford's Prayer for Healing of Memories

Lord Jesus, I ask you to enter into these persons who have need of your healing in the depths of their being. I ask you to come as a careful housekeeper might come into a house that has long been closed and neglected. Open all the windows, and let in the fresh wind of your Holy Spirit. Raise all the shades so that the sunlight of your love may fill this house of the soul. I rejoice that as the light of your love now fills this mansion of the soul, all darkness shall flee. In your name I speak to that darkness, gently telling it that it cannot abide here in these persons whom you have redeemed. See whether there are any ugly pictures on the walls, pictures of old distressful wounds of the past. Take them down and give to this memory-house pictures of beauty and joy. Out of all the ugliness of the past make a new beauty. Transform old sorrows into the power to comfort others who have sorrowed. Heal old wounds by your love and turn them into a love that heals the wounds of others.

Go back, Lord, through all the rooms of this memory-house. Open every closed door and look into every closet and bureau drawer and see if there be any dirty and broken things that are no longer needed in the present life. If so, take them completely away. I give you thanks, O Lord, for this is what you promise: "As far as the East is from the West, so far has he removed all our sins from us" (Psalm 13). Look upon any memories that may come up from the deep mind, and in your mercy forgive them. Go back even to the years of childhood and even the nursery and open windows long sealed and let in the gentle sunlight of your love. Make everything clean and beautiful within. Sweep away all dirt from the floor of this memory-room, even the confusion and horror and shame of ancient memories, perhaps of childish and uncomprehended sins, perhaps sins of parents. Take a clean cloth and wipe away every stain from the walls and furniture. Purge this, your child, with hyssop so that the heart may be clean. Wash this one that the soul which is created in your image may be whiter than snow. Look within the closets and under the furniture and see if there be any old unclean rags of memory that are no longer needed. Take them entirely away; gather them into your redemptive love so that the burden of them is no longer present.

Follow the soul of this your child all the way back to the hour of birth and heal the soul of the fear of being born into the world. Restore that bright memory of your eternal being and love, an unconscious infilling of the eternal radiance from which one is born. If, before birth, the soul was darkened by the fears and sorrows of the human parents, heal even these memories. I pray that you will restore the soul as you made it to be, and will awaken in it all those creative impulses and ideas you have placed there so that whatever your purpose may be for its human pilgrimage, that purpose may be fulfilled. "He restores my soul and leads me in the paths of righteousness for his name's sake" (Psalm 23). I give thanks, O Lord, knowing that this healing of the soul is your will, and is the very purpose of the giving of your life for us. Therefore, it is now being accomplished, and by faith I set the seal of your love and grace upon it. I ask all this in the name of Jesus Christ, your Son, Our Lord. Amen. So be it.

The Wounded Healer

Each of us is called to be a healer. The greatest healer in human history has been Jesus. We need to study Jesus' way in healing others, and endeavor to follow his example. One of the most striking aspects of Jesus, the healer, was that he himself was a wounded healer. He did not remain apart from the ills of the world, but actually immersed himself in the world's sufferings. Isaiah 53 describes how "by his wounds, we are healed. He was spurned and avoided by men, a man of suffering, accustomed to infirmity. Yet it was our infirmities that he bore, our sufferings that he endured. He was pierced for our offenses, crushed for our sins. Upon him was the chastisement that makes us whole. Because he surrendered himself to death and was counted among the wicked, he shall take away the sins of many, and win pardon for their offenses."

Henri Nouwen has written a book entitled *The Wounded Healer*. He insists that no one can help another without becoming involved, without entering with our whole person into the pain of the other person, without taking the risk of becoming hurt, wounded, rejected and even destroyed. We can only take away suffering by entering it, sharing it and then expressing the affirmation that there is life on the other side of darkness. We overcome another's fear by entering into that fear with the other person. If we ourselves have been wounded, and have discovered a source of healing in the midst of our wounds, then we are able to offer our experience as a source of healing to others. This is the price we have to pay to be a good healer.

God takes delight in bringing good out of the unfortunate circumstances of our life. Instead of being depressed by our present or past wounds, be they of body, mind, heart, will, emotions, or the wounds of soul called sins, we can take courage that these very wounds can be the source of our own healing powers, provided we accept them with love and trust in God. Not all wounds or sufferings are a source of healing. They can make us very bitter, resentful, and angry at God, and result in our ceasing to believe in God. Instead of losing faith and hope in time of suffering, we need to make a leap of blind faith, trust and love for God. This will require not only special grace from God, and our personal cooperation and consent, but often it requires the assistance of another human, wounded healer.

Here is where we can accomplish some of our best healing—encouraging others to make this leap of blind faith and trust in times of suffering.

Ministering to Dysfunctional Families

A dysfunctional family is one in which one or both parents fail to practice unconditional love towards their children and their spouse. Unconditional love exists when one consistently puts the needs of another ahead of one's own. Love is something we learn by being on the receiving end of love that is not subject to conditions or limitations. This kind of love is needed especially by children, most of all by very small children. It is needed throughout childhood and adolescence. If we have not had good experiences of being loved unconditionally, we will not know how to love others.

Probably the majority of households and families in this country are at least partially dysfunctional. A family will be dysfunctional if any one of the attributes given below applies to one or both parents. If both parents are dysfunctional, a child growing up in this environment will be challenged to learn a healthy way to live and raise a family. As a result, when married, they pass on the same dysfunctionalism to their own family. The absence of good experiences of unconditional love results in a very low self-esteem and a poor self-worth. Persons from dysfunctional families carry heavy complexes in all of their activities and relationships. They frequently experience deep insecurity, excessive anxiety, self-imposed guilt and shame, loneliness and rejection. They experience an inability to love, to make good judgments and decisions. Without the good example of well-functioning parents, they do not know the proper behavior of a spouse, parent, child, sibling, friend or neighbor.

Those of us who have been recipients of unconditional love from our family have a responsibility to give persons from dysfunctional families as many examples of unconditional love as we possibly can. We then become

247

surrogate parents to those who have been denied good experiences of being loved when they were growing into adulthood. People from dysfunctional families do not know how to love. They have to be taught and can only be taught by example. Our efforts to love people from dysfunctional families will frequently be rebuffed or might be taken advantage of. Sometimes such persons are merely testing us to make sure this love is genuine. We need to keep going out in love to such persons again and again. Those of us who have been blessed with a family life that was functional, and where both parents loved us unconditionally, have an obligation to teach others how to love. By our consistent, unconditional love we become a healer of the deep wounds experienced by members of dysfunctional families. Most of the examples given below are not due to deliberate fault on the part of the dysfunctional person. It is the cross that divine providence has placed on their shoulders. As a healer we are called upon to help them carry their cross.

Examples of Dysfunctionalism

- Alcoholism, drug addictions, any other form of addiction
- Mentally ill, mentally unstable, emotionally unstable
- Selfish, self-centered, egotistical, proud, vain, conceited
- Greedy, miserly, lacking in generosity and charity towards the poor
- Emotionally immature and childish, delayed adulthood
- Irrational, unreasonable, lacking common sense
- Unbalanced, extremist, fanatic, rigid, intolerant, perfectionist
- Undependable, unpredictable, compulsive behavior
- Lacking in gentleness or compassion, unforgiving, excessively demanding

- Violent, abusive sexually, physically, verbally, oppressive
- Negative attitude towards others, towards future, world, God, self
- Lazy, unable to hold down a job, unable to find work, workaholic
- Destitute, extremely poor, lacking the essentials of life
- Absence of one or both parents from the home
- Death of one or both parents while child is young, left orphan, abandoned
- Frequent or debilitating illness of either or both parents
- One or both parents still unredeemed in their Enneagram number
- Refugees from war-torn country

CHAPTER 16

JOURNEY OF FAITH

Carrying Out God's Plan for Us and the Whole Human Race

The image of a journey is frequently used to describe the spiritual life of a person on earth. The Old Testament uses three images of a journey to describe our relationship with God. The first is the journey from the slavery of Egypt to life in the promised land, a land flowing with milk and honey. This journey is a symbol of our victory over our slavery to addictions of various kinds, and our entrance into the promised land of freedom and wholeness. The second Old Testament journey is from exile in Babylon to a restoration of the temple in Jerusalem. This is a symbol of our deliverance from captivity to our excessive attachments, and our return to the freedom of the children of God. The third Old Testament journey is that from slavery to sin to the freedom of love of God.

Jesus in the Gospels frequently refers to the journey of faith to the Kingdom of God. Spiritual writers have used the image of a journey to describe our progress towards a union of love with God for all eternity. Another image to describe the journey of faith is that of a spiral staircase. As we climb the stairs we keep returning to the same point of view, but always at a higher level. As we proceed from one level to the next there is a definite number of steps that we must take in order to progress to a higher point of view.

In our journey of faith there are six distinct steps that we need to repeat again and again throughout our life on earth. We may think of them as the 6 Cs. They are Call, Conversion, Covenant, Celebration, Consolation,

Commission. The first step, CALL, describes the constant call and challenge from God to make a return of love to His offer of love. This call is persistent throughout our life on earth. God respects our freedom and never forces his love upon us, but constantly calls and invites us to an ever deeper love. This call comes in many forms. It comes especially during our prayer-time. It comes when we are reading Sacred Scripture or other spiritual books. It comes during retreats, or while listening to a sermon or in conversation with a friend. God is calling us every day of our life. We need to keep our hearts and minds open to these calls of grace. The primary purpose of prayer is to be alert to God and eager to hear these calls.

The second step in our faith journey is CONVERSION. This is the response we need to make to God's calls of grace. The Greek word for conversion is "metanoia," which is usually translated as "repent." Both John the Baptist and Jesus insisted that metanoia was the primary way to respond to the Incarnation of God in the human flesh of Jesus (Mark 1:4 and 1:15). Peter also on Pentecost Sunday insisted that metanoia was the primary way to respond to the resurrection of Jesus (Acts 2:38). Metanoia implies the willingness to change the direction of our life. This might be a total turn-about change or a change of lesser degree. The importance of this second step is that God is never satisfied with the present status quo in our relationship of love with God. God is always calling us to a higher, more intimate union of love. In order to respond properly to this constant call of God we must be always ready to make some change in the direction of our life. We need to keep asking ourselves, "What can I do to show a greater love of God?" "What change in my life can I make to attain a closer union with God?"

The third step of our faith journey is COVENANT. If we respond properly to God's call, and experience a closer union of love with God, the result will be the experience of a covenant of love between God and ourselves. A covenant is always mutual and never one-sided. It involves a total commitment of love on the part of both God and ourselves. This covenant of love is personal between God and us. There is also a community covenant between God and our church community. Thus it has both a vertical and horizontal dimension. God is ready and willing to go to any height and depth of love that we are ready and willing to go. God seeks a total, unconditional love for us but this is not possible unless we are willing to show a similar unconditional love for God. Such unconditional love may be described as the consistent desire to put the needs of the Beloved ahead of our own desires. This is how God wants to love us, but this is possible only when it is mutual, and when we try to love God unconditionally.

The fourth step of our journey of faith is CELEBRATION. God desires to express and celebrate this covenant of love with us, both as individuals and as a community. We celebrate the individual covenant of love with God each time we are united with God in prayer. This is especially true in our prayers of gratitude and praise. We celebrate the community covenant of love during each of the seven Sacraments, but especially during our community Sunday Eucharist. Each time we celebrate the covenant of love with God we experience a deeper union of love. This is why we need to repeat the celebration frequently.

The fifth step of our faith journey is CONSOLATION. St. Paul speaks of the consolations of the Holy Spirit as love, joy, peace, patience, kindness, generosity, faithfulness, gentleness and self-control (Gal 5:22-23). If we do a good job of hearing and responding to God's daily calls of grace, if we experience a true conversion of our life towards God, if we celebrate the covenant of love with God both personally and communally, then we can expect to experience these consolations of the Holy Spirit. If they are lacking in our life, it means that somewhere in our journey of faith, we have short-circuited the relationship of love with God. St. Teresa of Avila insisted that all the way to heaven should also be an experience of heavenly delight. This experience of heaven on earth will be found in one or more of the consolations of the Holy Spirit.

The final step of our journey of faith is COMMISSION. We should never be selfish in our possession of God's love. We must be ready to share it with others. One of the best ways to show our gratitude to God for the many gifts of love is to pass on this love to every person we meet. Jesus told his disciples on Easter Sunday, "As the Father has sent me, I also send you. Receive the Holy Spirit" (John 20:21-22). God sent Jesus to earth to reveal God's love, mercy, and compassion for all of us. Jesus now commissions us to reveal that love by the actions of our life, and we must pass it on to the whole human race. By our acts of unconditional love towards others, we co-create with God new energies of love on earth that will last forever. Thousands of years after we are dead and gone, our acts of love will still be generating new spiritual energy on earth, enabling countless other human beings who will follow us to practice a similar unconditional love.

If we are faithful to these six steps of love, we will surely carry out God's plan for us. At the same time, we will make a substantial contribution to the fulfillment of God's plan for the whole human race. Each time we repeat these six steps of our journey of faith, we will rise to a higher level of faith, hope and charity. At the same time, we will make it easier for all our fellow human beings to grow in love. By fulfilling God's plan for us, we take the whole human race another tiny step towards the fulfillment of God's purpose in sending Jesus Christ to earth - namely to establish the Kingdom of God and to expand the family circle of heaven to include the whole of creation.

The Uniqueness of Our Call

Every person's faith journey is unique and somewhat different from every other person that has ever lived. God throws away the pattern each time He creates a new person. This uniqueness is a manifestation of the infinite greatness of God. The wealth of possible patterns is unlimited. All of us are called to be saints, but sanctity for each one of us will be somewhat different from the sanctity of every other person. It is the task of the spiritual director to help each directee to discern the particular faith journey God is calling that person to follow. It is a serious mistake for the director to try to direct each person in the same way. We can learn much by reading and studying the lives of the saints, but it is a mistake to try to imitate exactly the life of any saint—including Jesus Christ and the Blessed Mother Mary. This is a mistake often made by members of a religious congregation who try to follow exactly the faith journey of the founder of their religious order. We must never forget or neglect our uniqueness.

The six steps of the journey of faith will be essential to the faith journey of every person, but always somewhat uniquely. God's call will be somewhat different from the call of every other person. Similarly, our response, our conversion, our commitment, our celebration of the covenant, our consolations, and our commission will be somewhat unique and different from everyone else's.

Desert Journey

The Israelites on their journey from Egypt to the promised land had to pass through the Sinai desert before reaching the land flowing with milk and honey. Similarly, all of us can expect that a part of our faith journey will pass through a barren desert before reaching the promised land of sanctity. This desert experience will be unique for each of us. For some it will come early in their faith journey, for others in the middle of their journey, for still others near the end of their journey. This desert experience is what St. John of the Cross calls the dark night. He describes several different dark nights. Thomas Green, a modern-day theologian, has several excellent books describing this dark night, how to recognize it, and how to persevere in it during our faith journey.

The Israelites spent forty years wandering in the Sinai desert before finally entering the promised land. Frequently they were tempted to return to the flesh pots of Egypt, and rebelled against the direction of Moses. The whole Book of Exodus in the Old Testament is a description of the trials of Moses and the Chosen People during their sojourn in the desert. This story of the Israelites in the Sinai desert is an excellent description of the trials and temptations every soul has to endure before reaching the promised land of spiritual maturity. Frequently, we are tempted to return to the old "flesh pots" of our former sinful addictions while enduring our desert journey. Just as it took all of forty years for the Israelites to traverse their desert journey, we can expect a similar long period of time to endure our dark nights before arriving at the peace and security of union with God.

We are told that the Israelites were guided by a pillar of fire during their forty years in the desert. This pillar of fire is the Holy Spirit, ready and willing to guide us on our desert journey to the promised land. At times they experienced the Holy Spirit as a dark cloud which came between them and their enemies. So too the experiences of darkness that we endure during our desert journey may be seen as God's way of protecting us from our enemies. The important thing is to maintain a constant openness to the Holy Spirit to show us the way we should go in the trackless deserts of our life.

During their sojourn in the desert God gave the Israelites the stone tablets of the Mosaic Law. These Ten Commandments were to govern their conduct. In the Sermon on the Mount of Matthew's Gospel (Chapters 5, 6, 7) we are given the rules that should govern our conduct. In the story of the golden calf we are told how the Israelites rebelled against the Ten Commandments. Today, our worship of money and possessions clearly shows that we are no different from the Israelites. We too have rebelled against the teachings of Jesus in the Sermon on the Mount, and are busy making and worshiping our golden calf.

What the Israelites lacked most during their desert journey was trust in God. They neither trusted God nor

God's agent Moses. Their lack of trust caused them to lose faith in God and in Moses. We, today, need to learn a lesson from the conduct of the Israelites in the desert of Sinai. We must hold on to our trust in God, despite all the apparent reasons we could lose faith. Trust is a gift of God, a grace. We need to ask God constantly for the gift of this grace of faith and trust. Like the widow in the 18th Chapter of Luke's Gospel, we must persist in our petitions to God for the grace of faith and trust. We need this persistence especially during the dark nights we must spend in our desert journey. At the end of this parable, Jesus asks, "When the Son of Man comes, will he find faith on earth?" Let us hold on to our faith and trust in God, and even ask God for more faith and trust. In the final chapter we will give some suggestions of where to begin to implement our present faith journey.

CHAPTER 17

WHERE TO BEGIN?

The world today is witnessing a crisis that could be greater than anything the human race has seen since the time of Alexander the Great. During the Christian era the nearest thing to our present situation was the collapse of the Roman empire around the year 400. The events of September 11, 2001 could mark the beginning of world-wide terrorist attacks leading to an all-out war between the Muslim and Non-Muslim worlds. Nuclear warfare could bring about a nuclear winter in which most of the population of the world would be killed. It could even result in the extinction of most living beings on the face of the earth. Biological and chemical warfare could result in unimaginable devastation. Just as Communism collapsed suddenly in Russia in 1989, our whole Capitalist economy could also collapse in the not too distant future. Environmentalists are warning us of the possible disasters to our planet. The total world population is increasing at an alarming rate, and this poses a threat of wide-scale famine and starvation. Racism and hatred between various ethnic and religious groups will probably grow worse in the years immediately ahead. Violence, oppression and discontent of various kinds throughout the world threaten the present status.

In view of all these possible disasters, each one of us needs to ask ourselves, "What can I do?" We must not stand around helplessly, awaiting the other shoe to fall. God has given each of us an intellect and a wisdom that enables us to know what to do in times of serious crises, such as faces us today. As the Chinese proverb tells us, "It is better to light one candle than to curse the darkness." So what are the candles we need to light at the present moment? I can think of a number of such candles: faith, hope, charity, prayer, almsgiving, fasting, and holiness. Let me conclude this book by commenting briefly on each of these "candles."

Faith

Faith or trust in God is the most important "candle" that we must light in the present crisis. Jesus Christ, in the four Gospels, recommends faith more often than any other answer. Faith, trust and belief are all synonyms to express our absolute certainty that God will never abandon the human species. God has a definite plan for us human beings, and no terrorists or other enemies of God will ever succeed in thwarting God's plans. God wishes us to be a part of the whole work of salvation. He has called each of us to contribute our love toward establishing the Kingdom of God on earth and expanding the family circle of heaven. Authentic love requires that we have freedom and power not to love. Many persons have used this freedom to go in the opposite direction of true love. God permits this abuse of freedom and love only to the extent where God is able to bring greater good out of the evil acts. "For those who love God, all things work together unto good" (Rom 8:28). This is our faith and our trust. God will never allow the human race to be destroyed by evil-doers. God is all-powerful, all-wise, all-good, all-loving and always faithful to His promises. Therefore, we need not be afraid that "everything is going down the tubes." Our faith and trust in God gives us the confidence that somehow, someway God will bring good out of terrible things that have happened or might happen in the future. This does not mean that we can sit back and presume that God will take care of us without our having to make any changes in our life. The recent events of history are a wake-up call for us as a nation and a people to amend our evil ways. Let us make the changes in our life that are needed. God will never abandon His people.

Jesus tells us that nothing is impossible if we have faith. "Put your trust in God. I solemnly assure you that whoever says to this mountain, 'be lifted up and thrown into the sea,' and has no inner doubts but believes that what he says will happen, shall have it done for him. I give you my word, if you are ready to believe that you will receive whatever you ask for in prayer, it shall be done for you." (Mk 11:22-24). This Gospel text is the origin of the expression, "faith can move mountains." The world is burdened with a mountain of evil that must be removed if we are to survive. Faith and prayer would seem to be the most important way to move this mountain of evil and convert it into a mountain of love.

Faith is an option which we are free to choose or reject. There are abundant reasons for discouragement regarding the future of the world today. If we are willing to put our trust in the promises of Jesus Christ, we have every reason to believe that God will rescue us from the mess we are experiencing. The Incarnation of God in Jesus of Nazareth, two thousand years ago, is proof that God can and does intervene in the history of the world. It was the faith of Mary that brought about the Incarnation of Jesus. We can believe and trust that the strong faith of each of us will bring about a new divine intervention in today's world.

Hope

Hope is the virtue that we need most when we think about the future. It is based upon our faith and trust in God. It enables us to have a positive attitude towards the future instead of a negative one. It enables us to overcome our fears and to be optimistic. It gives us the energy to tackle the problems at hand, having confidence that all will be well. Hope gets us up in the morning and enables us to face each day with enthusiasm. The promises of God regarding the future Kingdom of God on earth will surely be fulfilled. These promises give us reason to hope for a successful conclusion of the present crises the world is now facing. God will never disappoint our hopes and expectations if they are based on God's word.

There is a negative attitude among many persons today. If we live among people filled with skepticism, it is extremely difficult not to be contaminated by it. Negativity is a very contagious psychic illness. The remedy for it is hope. Hope has the power to send out waves of spiritual energy which will neutralize the vibrations of negativity and despair which plague our society. Like faith, we have the option either to hope or to despair in any one of five areas. They are our attitudes toward God, ourselves, others, the world, the future.

Hope, as a virtue, stands in the middle between presumption and despair. Presumption is imagining that God will take care of our needs without our doing anything. Despair is imagining that, no matter what we do, the situation is hopeless. Having hope means that we have confidence in God's grace, but we also accept the responsibility of cooperating with the grace God bestows upon us.

Charity

God intends that we live in a world community of faith, hope, and love. Our failure to do this has brought the present crisis and upheaval in the world. We will succeed in bringing order to our world only when we start putting God's intentions ahead of our desires. This new order must begin somewhere, and it is the responsibility of each one of us to start putting God's plans ahead of our desires. If we commit ourselves to do this each day, we will make a substantial contribution towards resolving our present crisis, and establishing God's Kingdom on earth. Evil is the exact opposite of love. Each time we practice Christian charity we counteract, neutralize, and convert evil into good. God's Kingdom is a kingdom of love. Any contribution of love which we make will take creation another step towards the fulfillment of God's plans for the human race.

The most difficult part of Jesus' teaching on charity is his command to love our enemies, to return good for evil, to pray for our enemies and to turn the other cheek. St. Paul tells us, "Be not overcome by evil, but overcome evil with good" (Rom 12: 21). Violence begets violence. Instead of projecting our negative shadow upon our enemies, we must take back our projections of evil, and accept ownership for our own evil tendencies. Secondly, we must never lose respect for our enemies. Regardless of the greatness of the evil they might have done, we must continue to believe in the basic goodness of all human beings. By our love of enemies we appeal to that basic goodness, and seek to activate it. Most people will claim that love of enemies will not work. However, in his book, *Engaging the Powers* (pages 244-251), Walter Wink lists 98 examples in history where non-violence and love did succeed in converting the enemy.

Prayer

We can always pray and ask God to intervene with the needed grace for the salvation of our wounded world. Jesus assures us that nothing is impossible to those who pray with faith and trust in God's power. Prayer is anything that helps our relationship of love with God. The Lord's Prayer gives us the model which we should follow in all our prayers. The first half of the Lord's Prayer deals with God's needs. Having given us the gift of freedom, God is now dependent upon our cooperation. We need to show reverence and respect for God, recognizing His supreme position as Lord of all creation. God needs our cooperation in order to bring about the Kingdom of God on earth. God needs us to put His will ahead of our will. If we place God's three needs first in all our prayers, we can be certain that God's destiny for the human race will be fulfilled.

The second half of the Lord's Prayer concerns our needs and the needs of all our fellow human beings. Again we are given here the model to be followed in all of our prayers of petition, namely, we put the needs of others on the same level as our personal needs. We avoid using the singular pronoun, I or Me, in our prayers. We use the plural pronoun, Us, in all our petitions. Thus we fulfill the second great commandment, "love your neighbor as you love yourself."

There is a deep mystery as to why prayer is so powerful. Jesus tells us in the Gospels, "There are certain evil spirits which can be cast out only by prayer" (Mark 9:29). In a very real way, God has put the destiny of the whole world into our hands. We are free to lead creation either toward good or evil. Prayer is the main way by which we head the human race towards God. It is not the only way but one of the more important ways. God has put into our hands tremendous power. By prayer we bring down God's blessing upon the whole world. Today many people by their evil conduct are bringing evil into the world. We are able to counteract this with the power of our prayer. Each time we unite ourselves to God in loving prayer we do this. Think of prayer as waves of love which we send out across the world. These waves have the power to disintegrate the powers of evil in the world and redirect their energy into love.

Almsgiving

Just as prayer keeps our tendency to exaggerate the power of our freedom in proper balance, so almsgiving counteracts our tendency to exaggerate the value and importance of money and material possessions. By giving alms we sacrifice possessions and avoid making a god out of money. Jesus insists that we cannot have two masters. It has to be either God or mammon. Love of money is a real threat to the lordship of God over our life. Almsgiving is a very practical way to fulfill the second commandment of love of neighbor. Whatever we call our own is only loaned to us by God and one day we will have to render an account of it. Almsgiving, therefore, is not giving to others something that belongs to us but rather distributing God's goods to help those most in need. Many Church Fathers claim that a failure to give alms is actually stealing from the poor.

Almsgiving is especially needed today as we witness an ever-increasing spread between the rich and the poor, the haves and the have-nots. If we are ever to resolve the crises facing today's world, we must start reversing the present trend and begin a more equal distribution of the resources of our planet. As individuals, our particular almsgiving may seem to be a mere drop in the bucket compared to what is really needed. The change in direction, however, must begin somewhere and we can hope that our generosity will encourage others to do likewise. Even if the amount of our offering is quite small, there are such desperate needs in so many places, that our pittance can actual prevent some person from starving to death or being deprived of the basic necessities of life.

Both the Old and New Testaments are quite impassioned in condemning the rich who turn a deaf ear to the needs of the poor. Mother Teresa insisted that we must give not only out of our abundance but give until it hurts. In other words, we need to deprive ourselves of things we now consider necessities for a full life in order to relieve the destitution of so many millions. Free enterprise, as it is generally understood, means that everyone may be as selfish as he likes in satisfying all of his acquisitive desires. This is the opposite of the teaching of Jesus in the Gospels. The unequal distribution of the wealth of the world could be resolved if people truly followed the teachings of the Gospels.

Fasting

The purpose of fasting is to bring discipline to the pursuit of bodily pleasure. Fasting is more than abstaining from food and drink. However, fasting from food and drink is especially important as a training ground for other acts of self-discipline. It is more difficult to use something in moderation than to give it up entirely. If we succeed in using food and drink in moderation, we will find it easier to practice the many other acts of self-discipline needed to lead a fully balanced life. Self-discipline is perhaps a better word than fasting.

Bodily pleasures are so attractive that they present a constant threat of becoming addictions. Thus we become slaves to pursuit of bodily pleasure. The high standard of living which we of the Western world insist upon maintaining and constantly increasing is concerned primarily with bodily pleasures and possessions. Fasting dethrones these pleasures from their place as lord and master of our lives. By a healthy regime of sacrifice and self-denial we are able to keep bodily pleasure in its proper place. A great many of the problems facing today's world are due to over-consumption, an absence of fasting and lack of self-discipline. Every act of fasting which we choose to undergo is a direct remedy to the mess in which we find ourselves today.

Fasting imposes the pursuit of a life-style more simple than the high standard of living to which most Americans are accustomed. It implies sacrifices we must make in order to stop the destruction of our earthly environment. If we want to save our planet and keep its ecology in balance, a rather strict regime of fasting and self-denial is necessary. Fasting is no longer a luxury that saints and holy people practice. It is a necessary requisite to prevent the continued rape of our planetary resources. We need to develop a new attitude towards abstaining from bodily pleasures. Instead of constantly seeking surfeit, we should see how far we can go in denying ourselves, and still be able to live a good and happy life. We must simplify our desires and our needs.

Evil spirits are not merely some cosmic, evil power which afflicts us. Each of our addictions may be seen as an evil spirit which leads us astray from the right path. Jesus says that there are certain evil spirits which can only be cast out by praying and fasting (Mt 17:21). Prayer obtains the needed grace and help from God to overcome our addictions. Fasting is the means we use to cooperate with God's grace in bringing our appetites for pleasure under control.

The prophet Isaiah ties together fasting and almsgiving. "This, rather, is the fasting that I wish. Share your bread with the hungry, shelter the oppressed and the homeless. Clothe the naked when you see them, and do not turn your back on your own. Then your light shall break forth like the dawn, and your wounds shall be quickly healed. Your vindication shall march before you, and the glory of the Lord shall be your rear guard. Then you shall call, and the Lord will answer. You shall cry for help, and he will say, 'Here I am.' If you bestow your bread on the hungry and satisfy the afflicted, then light shall rise for you in the darkness and the gloom shall become for you like midday. Then the Lord shall guide you always, and give you plenty even on the parched land. He will renew your strength, and you shall be like a well-watered garden" (Is 58:6-11).

Holiness

All of the above six candles may be summed up in the one word holiness. We are all called to be saints. Leon Bloy once remarked, "There is only one tragedy in life, the failure to be a saint." The call to sanctity is greater than ever in the world after September 11, 2001. Saints share abundantly in God's infinite power. Saints can use this divine power to change the whole course of history. Today's world needs saints more than any other group of people. Each of us is given the grace to become saints. Let us use and not abuse this grace.

APPENDIX A:
PERSONAL GROWTH PLAN

God is love and we were created in the image and likeness of God. The whole purpose of our existence on earth is to love. This love will be expressed by four relationships of love: love of God, love of other human beings, love of self, and love of nature. **EACH MORNING**, we should begin the day thanking God for another opportunity to practice love in each of these four areas. **SECONDLY**, we should spend five or ten minutes discerning how we might do a good job today in each of the four areas of love. **THIRDLY,** we need to petition God to give us the grace and help to fulfill the resolutions of love we have made. **DURING THE DAY**, we should fill any free moments with gratitude and love of God and with intercessory prayer for our loved ones and all people in need throughout the world. **EACH EVENING,** we should take a few minutes to review the events of the day, thanking God for the grace to have practiced love in each of the four relationships and asking forgiveness for any failures to love.

I. Love of God:

> Head: how can I grow in wisdom and knowledge of God today?
> Heart: how can I increase my desires and expectations of God?
> Hand: what actions can I do today to express my love of God?

II. Love of other human beings:

> What individual persons can I show a special love today?
> Is there anyone I need to forgive?
> Is there anyone I need to ask forgiveness?
> What can I do to reform and help the communities to which I belong?

What are the needs of society which are not being fulfilled?

What God-given talents do I have that might help fulfill these needs?

III. Love of myself:

What can I do to develop my inner self today?

What part of my unconscious shadow do I need to make conscious?

How can I maintain a good balance and order in all my activities?

How can I grow in the areas of **authenticity, significance, transparency** and **solidarity**?

What can I do to take good care of my body today?

IV: Love of nature (earth, environment, creation)

How can I show a love for animals today?

How can I make a wider distribution of food among the have-nots of the world?

How can I do a better job of preserving natural resources?

What beauties of God's creation can I enjoy today?

BIBLIOGRAPHY

Berne, Patricia H., and Louis M. Savary. *Dream Symbol Work: Unlocking the Energy from Dreams and Spiritual Experiences.* New York: Paulist, 1991. Print.

Berry, Thomas. *The Dream of the Earth.* San Francisco: Sierra Club, 1988. Print.

Bolen, Jean Shinoda. *Goddesses in Every Woman: A New Psychology of Women.* New York, NY: Harper & Row, 1984. Print.

---. *Gods in everyman: archetypes that shape men's lives.* New York: Quill, 1989. Print.

Borg, Marcus J. *Meeting Jesus Again for the First Time: The Historical Jesus & the Heart of Contemporary Faith.* San Francisco: Harper, 1994. Print.

Claremont de Castillejo, Irene. *Knowing Woman: A Feminine Psychology.* New York: Putnam for the C. G. Jung Foundation for Analytical Psychology, 1973. Print.

Clift, Jean Dalby., and Wallace B. Clift. *Symbols of Transformation in Dreams.* New York: Crossroad, 1986. Print.

Coleman, William V., and Patricia Coleman. *Whispers of Revelation: Discovering the Spirit of the Poor.* Mystic, CT: Twenty-Third Publications, 1992. Print.

Covey, Stephen R. *The Seven Habits of Highly Effective People.* Provo, UT: Franklin Covey, 1996. Print.

Crossin, John W. *Friendship: The Key to Spiritual Growth.* New York: Paulist, 1997. Print.

Day, Dorothy. *The Long Loneliness: The Autobiography of Dorothy Day.* San Francisco: Harper & Row, 1981. Print.

De Caussade, Jean Pierre. *Abandonment to Divine Providence.* Garden City, NY: Image, 1975. Print.

De Mello, Anthony. *Sadhana, a Way to God: Christian Exercises in Eastern Form.* Garden City, NY: Image, 1984. Print.

---. *The Song of the Bird.* Garden City, NY: Image, 1984. Print.

---. *Wellsprings: A Book of Spiritual Exercises.* Garden City, NY: Image, 1986. Print.

Dourley, John P., and C. G. Jung. *The Illness That We Are.* Toronto: Inner City, 1984. Print.

Eadie, Betty J., and Curtis Taylor. *Embraced by the Light.* Placerville, CA: Gold Leaf, 1992. Print.

Fischer, Kathleen R. *Women at the Well: Feminist Perspectives on Spiritual Direction.* SPCK, 1989. Print.

Estés, Clarissa Pinkola. *Women Who Run with the Wolves.* New York: Ballantine, 1992. Print.

Foster, Richard J. *Celebration of Discipline: The Path to Spiritual Growth.* San Francisco: Harper & Row, 1978. Print.

---. *Freedom of Simplicity*. San Francisco: Harper & Row, 1981. Print.

Fowler, James W. *Stages of Faith: The Psychology of Human Development and the Quest for Meaning*. San Francisco: Harper & Row, 1981. Print.

Fox, Matthew. *Original Blessing*. Santa Fe, NM: Bear, 1983. Print.

Frankl, Viktor E. *Man's Search for Meaning*. Boston: Beacon, 2006. Print.

Görres, Ida Friederike. *The Hidden Face: a Study of St. Thérèse of Lisieux*. New York: Pantheon, 1959. Print.

Goodier, Alban. *The Public Life of Our Lord Jesus Christ: an Interpretation*. New York: P.J. Kennedy & Sons, 1944. Print.

Green, Thomas H. *A Vacation with the Lord: A Personal, Directed Retreat*. Notre Dame, IN: Ave Maria, 1986. Print.

---. *Drinking from a Dry Well*. Notre Dame, IN: Ave Maria, 1991. Print.

---. *When the Well Runs Dry*. Notre Dame, IN: Ave Maria, 1979. Print.

Guardini, Romano. *The Lord*. Chicago: Henry Regnery, 1954. Print.

Guenther, Margaret. *Holy Listening: The Art of Spiritual Direction*. Cambridge, MA: Cowley Publications, 1992. Print.

Guzie, Tad W., and Noreen Monroe Guzie. *About Men & Women: How Your "great Story" Shapes Your Destiny*. New York: Paulist, 1986. Print.

Hutchinson, Gloria. *Six Ways to Pray from Six Great Saints*. Cincinnati, OH: St. Anthony Messenger, 1982. Print.

Johnson, Robert A. *He: Understanding Masculine Psychology*. New York: Perennial Library, 1989. Print.

---. *She: Understanding Feminine Psychology*. New York: Perennial Library, 1989. Print.

---. *We: Understanding the Psychology of Romantic Love*. San Francisco: Harper & Row, 1983. Print.

Johnston, William. *The Cloud of Unknowing and The Book of Privy Counseling*. Garden City, NY: Image, 1973. Print.

Julian of Norwich, Elizabeth Spearing, and A. C. Spearing. *Revelations of Divine Love (short Text and Long Text)*. London: Penguin, 1998. Print

Jung, Carl G. *Memories, Dreams and Reflections*. New York: Vintage, 1989. Print.

Keating, Thomas. *Invitation to Love: The Way of Christian Contemplation*. Rockport, MA: Element, 1992. Print.

---. *Open Mind, Open Heart: The Contemplative Dimension of the Gospel*. New York: Amity House, 1986. Print.

Kelsey, Morton T. *Christianity as Psychology: The Healing Power of the Christian Message*. Minneapolis: Augsburg Publishing House, 1986. Print.

---. *Companions on the Inner Way: The Art of Spiritual Guidance*. New York, NY: Crossroad, 1983. Print.

---. *Encounter with God; a Theology of Christian Experience*. Minneapolis: Bethany Fellowship, 1972. Print.

---. *The Other Side of Silence: A Guide to Christian Meditation*. New York: Paulist, 1976. Print.

Küng, Hans. *Theology for the Third Millennium: An Ecumenical View.* New York: Doubleday, 1988. Print.

Kunkel, Fritz, Elizabeth Kunkel, and Ruth Spafford Morris. *Creation Continues.* Waco, TX: Word, 1973. Print.

Lawrence, Brother. *The practice of the presence of God: conversations & letters of Brother Lawrence.* Oxford: Oneworld, 1993. Print.

Leonard, Linda Schierse. *The Wounded Woman: Healing the Father-daughter Relationship.* Boulder: Shambhala, 1983. Print.

Lewis, C. S. *Mere Christianity.* New York: MacMillan, 1952. Print.

Linn, Matthew, Sheila Fabricant Linn, and Dennis Linn. *Healing the eight stages of life.* Mahwah, NJ: Paulist Press, 1988. Print.

MacNutt, Francis. *Healing.* Notre Dame, IN: Ave Maria, 1974. Print.

May, Gerald G. *Addiction and Grace.* San Francisco: Harper & Row, 1988. Print.

---. *Care of Mind, Care of Spirit: Psychiatric Dimensions of Spiritual Direction.* San Francisco: Harper & Row, 1982. Print.

Merton, Thomas. *Conjectures of a Guilty Bystander.* Garden City, NY: Doubleday, 1966. Print.

Michael, Chester P. *A New Day.* West Conshohocken, NJ: Infinity, 2010. Print.

---. *An Introduction to Spiritual Direction: A Psychological Approach for Directors and Directees.* New York: Paulist, 2004. Print.

---. *The Human Side of Jesus.* Charlottesville, VA: Open Door, 2001. Print.

Michael, Chester P., and Marie C. Norrisey. *Prayer and Temperament: Different Prayer Forms for Different Personality Types.* Charlottesville, VA: Open Door, 1991. Print.

---. *Arise: Jungian Insights for the Christian Journey.* West Conshohocken, NJ: Infinity, 2011. Print.

Miller, William A. *Make friends with your shadow: how to accept and use positively the negative side of your personality.* Minneapolis: Augsburg Pub. House, 1981. Print.

---. *Your golden shadow: discovering and fulfilling your undeveloped self.* San Francisco: Harper & Row, 1989. Print.

Myss, Caroline M. *Anatomy of the spirit: the seven stages of power and healing.* New York: Three Rivers Press, 1996. Print.

Nouwen, Henri J. M. *The road to daybreak: a spiritual journey.* New York: Doubleday, 1988. Print

---. *The wounded healer: ministry in contemporary society.* Garden City, N.Y.: Doubleday, 1972. Print.

O'Murchú, Diarmuid. *Quantum theology: spiritual implications of the new physics.* New York: Crossroad, 2004. Print.

Pearson, Carol. *The hero within: six archetypes we live by.* San Francisco: Harper & Row, 1989. Print.

Peck, M. Scott. *People of the lie: the hope for healing human evil.* New York: Simon and Schuster, 1983. Print.

---. *The different drum: community-making and peace.* New York: Simon and Schuster, 1987. Print.

---. *The road less traveled: a new psychology of love, traditional values, and spiritual growth*. New York: Simon and Schuster, 1978. Print.

Pennington, M. Basil. *Centered living: the way of centering prayer*. Garden City, N.Y.: Doubleday, 1986. Print.

---. *Centering prayer: renewing an ancient Christian prayer form*. Garden City, N.Y.: Doubleday, 1980. Print.

Perrin, Norman. *Rediscovering the teaching of Jesus*. New York: Harper & Row, 1967. Print.

Powell, John, and Loretta Brady. *Will the Real Me Please Stand Up? So We Can All Get to Know You! : 25 Guidelines for Good Communication*. Texas: Argus Communications, 1985. Print.

Rolheiser, Ronald. *The holy longing: the search for a Christian spirituality*. New York: Doubleday, 1999. Print.

---. *The shattered lantern*. New York: Crossroad, 2001. Print.

Sanford, John A. *Dreams: God's forgotten language*. Philadelphia: Lippincott, 1968. Print.

---. *Healing and wholeness*. New York: Paulist Press, 1977. Print.

---. *The invisible partners: how the male and female in each of us affects our relationships*. New York: Paulist Press, 1980. Print.

Savary, Louis M., Patricia H. Berne, and Strephon Kaplan Williams. *Dreams and Spiritual Growth: A Christian Approach to Dreamwork*. New York: Paulist, 1984.

Teilhard de Chardin, Pierre. *Building the earth*. Wilkes-Barre, Pa.: Dimension Books, 1965. Print.

---. *Christianity and evolution*. New York: Harcourt Brace Jovanovich, 1969. Print.

---. *The divine milieu; an essay on the interior life*. New York: Harper, 1960. Print.

Therese, of Lisieux, St. *Story of a soul: the autobiography of Saint Thérèse of Lisieux*. Washington, DC: ICS Publications, 1996. Print.

Tyrrell, Bernard. *Christotherapy: healing through enlightenment*. Eugene, OR: Wipf and Stock, 1999. Print.

Underhill, Evelyn. *Mysticism, a study in the nature and development of man's spiritual consciousness*. New York: Noonday Press, 1955. Print.

Whitmont, Edward C. *The symbolic quest*. Princeton, N.J.: Princeton University Press, 1969. Print.

Wilkinson, Bruce. *The Prayer of Jabez: Breaking through to the Blessed Life*. Sisters, Or.: Multnomah, 2000. Print.

Wink, Walter. *Engaging the Powers: Discernment and Resistance in a World of Domination*. Minneapolis: Fortress, 1992. Print.

---. *Naming the Powers: The Language of Power in the New Testament*. Philadelphia: Fortress, 1984. Print.

---. *The Powers That Be: Theology for a New Millennium*. New York: Doubleday, 1998. Print.

---. *Unmasking the powers: the invisible forces that determine human existence*. Philadelphia: Fortress Press, 1986. Print.

Zukav, Gary. *The seat of the soul*. New York: Simon and Schuster, 1989. Print.

INDEX

A

Act of contrition, 158, 160
Advertising, 54
Agapic love, 108, 191, 195
"Ah-Ha" verses, 130, 140, 188
Almsgiving, 2–3; as antidote for attachment, 7, 43–44; need for, 262–263
Anatomy of the Spirit (Myss), 208
Apocalyptic worldview, 18, 19
Aquarian worldview, 24–27
Aristotle, 10
Assumptions, examining, 13, 14–15
Augustine (saint), 13; just war theory, 45; peace defined by, 97; prayer method, 134, 135–136
Authenticity, 99; first Beatitude, 53; in Little Way of Spiritual Childhood, 175–176, 197; as pursuit of truth, 213; as quality of maturity, 198

B

Balance of opposites: action and contemplation, 201–202; awesome and fascinating aspects of God, 186–188; change and status quo, 202–203; consciousness and unconscious, 199; counsel and fortitude, 204; femininity and masculinity, 199–200; freedom and submission, 204–206; fulfillment and diminishment, 196–197; life and life after death, 190–192; meekness and mercy, 206–207; nature and grace, 188–190; perceiving and judging functions, 200–201; self-development and renunciation, 193–196; spiritual childhood and spiritual maturity, 197–198; three commandments of love, 183–186; in worldview, 24–25, 26, 181–183
Baltimore Catechism, 158, 160

Baptism, Sacrament of, 164–167
Beatitudes, 1, 22. *See also* Kingdom of God; eighth, 63–67; fifth, 81–88; first, 53–59; fourth, 74–81; second, 60–63; seventh, 96–102; sixth, 88–95; third, 67–74; as worldview of Jesus, 52–53
Benedict (saint), 133
Benson, Robert Hugh, 94–95
Berakah, 145–147, 156
Berry, Thomas, 36, 37
Bible, 1; "Ah-Ha" verses, 130, 140; Augustinian prayer, 135–136; authorship of, 128–129; Franciscan prayer, 137; how to use in prayer, 130–133; Ignatian prayer, 134–135; interpretation of, 19–20, 128–129; Lectio Divina, 133–134, 140; as revealing aspects of God, 131–132; Thomistic prayer, 136–137; transposition, 135–136; as Word of God, 139; worldview of, 128–133
Bin Laden, Osama, 29, 35
Blind faith, 4, 8, 9
Bloy, Leon, 265
Breaking of bread, 149
Briggs, Katharine, 200
Bultmann, Rudolph, 18

C

Cassian, John, 133
Catherine of Siena (saint), 187
Catholic Catechism, 20
Catholic Worker Movement, 45
Charity, 260–261
Chesterton, G. K., 107
Christ the Sacrament of the Encounter with God (Schillebeeckx), 132
Christian Church, 103; co-relational Einsteinian structure, 109, 111, 114–121; horizontal Copernican structure, 109, 111–114, 120–121; importance of structure,

119–120; mission of, 108–109; pyramidal Ptolemaic worldview, 109–111, 120–121

The Church in the Modern World (Second Vatican Council), 21, 116

Communal Penance Service, 162–163

Communion, 123–124, 144, 151–152. *See also* Eucharist

Confession. *See* Penance, Sacrament of

Confirmation, Sacrament of, 164–167

Constantine (emperor), 33, 45

Copernican worldview, 112; characteristics of, 120–121; as Christian worldview, 18; Church shift to, 109; described, 21, 113–114; *vs.* Ptolemaic worldview, 110–111

Copernicus, 20, 112

Counsel, Gift of, 89

D

Day, Dorothy, 45

Deist worldview, 18–19

Demons, 40–51. *See also* fallen spiritual powers; three Ps; addictions, 41–42, 264; antidotes for, 42–44; capital sins, 41; desert, 41; evil spirits, 41; exorcism, 40; in modern world, 41, 44; redeeming, 46–49; stages, 47–48

Destitution, 29, 35–36

Detachment, 54–57, 194, 196

The Divine Milieu (Teilhard de Chardin), 92–95, 193–194

Divino Afflante Spiritu (Pius XII), 20

Dreams: animals in, 226–229; collective meanings, 230–231; commonsense in interpreting, 234–236; completing unfinished, 233–234; death in, 219–220, 229; dialoguing with characters in, 224–229; discerning God's will through, 217–219; Dream Ego, 217–219, 221, 224, 235; meaning of images in, 229–231; nightmare characters in, 226–229; objective interpretation of, 231–233; precognitive, 231–232; prophetic, 232; putting in

perspective, 221–222; relationship, 232–233; remembering, 217–218; subjective interpretation of, 222–224; understanding language of, 219–220; value of, 218–219

Dysfunctionalism, 247–249

E

Ecological pollution, 29, 36–37

Einstein, Albert, 21, 117

Einsteinian worldview: characteristics of, 120–121; as Christian worldview, 18; Church shift to, 109, 111; described, 21, 116–120

Emath, 77

Enantiodromia, 24

Engaging the Powers (Wink), 46, 261

Eucharist, Sacrament of, 123, 124. *See also* Communion; healing; appealing to all temperaments, 142–143; Berakah, 145–147, 156; development of, 148–150; dimensions of, 143–145; elements for good, 154; Jesus and, 155–157; lost symbolism of, 150–152; parallels between Passover and, 147–148; place in worldview, 141–143; as powerful healing method, 243–244; presence of Risen Christ in, 153–154; recapturing personal meaning in, 152–155

Evely, Louis, 18

Evil: causes of, 237; charity *vs.*, 260–261; Jesus' attitude towards, 40, 44–45; overcoming with good, 62–65; spirits, 41, 47

Exorcism, 40, 103, 239

F

Faith, 250–256, 258–259; aspects of, 190; blind, 4, 8, 9; call, 250, 251, 253–254; carrying out God's plan, 250–253; celebration, 252; commission, 253; consolation, 252–253; conversion, 251; covenant, 251–252; journey images, 250; passing through desert, 254–256; uniqueness,

253–254
Fallen spiritual powers, 28, 32–34.
    See also demons
Fanaticism, 181
Fasting, 3, 7, 32, 43, 196, 263–265.
    See also self-denial; self-
    discipline
Fear of the Lord, 186–187
Feasting, 196
Flanigan, James, 35
Francis de Sales (saint), 210
Francis of Assisi (saint), 134
Freud, Sigmund, 38
Fundamentalist worldview, 18, 19–20

G

Galileo, 20, 112
Gandhi, Mahatma, 107–108;
    influence on history, 6, 14; non-
    violent redeeming love, 33, 45,
    48–49, 107–108; singleness of
    purpose, 94
Genesis 3, rereading, 49–51
Gifts, of Holy Spirit, 89
Global issues, 28–29
God. *See also* Holy Spirit; Jesus
    Christ: aspects of, 131–132, 215;
    attributes of, 77, 98–99; balance
    of awesome and fascinating
    aspects, 186–188; dependence
    upon, 53, 57–58; divine plan of,
    1, 35, 38, 122–124; immanent
    closeness of, 186, 187; as
    meekness example, 68–69;
    seeing, 88–89; transcendence
    of, 186–187; transparency of,
    186; true nature of, 105–106; as
    truth, 212–213; unconditional
    love, 2, 106; worldview of, 122–
    124
Goerres, Ida F., 170
Good news, 106
Goodness, 24
Grace, 38, 39, 126, 188–190
Green, Thomas, 254
Guigo II, 134

H

Healing, 237–249. *See also*
    Eucharist, Sacrament of;
    Penance, Sacrament of; areas
needing, 240–241; bodies, 239;
causes of evil, 237; correcting
worldview, 237–238; of demonic
oppression, 239; dysfunctional
families, 247–249; family tree,
243–244; forgiveness of sins,
238; laying on of hands, 239,
241; of memories, 238–239,
241–242, 244–245; methods,
238–239; sickness types, 237;
virtues to help, 238; wounded
healer, 245–247
Healing the Family Tree (McAll), 243
Heliocentric worldview, 112
Heraclitus, 202
Heresy, 181
Hesed, 77
The Hidden Face (Goerres), 170
Hippocrates, 142
Hitler, Adolph, 14, 93
Holiness, 74–81, 265; areas of
    justice, 74–75, 79–81; barrier to,
    76; becoming saint, 74–75, 76;
    desire for, 77; example of, 78–
    79; fulfilling potential for good,
    79–80; love of others, 75
Holy Spirit. *See also* God; Jesus
    Christ: as feminine aspect of
    God, 165; openness to, 164–
    169; role in God's plan, 167–
    169; as sleeping giant, 164–167;
    wisdom as gift of, 192
Holy water, 166
Hope, 259–260
Humility, 173, 187

I

Idolatry, 6, 15–16, 28, 30–31
Ignatius of Loyola (saint), 134–135,
    188–189, 212
Incarnation, 89–90, 122–124

J

James, William, 55
Jefferson, Thomas, 18
Jehovah's Witnesses, 19
Jesus Christ, 5–6. *See also* God;
    Holy Spirit; attitude towards evil,
    40, 44–45; Beatitudes, 52–53;
    Eucharist and, 155–157; as
    healer, 245–246; as king, 105;

as meekness example, 69, 73; ministry of table fellowship, 156; non-violence, 107–108; peace-making efforts of, 100–101; and physical/material world, 22; as priest, 104; as prophet, 104–105; simple lifestyle, 22, 175; suffering of, 62–63; temptations in desert, 41; twelve aspects of mission, 103–108; worldview of, 1, 21–24

Jesus prayer, 137–138
John of the Cross (saint), 54, 254
John (saint), 118
John XXIII (pope), 6
Jung, Carl G., 24, 25; anima/animus, 199–200; authenticity, 213; Collective Unconscious, 230; dream archetypes, 220; on interpreting dreams, 230; qualities of mature person, 198; synchronicity, 226; unconscious, 199

Jungian depth psychology, 25
Jungmann, Josef, 112
Justice. *See* holiness

K

Kerygmatic theology, 112
Kiersey, David, 142
King, Martin Luther, Jr.: influence on history, 6, 14; non-violent redeeming love, 33, 45, 48–49, 107–108; singleness of purpose, 94
Kingdom of God, 2. *See also* Beatitudes; Omega Point; in co-relational church model, 115–116; in horizontal church model, 112, 113–114; Jesus' worldview as, 23–24; meaning of, 156; power over evil, 103; in pyramid church model, 113
Knowledge, Gift of, 89, 189–190

L

Law of polarity. *See* balance of opposites
Laying on of hands, 160, 239
Lectio Divina, 133–134, 140, 142, 202

Life after death, 190–192
Little Way of Spiritual Childhood, 170–180, 197–198; authenticity, 175–176; dependence upon God, 173; desire to be forgotten, 174; humility, 173; immense desires, 178–180; joyful acceptance, 174; littleness consequences, 173–175; reaching sanctity with, 172–173; simplicity, 175–176; unlimited confidence in God, 176–178; worldview of saints, 170–172
Logos, 212
Lord's prayer, 138–139, 184, 261
Lord's Supper, 147–148, 150
Love, 2, 3; agapic, 108, 191, 195; authentic, 211, 258; balance among commandments of, 183–186; divine, 211; enemies, 39, 44–45; of family, 247–248; God, 106, 158, 159; neighbor, 106, 158, 159; self, 106, 158, 159; unconditional defined, 184, 247
Lumen Gentium (Second Vatican Council), 110–111

M

Martyrs, 108
Maslow, Abraham, 191
McAll, Kenneth, 243
Medieval worldview, 10, 12, 15, 21–22, 26
Meekness, 67–74, 212; anger and, 71, 72; balance with mercy, 206–207; choosing last place, 73; compassion, 72; examples of, 68–70; farsightedness and, 74; love of others, 73; meaning of, 67–68; nonviolence, 71; patience, 72–73; praying for, 72; signs of, 68; weakness *vs.*, 67
Mercy, 81–88; balance with meekness, 206–207; bruised reed, 84; corporal works of, 85, 86; facing own healing needs, 85; forgiveness, 82; as healing, 82; as higher justice, 88; judgment, 83; meaning of, 81; ministering to others, 83–84; openness to others, 82, 83; similarities to meekness, 81; smoldering wick, 84–85; spiritual

works of, 85–87
Metanoia, 28, 103, 158, 251
Missionaries of Charity, 6
Mosaic law, 106–107
Moses, 70, 106, 149, 255, 256
Mother Teresa, 6, 94, 263
Myers, Isabel Briggs, 200
Myers-Briggs Type Indicator, 200–201
Myss, Catherine, 208

N

Narcissism, 44
Natural resources, diminishing, 29, 37
Negativity, 259–260
Nonviolence, 32–34
Nouwen, Henri, 85, 246
Nuclear proliferation, 15–16, 29, 34–35, 50

O

Omega Point, 92, 113. See also Kingdom of God

P

Parables, 107
Paschal Mystery, 108, 192, 220, 229
Passivities of diminishment, 194
Passivities of growth, 193
Passover, 147–148
Paul (saint), 114, 118
Peace-making, 96–102; with God, 97, 98–99; in human relationships, 97, 99–102; international relations, 102; power of love, 96–97; refusal to use violence, 100–101; within self, 97–98; tolerance of differences, 101; tranquility of order, 97
Penance, Sacrament of, 158–163. See also healing; act of contrition, 158, 160; Communal Penance Service, 162–163; examining conscience, 158; four love relationships, 158, 159; frequency of confession, 159; laying on of hands, 160; new regulations for, 159–160;

reasons for neglect of, 161–162; resolution of amendment, 158, 159, 160–161
Personal Growth Plan, 1, 2, 125–127, 161, 266–267
Peter (saint), 114
Piety, 186–187
Pius XII (pope), 20
Please Understand Me (Kiersey), 142
Pleasure. See three Ps
Possessions. See three Ps
Poverty, of spirit. See spiritual poverty
Power. See three Ps
Pragmatism, 44
Prayer, 2, 7, 261–262; as antidote for demons, 43; Augustinian, 135–136, 137; Berakah, 146–147; centering, 137–138; as dialogue with God, 129–130; discernment, 125–126; five bases of, 125–127; Franciscan, 137; gratitude, 125; for healing of memories, 244–245; how to use Bible in, 130–133; Ignatian, 134–135; intercession, 126; Jesus, 137–138; as listening, 187–188; of liturgical year, 135; Lord's, 138–139; meditation, 129–130; petition, 126; review, 126–127; Thomistic, 136–137; as work of mercy, 87
Prayer and Temperament (Michael and Norrisey), 134, 136, 142
The Prayer of Jabez (Wilkinson), 132–133
Projection, 26
Psalms, 131
Ptolemaic worldview, 110–111; characteristics of, 120–121; as Christian worldview, 18; described, 20; shift from, 109
Ptolemy, Claudius, 20
Purity of heart, 88–95; absence of egocentricity, 91; connection to suffering, 90–91; developing, 95; power to love, 91–92; seeing God, 88–89, 91, 95; single eye, 93–94; Teilhard de Chardin on, 92–95; Virgin Mary as example, 89–90

Q

Quakers, 45

R

Reason, human, 12–13, 15
Redemptive violence, 44–45
Remythologizing, 7
Resolution of amendment, 158, 159, 160–161
Rolheiser, Ronald, 44

S

Sacraments, 1, 252. *See also under specific types*
Sanford, Agnes, 239, 244–245
Schillebeeckx, Edward, 132
SDI. *See* Spiritual Direction Institute (SDI)
Secular worldview, 5, 9–10; changing, 12–13; contamination by, 6–7; disillusionment with, 12; faulty assumptions of, 15–16; history of, 10–12; mistakes of, 15–16, 26; origin of, 10–12; spiritual *vs.*, 11–12
Self-denial, 42, 43, 55–56, 183, 194–196. *See also* fasting
Self-discipline, 32, 204–205, 263. *See also* fasting
Self-evident truths, 4–5
September 11, 2001, 257, 265; as call for change, 29, 33–34, 35, 37; use of unconscious negative shadow energies, 38–39; worldview after, 28–29
Seven Industrial Nations, 35
Seven truths, 208–216; after-death experiences and, 215–216; all is one, 208–209; in beliefs of all religions, 215; honor one another, 209–210; honor oneself, 210–211; live in present moment, 214; love is divine power, 211; order of pursuit, 215; seek only truth, 212–214; surrender personal will to divine will, 211–212
Seventh Day Adventists, 19
Shadow, 26–27, 29, 36
The Shattered Lantern (Rolheiser), 44

Significance, 198
Simplicity, 175–176
Six Cs, 2, 250–253
Solidarity, 198
Spiritual Childhood. *See* Little Way of Spiritual Childhood
Spiritual Direction Institute (SDI), 1
Spiritual maturity, 197–198
Spiritual poverty, 53–59, 173; dependence upon God, 53, 57–58; detachment, 54–57; as prayer preparation, 58
Spiritual values, secular values *vs.*, 11–12
The Story of a Soul (Therese of Lisieux), 170
Suffering, 60–67; accepting, 63–64; breaking proud streak, 61–62; contrition, 66; of Jesus, 62–63; letting go of past, 66; persecution, 63–67; reasons for, 62; rejoicing in, 66–67; sensitivity to, 64; viewed as evil, 60–61

T

Teilhard de Chardin, Pierre, 113; divinization, 193–194; purity of heart, 92–95; search for truth, 212–213
Teresa of Avila (saint), 252
Terrorism, 28, 29–30, 34–35
That Man is You (Evely), 18
Therese of Lisieux (saint), 1, 69, 78–79; as Doctor of the Church, 170; doctrine of Spiritual Childhood, 171–172, 197–198; on humility, 173; on immense desires, 178–180; religious name, 174–175; spiritual darkness, 177–178; teachings in autobiography, 170–172
Thomas Aquinas (saint), 10; on meekness, 71; peace defined, 97; prayer method, 134, 136–137; virtue and balance, 181
Three Ps, 5, 17, 28, 29. *See also* demons; as demons, 41; detachment from, 54–57; Jesus tempted by, 205–206; pleasure worship, 28, 31–32; power worship, 28, 31
Transparency, 198

U

Ultimate reality, 16–18; Christian belief in divinity of Jesus Christ, 17–18; human race, 17; impersonal force, 17; influence on worldview, 16; nameless void, 17; personal God, 17; physical universe, 17
Unbridled restlessness, 44
Unconditional love. *See* love
Understanding, Gift of, 89, 189–190

W

The Way of a Pilgrim (Anonymous), 137–138
Why Do Bad Things Happen to Good People (Kushner), 18
Wilkinson, Bruce, 132–133
Wink, Walter, 32, 33, 46, 47–48, 261
World hunger, 29, 35–36
Worldview. *See also under specific types*: after September 11, 2001, 28–29; in America, 9–10; birth of, 7–9; changing, 12–13; correcting, 237–238; defined, 4; developing Christian, 21–24; of God, 122–124; healing, 1–2; individual importance, 13–15; of Jesus, 1, 21–24; new, 5–7; of saints, 170–172; tentative nature of, 5
The Wounded Healer (Nouwen), 85, 246
Wright brothers, 93–94